ELEANOR OF AQUITAINE: PATRON AND POLITICIAN

Symposia in the Arts and the Humanities, No. 3

Sponsored by the College of Humanities
and the College of Fine Arts

The University of Texas at Austin

Eleanor of Aquitaine

Patron and Politician

edited by William W. Kibler

University of Texas Press, Austin

Library of Congress Cataloging in Publication Data
Main entry under title:

Eleanor of Aquitaine, patron and politician.

(Symposia in the arts and the humanities; no. 3)
Rev. versions of papers presented at a symposium held
at the University of Texas at Austin, Apr. 23–25, 1973.
Includes index.
1. Eleanor, of Aquitaine, Consort of Henry II, 1122?-
1204—Congresses. 2. England—Intellectual life—Medieval period, 1066–1485—Congresses. 3. France—Intellectual life—Congresses. I. Kibler, W.W. II. Series.
DA209.E6E43 942.03′1′0924 75–16080
ISBN 978-0-292-74123-2

First paperback printing, 2012

Contents

Illustrations

In Memoriam: Raphael Levy

On July 23, 1969, the career of Raphael Levy came to an end. It was a career completely dedicated to work: work for his family, for his religion, for his profession. Raphael Levy was a man of peace, a gentle man, kind and considerate of others. Calm pride, love, and faith characterized also his self-image as a Jew. But his compassion and sympathy were extended to all men.

After receiving his bachelor's degree before his twentieth birthday, Raphael Levy won his master's degree two years later and in another two years earned his Ph.D. Both undergraduate and graduate work were carried on at Johns Hopkins University, in Levy's native Baltimore. But study and research took him to Europe many times, with the financial support of grants from the John Simon Guggenheim Foundation, the American Council of Learned Societies, Johns Hopkins University (Johnston Scholarship), the American Philosophical Society, and the University of Texas Research Institute.

Levy's teaching career was spent at the University of Wisconsin, the University of Baltimore, Louisiana State University, and the University of Texas at Austin. It covered a period of forty-five years. During that time his scholarly production was maintained at a high level: nine books and over a hundred articles, published both in this country and abroad. A large number of book reviews attest to the wide-ranging study of this scholar. The library he left was a marvelous thing to behold: each book was carefully wrapped in an envelope or a carton, together with any review of it that had appeared and any pertinent reference to it. Thus each item on his shelves was more than a book; it was a collection of information on a given topic. Such meticulous attention to relevance of material characterized his work, and his library was truly a working library.

By his will Raphael Levy gave the portion of his collection of books dealing with medieval French language and literature, Judaeo-French, and related subjects, without reservation, to the Hebrew University in Jerusalem. Through the Friends of the Hebrew University, over 1,500 volumes were sent to Israel. It has been characterized as a "princely" gift, because of the great care of the selection as well as the intrinsic value of many of the items.

The major parts of Raphael Levy's teaching career fell in a period when interest in philology and particularly in Old French was at a low ebb. His influence as a teacher is, then, not to be measured in the number of graduate students who worked for their degrees in this field he had chosen for his specialization. Rather, large numbers of graduate students in many fields came under his influence and became his friends through the years during which Levy taught the course and gave the examination in the reading knowledge of Old French for the graduate degree. In this work Levy was expert and, as always, conscientious and helpful. Unlike some who devote their energies to the scientific study of language, he was sensitive to literature, both of the French middle ages and the contemporary scene.

Between 1946 and 1966, Levy gave twenty-seven addresses before such groups as the Modern Language Association, the South-Central Modern Language Association, the Alliance Française of Houston, and local organizations.

The world of French lexicography, French-Hebrew linguistic relationships, and medieval studies has lost an outstanding and indefatigable worker. The gap left in the ranks is not entirely empty, however, for younger men will come forward to continue the work, inspired and guided by the scholarly publications of Raphael Levy.

Ernest F. Haden
James F. M. Stephens, Jr.
Stanley N. Werbow

Major Books by Professor Raphael Levy

The Astrological Works of Abraham ibn Ezra. The Johns Hopkins Studies in Romance Literatures and Languages, vol. 8. Baltimore, Md.: Johns Hopkins Press, 1927.

Recherches lexicographiques sur d'anciens textes français d'origine juive. The Johns Hopkins Studies in Romance Literatures and Languages, extra vol. 5. Baltimore, Md.: Johns Hopkins Press, 1932.

Répertoire des lexiques du vieux français. New York: Modern Language Association of America, 1937.

The Beginning of Wisdom, edited in collaboration with Francisco Cantera. The Johns Hopkins Studies in Romance Literatures and Languages, extra vol. 14. Baltimore, Md.: Johns Hopkins Press, 1939.

Chronologie approximative de la littérature française du moyen âge. Beihefte zur Zeitschrift für romanische Philologie, vol. 98. Tübingen: M. Niemeyer, 1957.

Contribution à la lexicographie française selon d'anciens textes d'origine juive. Syracuse: Syracuse University Press, 1960.

Trésor de la langue des Juifs français au Moyen Age. Austin: University of Texas Press, 1964.

In addition to these major contributions, over one hundred scholarly articles were published in American and foreign journals.

Acknowledgments

The Symposium on the Court of Eleanor of Aquitaine would not have been possible without the aid and encouragement of many individuals, colleges, and departments. The coordinator's greatest debt of gratitude is to Dean Stanley N. Werbow of the College of Humanities at the University of Texas at Austin, for continued moral and monetary support. Many members of the university's Medieval Studies Committee contributed their time and talents. Funding for the symposium and this volume was made possible by grants from the Graduate School, the Colleges of Humanities and Fine Arts, and the Departments of French-Italian and History of the University of Texas at Austin.

Eleanor of Aquitaine

Introduction

WILLIAM W. KIBLER

The twelfth century in France and England was an age of artistic and intellectual awakening; the invasions of Western Europe from the north had ceased in the preceding century, and a time of relative peace, both internal and external, led naturally to a new concern with the quality of life. The concept of a "Twelfth-Century renaissance" has inspired a number of recent volumes evaluating the period's contributions in theology, in the methods of theological discussion and the systematization of theological thought, in logic and grammar, in canon law, in the development of universities, in art and architecture, in music, in Latin and vernacular poetry, in new economic considerations, and in the beginnings of the modern state. The diversity of these trends may cause us to overlook the fact that most of this activity was centered at the University of Paris and at the royal courts of France and England and was due largely to a close cooperation between the universities and the lay feudal society. The "renaissance," particularly in its literary aspects, began in the Poitou-Aquitaine region of southern France in the early years of the century; a quickening of activity in the north of France and in England was not evident until around mid-century. This chronology corresponds closely with that of the principal subject of this volume, Eleanor of Aquitaine, who was married in 1137 to King Louis VII of France. Barely eight weeks after the annulment in March 1152 of her first marriage on grounds of consanguinity, Eleanor wed Henry, Duke of Normandy, who in 1154 succeeded his father to become Henry II Plantagenet, King of England. Wife of two kings and mother of two others, political activist and artistic patron, Eleanor of Aquitaine steered a path through the twelfth century that might forever put the lie to the notion that women had no place in a man's world until the middle of the twentieth century. Her figure stands out even from a crowd which includes Thomas Becket, John of Salisbury, Abelard, Abbot Suger, Chrétien de Troyes, and Bernard of Clairvaux.

Eleanor never reigned personally, never cut or laid a stone, never (as far as we know) wrote a poem or composed a note of music; yet her personal court and that of her second husband, Henry II Plantagenet, were the centers of an intense artistic life, seldom rivaled in the history of Western civilization. Today, when learning is so general and intellectual life so decentralized, it is difficult to conceive the effect one stimulating personality could have on the life of a whole century and of nearly an entire continent. Today, too often, even medievalists tend to compartmentalize their view of medieval society and to study its literature *or* its art and architecture *or* its music *or* its history. Although specialists in one field often must call upon the knowledge of those in others, only too rarely do we have the opportunity to view a civilization in all its cultural ramifications. Eleanor of Aquitaine is at the heart of an entire civilization. A shrewd and dedicated politician, a patron of the arts in the broadest sense, a lover of gaiety—Eleanor was all these and more. In an effort to assess her importance within her own century and in those to follow, the University of Texas invited distinguished medievalists from this country and abroad to meet in Austin for discussion on April 23–25, 1973. The essays in this volume are revised versions of the papers presented at the symposium. Eleanor's wide-ranging interests and influence can be seen from the topics and fields covered: history, music, sculptural and pictorial arts, French and Provençal literature, English literature. Although some of the essays have been modified as a result of the work sessions of the symposium, there has been no attempt to reach a unified view of so complex a personality as Eleanor's. The essays thus present divergent and at times frankly contradictory interpretations of Eleanor's significance, and the reader is encouraged to form his own synthesis.

The opening essay, by Elizabeth A. R. Brown of the City University of New York, considers three aspects of Eleanor's historical impact: as parent, queen, and duchess of Aquitaine. Brown rejects the romantic mandorla which so often surrounds this intriguing personage and presents to us a woman in whom "the domineering rather than the nurturant side of motherhood was strongest" and who was "far more concerned with the realities of political life than with matters cultural and intellectual." For the first time, Brown uses Eleanor's and Henry's childhoods to attempt to understand their adult reactions to one another, to their children, and to their land. In her view, Eleanor emerges as a tenacious, vigorous, and clever woman who refused to capitulate to the whims of her husbands and who until her death at the very advanced age of eighty-one "remained intoxicated with the exercise of power and political maneuvering, at which she excelled."

While Brown concentrates on Eleanor's influence as parent and politician and minimizes her potential contribution as patron, other scholars found that her activities in the cultural realm, although not always so easily documentable as those in the political one, were nonetheless pervasive in several domains. Moshé Lazar of Tel Aviv University sees Eleanor's court as "a melting pot for various folkloric and narrative traditions and a fertile ground for the confrontation or the synthesis of different concepts of love," especially after her marriage to Henry. The frequent peregrinations of her court, from Poitiers (1152–1154), through Normandy, Maine, and Anjou (1154, 1158, 1159–1162), to England (1154–1156, 1157–1158, 1163–1164), and back to Poitou and Aquitaine (1166–1173), are seen by both Lazar and Larry M. Ayres as the source of what the former terms "one of the most enriching cultural exchanges and cross-fertilizations in history."

In his essay, Lazar enters once again into the arena of "the courtly-love question," challenging, as he did in his seminal study, *Amour courtois et Fin'amors dans la littérature du XIIe siècle* (Paris: C. Klincksieck, 1964), the view that courtly love represented from its inception a sublimation of sexual, earthly desires to an other-worldly end. He opposes the lumping of the many varied and often contradictory expressions of love throughout the Middle Ages together under the too convenient term *courtly love* and proposes instead a threefold division of love as it is expressed in the literary works of the twelfth century:

1. *Fin'amors*, "a new mode of love and the central theme of the Provençal troubadours' poetry."

2. Tristan-love, "a mode of tragic love [which includes] the characteristic and constitutive elements of *fin'amors*."

3. Conjugal courtly love, an *anti-fin'amors* which refuses the adulterous relationship characteristic of the first two modes.

Lazar defines the troubadour love ethic as essentially this-worldly, adulterous, and a-Christian, and he refuses to attempt to reconcile this attitude with the Christian ethic under which the troubadours lived, for this existence of two opposing truths—one here, on the level of daily morality, and the other on the level of faith—was not untypical of medieval thought patterns. Eleanor and her daughter Marie de Champagne are to be seen as exponents of the first two modes of love, while Chrétien de Troyes's personal preference was for the third.

Poetry in the twelfth century, Rebecca A. Baltzer of the University of Texas reminds us, must never be dissociated from the music which accompanied it. Citing vernacular and Latin texts, Baltzer shows us the important role which music played in courtly society of the day. Almost no music was written down in the twelfth century, but the oral tradition was strong, and many early works are preserved in thirteenth-century manuscripts. Much of this music can be associated either directly or indirectly with Eleanor and her descendants or with historical events involving members of her entourage and that of her husband Henry. "No other medieval monarch inspired so much music as did Eleanor and her family," Baltzer concludes, and "without her, the course of history *and* the course of music would be entirely different."

Not content with the traditional view that Eleanor's artistic patronage began only after she became the bride of Henry II Plantagenet and Queen of England, Eleanor S. Greenhill of the University of Texas points to varied evidence—historical, artistic, and literary—which suggests royal patronage for the rebuilding of the Abbey of Saint-Denis: royal patronage which Abbot Suger, for various reasons, neglects to mention in his writings. Saint-Denis was, first and foremost, a royal abbey, where a long line of Frankish sovereigns lay buried and where the patron martyr was revered as *dux et protector* of the realm. Failure on the part of the king to support its refurbishment would surely have been "*lèse majesté* of the grossest sort." Furthermore, Suger's records show a constant preoccupation with finances and a number of "miraculous" gifts which, Greenhill quite plausibly argues, were none other than royal bequests. It was, moreover, Aquitaine's money which enabled this patronage. The style of Saint-Denis has long been seen to reflect a *renovatio imperii Karoli Magni*, but Greenhill points out that its true model was not the Carolingian church at Aachen but Santiago de Compostela, and that therefore Saint-Denis is in truth built *ad similitudinem scilicet ecclesiae beati Jacobi*. What links Charlemagne to Spain and to Santiago is the tradition of the *chansons de geste*, reflected particularly in the *Chronicle of Pseudo-Turpin*. This false document was written contemporaneously with the construction of Saint-Denis and links it directly to Santiago. The *Chronicle of Pseudo-Turpin* is likewise an important link associating Eleanor with the spirit of reconstruction. Eleanor's forebears had long had a special interest in the pilgrimage of Santiago, and her father was even buried under the altar of Saint James in the Santiago cathedral. When Saint-Denis was being rebuilt to the greater glory of Charlemagne, who better than Queen Eleanor could associate Charlemagne, Santiago, and Saint-Denis? Moreover, study of the phases of construction at Saint-Denis shows difficult progress and shaky finances before Eleanor's arrival in Paris, then a great spurt of "miraculous" interventions and construction in the 1140's, followed by a marked slowdown after the divorce. When one adds to this the presence at Saint-Denis after 1140 of sculptors from the southwest of France, the possibility that Eleanor's hand was felt in the rebuilding of the royal abbey can no longer be lightly dismissed.

Although the problem of Eleanor's influence on the arts while Queen of the Franks remains problematical, the possibility of her having exerted some influence while Queen of England is more capable of documentation. Larry M. Ayres, of the University of California at Santa Barbara, suggests that British pictorial art of the second half of the twelfth century is deeply indebted to artistic developments in the west and southwest of France and that the style associated with the Angevin region becomes more discernible in the art of English centers precisely during the reign of Eleanor and Henry II Plantagenet. Using stylistic comparisons of manuscript illuminations as the basis for his findings, Ayres considers three aspects of the relationship between English painting and that of the Continent. Examining the work of the Apocrypha Master in the famous Winchester Bible, he shows that this particular artist, working in the late 1170's or early 1180's, shows definite archaizing tendencies in his modeling. He does not use the then-current "damp-fold style" but rather prefers what Ayres calls "Angevin style," a style which originated in southwestern France and which only pervaded English painting after the ascendance of Eleanor and Henry in 1154. With regard to "Channel style," it is less easy to determine the direction of influence, but it too attests to an increased interchange of artistic ideas between France and England during this period. Finally, a third relationship between England and the Continent is seen in the classicizing trend of the early 1180's. Seeking the origin of this trend, Ayres pointedly reminds us that it may be related to the marriage of Joanna, daughter of Henry II and Eleanor, to William II of Sicily in 1177.

In the final and farthest-ranging essay, Rossell Hope Robbins of the State University of New York at Albany assesses the influence of the love poetry popularized in the English court at the time of Eleanor and Henry on subsequent movements in English letters, from about 1100 to 1530. Court literature written in French in England falls roughly into two periods: 1100–1350, when the courtly lyric and romance genres were most firmly entrenched, although much of the Anglo-Norman production did not treat the love themes; and 1350–1500, when the *nouvelle vague* style of Machaut and his school was triumphant. Concurrent with the early period of French court literature, there was written much Latin material (generally of a nonliterary nature) and some noncourt literature in English, composed largely for the "lewed" populace. After the watershed year of the Black Death, 1349, popular literature continued to spread, but most attention is given to the two trends in English court literature: the Alliterative Revival (1350–1400) and the Chaucerian School (1370–1530). Robbins recalls that the Alliterative poets used French romance as their model more frequently than is sometimes realized, and we find conventional courtly themes in the poetry fully two decades before Chaucer. While the Alliterative poets were influenced by the romances, Chaucer took as his model the new poetry of Machaut, typified by the *dits amoureux*. Both branches of English courtly literature, however, show at least the indirect influence of the love themes and styles of Eleanor's day. In closing, Robbins asks us to ponder the problem of Chaucer's earliest poetry: is it not likely that at an essentially French-speaking court he would have written lyrics in the French manner *in French*?

While a symposium of this sort, bringing together scholars from such varied disciplines, cannot possibly pretend to unanimity of view, it does focus attention on the exceptional range of areas in which the queen's eclectic interests played. In music, the direct effect of her life and that of her relatives is easily traceable in the lyrics. Her influence in the political sphere can be measured from extant records and testimony, but even here speculation is necessary if we are fully to appreciate her impact on her husbands and sons. In the field of literary criticism, we find a controversy still raging over the meaning of courtly love and over Eleanor's possible role in the formulation of the love codes of the twelfth century. Lazar and Robbins both accept the validity of the concept of courtly love and the probability of Eleanor's having had a significant role in its development, while Brown would dismiss this as idle and unsubstantiated speculation. In the fine arts, Eleanor's influence is perhaps even more difficult to trace directly, but the chains of coincidences brought forward by Greenhill and Ayres must henceforth be seriously considered in any evaluation of her impact.

1. Eleanor of Aquitaine:

Parent, Queen, and Duchess

ELIZABETH A. R. BROWN

Eleanor of Aquitaine was an extraordinary person, who has intrigued a remarkably varied group of writers and commentators—gossipmongers, serious historians of literature and of political and institutional development, and the most romantic of novelists. Exaggeration and anachronistic fantasy are apparent in many of the accounts of her life, suggesting that those who have observed and studied her have not done all they might to establish sound foundations for their statements. The process of gaining reliable information and reaching satisfactory conclusions about her is, indeed, exceedingly difficult, and the tendency of those who have studied her to trust their imaginative insights more than is perhaps warranted is understandable. H. G. Richardson, dedicated scholar and archivist that he was, saw the chief problem as arising from historians' failure to deal with "the not inconsiderable bulk of record material."[1] The importance of analyzing the documents is unquestionable, but the avenue of approach to the historical Eleanor has been most effectively blocked by writers who have used Eleanor as a vehicle for expressing their own prejudices and assumptions and by those who have filled books and articles ostensibly dedicated to Eleanor with cultural and political events only loosely connected with her life, instead of focusing on Eleanor and her family.[2]

The work of many modern historians demonstrates the second failing,[3] while the Victorians provide rather delicious examples of the first. Mary Anne Everett Green, writing in the middle of the last century on the princesses of England, applied her own age's standards of motherhood to Eleanor when she proclaimed her "far from being a pattern with regard to the training of her children. She seems to have indulged their every wish, and not even to have thwarted their caprices, while the frequent migrations of the royal nursery must have been a sad impediment to any set plans of education,—if such were attempted." She concluded that Eleanor's daughters were more fortunate than her sons: "they appear to have escaped uninjured from such injudicious treatment, perhaps from their having left home when quite young."[4] Bishop William Stubbs thought that Eleanor had been unfairly judged. "I do not speak of her moral qualities," he hastened to add; "although probably her faults have been exaggerated, she can hardly be said to shine as a virtuous woman or a good wife."[5] He went on, however, to blame her for what he called "her" quarrel with Henry II, which he said "long retarded the reforming schemes of his great administrative genius."[6] Agnes Strickland, the historian of the English queens, was more interested in Eleanor's qualities of leadership than her domestic failings. Having described her (without a shred of evidence)[7] as leading a dress parade of female warriors armed to the teeth after taking the cross at Vézelay from Saint Bernard, she remarked of her participation in the crusade, "Such fellow-soldiers as queen Eleanora and her Amazons would have been quite sufficient to disconcert the plans and impede the projects of Hannibal himself."[8] Contemporary historians are not immune from Victorian inclinations and opinions, and Richardson and his colleague G. O. Sayles say of Eleanor, "It may be that she was cursed by fate in being born a woman."[9]

Such evaluations as these must be disregarded if Eleanor herself is to be understood. Scanty and disordered as the evidence may be, it is still possible to use it to discern the woman who lived, bore children, and ruled eight centuries ago.

In terms of centennials Eleanor would, I feel sure, be happy that a symposium was held to celebrate her importance in April of 1973 rather than a year later: 1173 was for her a far more pleasantly memorable year than 1174. The earlier year found her raising resistance in Aquitaine as, supported by her sons Henry, Richard, and Geoffrey, and by her former husband, Louis VII, she led the attack against her husband, Henry II. Then were manifested the traits that seem most characteristic of her— her passionate courage, her determined control over her offspring, her tenacity, her cleverness. The following year found her in England, her husband's prisoner, destined to remain for a decade and a half the instrument of his will and not to re-emerge until 1189 as the influential figure she had formerly been. In 1173 various facts were demonstrated: first, that Eleanor loved power and the machinations of politics; second, that in her the domineering rather than the nurturant side of motherhood was strongest; third, that she was far more concerned with the realities of political life than with matters cultural and intellectual.

Though it may be easiest to describe the adult Eleanor and to isolate her aims and interests at that period of her life, her background and childhood cast light on the adult she became and provide a perspective for examining the significant themes and patterns of action which emerge from and give unity to her life and which, in large part, determine her historical significance. She was born in 1122, probably near Bordeaux,[10] the first child of William, tenth duke of Aquitaine and eighth count of Poitou, and of his wife Aenor of Châtellerault.[11] Her father was in his early twenties, her mother presumably also young, and still living was her grandfather William IX, who did not die until 1127, when Eleanor was five.[12] For the first years of her life Eleanor and her parents were under the actual control and certain influence of this man, whose reputation has for many reasons outshone that of Eleanor's own father, known chiefly for his enormous appetite.[13]

It is worth dwelling on the deeds and characteristics of William IX, since his actions and attitudes seem to have affected Eleanor as both child and adult. William became duke when not yet fifteen, and, despite the difficult circumstances of his accession, he managed to establish control over his lands. A participant in the First Crusade, he was better remembered in his own times for his territorial ambitions, directed chiefly against Toulouse,[14] for his conflicts with the churches of his lands, and for his amorous exploits than for his service to the cause of God in the East.[15] Renowned for his brilliant love poems, he was ambivalent toward and sometimes quite contemptuous of women. Although the beginning of the rise of the status of women has been connected with his expressions of submission and devotion to them in his poems,[16] he actually treated the women with whom he came in contact rather shoddily. After sending two wives packing, he had a notorious affair with the *vicomtesse* of Châtellerault, and then, perhaps to placate and honor the *vicomtesse*, he proceeded to marry her daughter to his son. The circumstances of William's life indicate that his attitude toward women may be most accurately reflected in the poem in which he wrote of the distant and adored love, never seen, with whom he could dispense quite easily because of the nicer, prettier, and worthier one he actually knew.[17] All William's literary efforts suggest that he judged a woman's place to be properly in the bedchamber or on a pedestal rather than in the council chamber—that, in short, his feelings about the opposite sex were dominantly sensual and exploitative and fundamentally insecure.[18] William's castoff wives took refuge in and he himself patronized the monastery of Fontevrault, the house founded by Robert d'Arbrissel, in which women prayed while men worked, and over which an abbess ruled supreme.[19] Given William's attitude toward women, it is not surprising that his wives should have found the principles of Fontevrault congenial and comforting. On the other hand, his own benefactions were no greater than the promptings of a minimally aroused conscience might be expected to produce. Furthermore, William either wrote about or actually set up an "abbey" of courtesans at Niort modeled rather tastelessly on Fontevrault, which hardly suggests serious respect for the institution.[20] In any case, authority in the cloister, like activity in the bed, left masculine control of the world's affairs unimpaired.

Eleanor's mother and father were far less flamboyant and impressive, and apparently far more moralistically inclined, than William IX. William X was linked with Cercamon and Marcabru, two poets of *fin'amors* who were not beyond sermonizing and whose outlooks were distinctly more restrained—although not necessarily less misogynistic—than those of William IX.[21] When Eleanor was thirteen, a confrontation between William X and Saint Bernard resulted in the duke's total and humiliating repentance.[22] Two years later William died a penitent and pilgrim before the altar at Santiago de Compostela.[23] In 1137 Eleanor and her younger sister, Petronilla, found themselves alone, since, some seven years before, their mother and their brother, Aigret, had died.[24]

Eleanor became duchess of Aquitaine and countess of Poitou at the same age as her grandfather had become duke and count, and, coincidental as this may be, her later life shows the influence of his traits of character, values, and accomplishments. Like him she was determined, independent, and jealous of any threat to her power. Like him she hungered for Toulouse and spent great effort trying to secure control of the area. Like him she went on crusade. She too supported Fontevrault, but her dedication to the house was different in quality, intensity, magnitude, and duration from that of William, and it seems clear that she found in that citadel of feminine authority a source of inspiration and reassurance. Henry II may, at a later date, have wished and even attempted to put her safely away within its walls,[25] but she was not to be relegated to the status of her grandfather's wives. Her hesitant attitude toward her roles as female and mother may well be connected with William IX's tendency to treat women as objects, an attitude reinforced by the moralizing misogyny of William X's poets. A spirited and sensitive woman exposed to these views might well be led to question the value of and finally reject traditional female goals and to turn to masculine spheres of activity to demonstrate her influence and importance. She certainly did nothing to patronize or propagate the work of the *fin'amors* poets whose views reflected her grandfather's antifeminist biases.

Eleanor's feelings about herself and her sex must have been affected, not only by her grandfather's attitudes, but also by events occurring in the years after her father's death. At first, all went well. William X had provided before leaving on pilgrimage and even at the moment of death[26] that his daughter and all his territories should be put under the guardianship of Louis VI, king of France, and, when news of this decision reached the king, he decided to marry Eleanor to his son Louis.[27] The union, celebrated in the summer of 1137, was advantageous to both parties. Eleanor's control over the restless lords of Aquitaine was established in a manner no other act could have guaranteed, while the monarchy gained power in an area formerly exempt from its control, as well as the prospect of the eventual incorporation into the royal domain of a land whose sovereignty was securely established.[28] Eleanor's husband, little older than herself, had six years earlier been catapulted into the position of royal heir on the death of his older and greatly admired brother Philip,[29] and his handsomeness,[30] his own attraction to his beautiful wife,[31] and the fact that the sudden passing of Louis VI made Louis VII and his bride rulers of France must have made Eleanor content with her new position. Furthermore, the first years of the marriage saw Eleanor's power confirmed, as her husband led expeditions in her interest against Poitiers and Toulouse and as she saw her sister married to the royal seneschal, despite his existing union with a woman of the house of Champagne.[32]

There were, however, darker sides to the picture. Eleanor resented rival influences , and she openly derided Thierry Galeran, an adviser Louis had inherited from his father.[33] Thierry was a eunuch, and her animosity against him may be attributable not only to his sway over her husband but also, at a deeper level, to her own barrenness. For, although Eleanor had become pregnant soon after her wedding, she had aborted, and the marriage had subsequently been sterile. Eleanor did not voice her despair until an interview with Saint Bernard in 1144, when she cried out to him that the Lord had sealed her womb,[34] but her interest in armies, expeditions, rivalries, and intrigue may have been a defensive shield raised against the discouragement and self-doubt caused by her failure to produce a child. Her self-confidence was also undermined in 1142 and 1143, when her sister was excommunicated, when France was put under interdict, when a campaign against the count of Champagne resulted in the awful holocaust of Vitry. She and Louis were shaken by these events, and the way was paved for the negotiation of a settlement. The consecration of Saint-Denis in June 1144 was important, not only because it saw the conclusion of a peace involving king, church, and count, but also because it brought Eleanor into contact with Saint Bernard, who promised her that, if she worked for peace, she would bear a child. The prophecy was fulfilled, and within a year Eleanor had a daughter. It is perhaps indicative of Eleanor's attitude toward herself and her femininity that the daughter was given the majestic name Marie, after the queen of heaven, mother of Christ, and chief patron of the house of Fontevrault.[35]

Maternal concerns could not fully occupy Eleanor, and her decision to take the cross and accompany her husband on crusade, made in the spring of 1146, was probably the culmination of interest in the expedition aroused at the time it was first discussed, in December 1145.[36] Without the support of Louis VII the expedition would never have been launched,[37] and it is difficult to imagine that the granddaughter of William IX would not have been an enthusiastic advocate of a project in the tradition of William's earlier enterprise.

Eleanor was twenty-five when the crusading army left for the East in the summer of 1147, and the two years between the army's departure and its return marked for her a period of readjustment of ambition and perspective. In Constantinople she was exposed to the glories of the Byzantine court; later she encountered the dangers of battle; in Antioch she renewed acquaintance with her uncle Raymond of Antioch, only eight years older than herself, a handsome, cultivated prince.[38] Ties of sympathetic affection at once developed between them, and in Antioch they were constantly together, arousing, it was said, the king's suspicions.[39] The nature of the suspicions and their foundation in fact are at this remove impossible to fathom, but, when Louis determined to depart for Jerusalem rather than assist Raymond in attacking other objectives, it became clear that Raymond did not want to be separated from Eleanor, nor she from him. Louis insisted that she come, and he was met with her stinging retort that their relationship was totally illicit because of the blood ties linking them. The king might well have left her on the spot had it not been for his counselors, particularly Eleanor's enemy Thierry Galeran. They convinced the king to take a firm stand and force Eleanor to accompany the royal host. The queen was bested, and the incident gives a foretaste of later occasions on which her aggressive, headstrong determination resulted in decisive, if temporary, defeat.

However fiery her attack on Louis, Eleanor was outwardly docile for the next four years. She accepted the peace the pope arranged between Louis and herself on their return to the West, and she dutifully produced another daughter, Alix.[40] As in the case of the confinement later imposed on her by Henry II, however, Eleanor's compliance between 1148 and 1152 was only superficial. The patience, calculation, and tenacity with which she awaited the opportune moment to assert herself were as evident then as they would be between 1174 and 1189. Her chance came after the death of the influential Abbot Suger in January 1151, when, in the following summer, her path crossed that of the young, energetic

Henry Plantagenet,[41] and when, in the fall of 1152, the death of Henry's father, Geoffrey, made him count of Anjou.[42]

Physical attraction and a thirst for power drew Eleanor and Henry together, despite the eleven-year difference which separated the queen and the young count. Eleanor's prestige, authority, and widespread holdings offered Henry the prospect of valuable and much-needed assistance, for he was determined to win the kingdom of England, a goal he had cherished for a decade, since he was nine.[43] For Eleanor, attachment to Henry meant the likelihood that she would simply exchange one royal title for another; it also meant that Aquitaine would be disengaged from Capetian control and would once more be truly sovereign territory. Eleanor may have hoped and expected, by virtue of her age and established position, to be able to dominate Henry, but in making her assessment of the situation she would have been well advised to consider Henry's background and consequent expectations. Disquieting as his line's alleged descent from Satan may have been, other, more easily verifiable facts might have given her pause.[44] Henry was the product of an alliance remarkably similar to the one he would have with Eleanor. His mother, Matilda, heiress of Henry I of England and widow of the Emperor Henry V, was eleven years older than his father when she married the fourteen-year-old Geoffrey; but, despite his wife's seniority and status, Geoffrey had at once asserted himself. Having dispatched her to Rouen, he received her back only under pressure exerted by the barons of England.[45] From that point on Matilda was clearly subordinate to the husband to whom she bore three sons, although—as would later be true of Eleanor—she eventually emerged to advise her son during the fifteen years she lived after her husband's death.[46] Henry's attitude toward marriage, wives, and women in general was, as later events showed, indelibly affected by his father's example, and he may well have hoped from the outset to be able to control Eleanor as his father had managed his own mother.

Eleanor was a curious blend of impulsiveness and calculated shrewdness. By the time she and Louis VII decided to separate, she seems to have known precisely what she would do when the divorce was final.[47] The marriage was dissolved in March 1152, and Eleanor at once left her husband of fifteen years and her two daughters, then seven years and eighteen months old, to return to Poitiers. Having escaped the clutches of two lords (one of them Henry's younger brother Geoffrey), each of whom wanted desperately to make her his,[48] Eleanor quickly sent messengers to Henry to tell him that she was free and that she wished to marry him.[49] Henry hastened to her—inspired, according to Gervase of Canterbury, primarily by a desire for her *dignitates*—and on May 18, 1152, the two were married.[50]

Henry had the anger of Louis VII to face and the kingdom of England yet to conquer,[51] and he was intelligent enough to move cautiously in establishing his relationship with Eleanor. He may have introduced his former tutor into her household as chancellor before the end of 1152,[52] but he did not assume the title of duke of Aquitaine until early 1153,[53] after having left Eleanor pregnant on the Continent and having achieved his first victories over his rival's forces in England. Military success bolstered his self-assurance, as did the birth in August 1153 of a son, named William after both Henry's and Eleanor's ancestors.[54] The death in the same month of the eldest son of Henry's English opponent, King Stephen, also advanced his cause.[55] In November 1153 the Treaty of Winchester assured him that England would one day be his, and in January the barons of England did homage to him.[56] Then, having through his own efforts secured his position in England, he turned his attentions to Eleanor and at Easter 1153 brought her from Poitiers to Normandy.[57] The move north signified a subtle shift in the balance of power between them, and the shift increased when Stephen died in October 1154 and when, in December, Henry and Eleanor were crowned king and queen of England.

Eleanor was again pregnant, and on November 6, 1155, she bore another son, Henry. Childbirth dominated the next years, and the speed with which child followed child—Matilda in 1156, Richard in 1157, Geoffrey in 1158, Eleanor in 1161, Joanna in 1165, and John in 1166— suggests that Eleanor was not nursing her children herself, although mothers of the higher classes sometimes did so in the late twelfth century.[58] On the other hand, Eleanor does not seem to have been a completely neglectful mother, for on her frequent travels selected children, generally the eldest, often accompanied her.[59]

Eleanor's involvement with her offspring was, however, subordinate in importance to the political activity she loved. During the years when she was having children she was most formally involved in government, for it was then that she served as official regent of England when Henry was abroad.[60] She was also doubtless responsible for the campaign against Toulouse undertaken in 1159 by Henry II, repeating the similar move made by Louis VII when Eleanor was his wife, and with as little success. The resentment caused by the expedition made Henry regret his involvement with Eleanor's ambitions, and no impulse to advance her claims moved him again until 1173. Then, shortly before the outbreak of the rebellion of Eleanor and their sons, Henry secured for himself, his eldest surviving son, Henry, and Richard, as count of Poitou, the homage of the count of Toulouse.[61] Eleanor may well have been angered at being excluded from the transaction—and also at the fact that Toulouse was not attached directly and exclusively to Aquitaine. The rebellion erupted remarkably quickly afterward, and it seems likely that the ceremony increased Eleanor's determination to incite her sons to rise.[62]

These events lay ten years in the future in 1163, the year when Eleanor's formal involvement in the government of England apparently ended.[63] Between 1163 and 1170 Henry, then in his thirties, was in his prime. Involved in the Becket affair, he firmly controlled the decisions that were made, as Eleanor was relegated to less centrally important functions, appearing at Christmas courts, traveling, producing her daughter Joanna and her last son, John.[64] The decision to name these last two children after the patron saint of the male house of Fontevrault—rather than give them traditional family names associated with Henry's or Eleanor's ancestors—may well reflect a desire on Eleanor's part, prompted by her decreased political importance, to assert, in some small way, her continued influence.[65]

In 1168 came a striking change, as, at Henry's wish, Eleanor assumed active and authoritative control of her duchy of Aquitaine. She was then forty-six, and the thirty-five-year-old, virile, and assertively amorous ruler must have been delighted to see his wife occupied abroad, leaving him to pursue undisturbed his own interests, political and amatory.[66] From this time on, Eleanor's ambitions were centered on her children and their fortunes, and she seems to have been more concerned with using them to attack Henry than with guiding and supervising their development. Traditionally maternal impulses were even less apparent then than earlier, and her last child, John, was sent off to Fontevrault for five years before being lodged in his brother Henry's household.[67] The unsettled circumstances of John's first years could hardly have failed to affect his sense of self-confidence and trust, even if we assume with Green that it was on the whole better for a child of Eleanor's to be protected from, rather than exposed to, her oversight.[68] In any case, whatever its impact on John, the move meant that Eleanor was free to indulge in the maneuvers she most enjoyed.

In January 1169 Henry divided his Continental territories among his sons, and Eleanor was doubtless delighted to see her sons endowed with titles and territorial claims, as her daughters were being engaged and married to such powerful princes as Henry of Saxony, Alfonso of Castile, and William of Sicily.[69] The twelve-year-old Richard was assigned Aquitaine as his portion, and he became his mother's companion and consort in the duchy.[70] In June 1170 Eleanor supported the coronation of the young Henry at York,[71] and later events show the practical value, for her schemes to undermine her husband's authority, of having her son a crowned and anointed king, a practice which followed Capetian rather than English tradition. In sum, 1170 was a bad year for Henry II, for December brought the murder of Becket; but the king's miscalculation in having his ambitious son crowned was Eleanor's good fortune. Her position was further strengthened with the young Henry's second, incontestably legitimate coronation in the fall of 1172.[72] By the spring of 1173 the young king had taken refuge with Eleanor's first husband, Louis VII of France, and then began the war which resulted in Eleanor's imprisonment in England in 1174.

This account of Eleanor's concerns between 1168 and 1173 is a rather somber one, overcast by strains of jealousy, rancor, and intrigue. Others have presented a quite different account, depicting the queen presiding over a glorious court at Poitiers, surrounded by her French daughters (neither of whom is in fact known ever to have been there) and her other children, involved in what Régine Pernoud has called "the keen and subtle arguments of the courts of love."[73] Richard le Poitevin's lament, written during Eleanor's captivity, provides convincing testimony that Eleanor's entourage was on occasion a pleasant company, enjoying music and other beguiling pastimes;[74] serious love affairs and chance amours surely flourished;[75] over dinner and in the royal halls there was certainly gossip, as well as discussion of the etiquette and protocol of love. Still, there is no evidence that talk about these matters was institutionalized into formal "debates on courtly love presided over by a noble Lady."[76]

The dicta cited in Andreas Capellanus's treatise on love are not conclusive on this question, and in any case the book is pointedly humorous and ironic.[77] The statements attributed to Eleanor herself, in view of their inescapable relevance to the facts of her own life, must have amused those who read them, who were doubtless acquainted with the gossip and abusive tales told of her and her activities, notably by Gerald of Wales.[78] That noble birth is no guarantee of *probitas*; that a lover who claims to be deserting his lady for a new love may simply be testing his lady's faith and constancy; that a woman should refuse to love an unworthy younger man in hopes of improving his character if she can have instead an older knight of proven worth; that love between those too closely related is wrong and illicit[79]—all these judgments have unmistakable pertinence to Eleanor's career. She was a noble princess whose own virtue was a subject of dispute,[80] whose two royal husbands—both of them her close relatives, and one much younger than she— brought her only grief, and whose second husband's shocking exploits with his mistress in England while his wife was on the Continent were notorious. In view of Eleanor's sad experiences, the pronouncements could hardly have been viewed as precepts about how to love, but must have been seen as advice about what sorts of relationships were best avoided. The irony of the whole book and its linkage with Eleanor's own life is established beyond much doubt by the single date it contains—May 1, 1174[81]—when Marie de Champagne, Eleanor's daughter, is said to have written a detailed letter to the noblewoman A. and to Count G., affirming that love cannot exist between man and wife.[82] What better testimony to the wisdom of this judgment than the fact that in the spring of 1174 Eleanor—whose French name, Alienor, begins with the letter A—was being held by her husband in close guard at Chinon before being sent ignominiously to England early in July?[83]

If Andreas's book is rejected as a reliable source of evidence, there is nothing else to support the thesis that Eleanor was occupied with games of amatory debate between 1168 and 1173. Furthermore, there is no indication that at this or any other time she was a leading patron of literature and art, and it seems rather to have been her husband Henry II who enjoyed preeminence as a promoter of culture.[84]

In supporting and perhaps initiating the rising of 1173,[85] Eleanor had gone too far, and Henry's decision to keep her under surveillance in England is understandable. If at first he contemplated divorcing her he shrewdly decided against this course of action, perhaps remembering the problems which separation had caused for Louis VII.[86] He also rejected any thoughts he may have had of putting her away as a nun at Fontevrault.[87] Although her earlier plottings connect her inescapably with it, captivity meant that she cannot have been personally associated with the war among her sons which occurred in 1183 and which ended only with the death of the young Henry on June 11, 1183.[88] Henry may have expressed as a dying wish the hope that his father would release Eleanor, but the king was too clever to do this. Eleanor was permitted to tour her dower lands, but, since she was immediately returned to confinement, it seems clear that Henry II calculatedly staged the tour to defend himself against French claims involving dower rights of young Henry's widow, the sister of Philip Augustus of France.[89] In 1184 Eleanor appeared at court several times, to see her daughter Matilda, in exile in England with her husband, Henry of Saxony, and to hear the news of Henry's successful intervention on their behalf,[90] but she was brought forth at Henry's command, to do his pleasure and witness his triumphs. The next year Henry summoned her to Normandy, and her usefulness to him—as well as the awe with which she was still viewed—was again demonstrated when, after ordering Richard to restore Poitou and its appurtenances to Eleanor, Henry warned him that, if he delayed, "the queen his mother would lay waste all his lands with a great army."[91] The threat had its intended effect, and Richard immediately capitulated.[92]

Eleanor did not return to England until 1186, and little is known of her life over the next three years. There is no indication that she enjoyed complete freedom, but she continued to influence her sons, as, in 1188, Richard took up her vendetta against Toulouse, attempting to conquer the county in his mother's name.[93] Even more to her taste, shortly after this, Richard and John joined in a final conspiracy with Philip Augustus against Henry II, who died, disheartened and beaten, in July 1189.[94] The king's feelings about his wife at the end of his life are unknown, but his burial at Fontevrault—a place, according to Gerald of Wales, "obscure and by no means suited to such great majesty"[95]—signified her final triumph over him.

Henry's death brought Eleanor's release, and William Marshal recorded that on his return to England he found her "*delivree*" and in a better state than she had been for some time.[96] She immediately proceeded on a ceremonious perambulation with her royal court; and, in an act whose relevance to her own misfortunes is clear, she ordered general, if quite controlled, amnesty for prisoners;[97] she also commanded that all free men in the kingdom should swear oaths of fealty to Richard as their liege lord.[98] Before Richard returned to England she seems to have been chiefly responsible for governing the kingdom, supervising defense and the administration of justice, and intervening through the justiciar as she saw fit.[99]

These actions foreshadowed the influence Eleanor exercised throughout Richard's reign. If her fifties and early sixties had been spent in a deferred, involuntary moratorium, her late sixties and early seventies saw her compensating for the long period of enforced inactivity and subjugation with a burst of what psychologists might call hypergenerativity. Her power reached its apogee, and some of her deeds fulfilled and even surpassed the goals cherished by her late husband.

After being invested in December 1189 with a grand array of dower lands,[100] Eleanor demonstrated her influence over Richard before he left on crusade—perhaps in hopes of increasing her own scope for action—by persuading him to dispense John from an oath not to return to England for three years following Richard's departure.[101] In an even grander display of her power in matters domestic and political, she then arranged, and perhaps personally negotiated, the marriage of Richard and Berengaria, daughter of the king of Navarre. Thus she set aside his long-standing engagement to Alice, daughter of Louis VII and sister of Philip Augustus.[102] If Henry II had, as the gossips said, actually dallied with Alice, Eleanor may have been motivated by disgust and spite. The move, however, also gave notice that her son could afford to brook the displeasure of Louis VII's son Philip, and the detention of the rejected Alice until 1195 also flaunted Richard's independence.[103] Equally important, on quite another level, the marriage with Berengaria was in the tradition of those alliances forged earlier by Henry II and Eleanor to link their offspring with families outside the orbit of France.

When Eleanor returned to the Angevin dominion from delivering Berengaria to Richard in Sicily, she learned of the troubles John was causing in England. In February 1192 she landed in England, and she acted with prompt and characteristic vigor to bring her wayward son to heel. She and the justiciar informed him that if he went to France—where he could have allied with Philip Augustus, who had abandoned the crusade—they would "seize his lands and fortresses and take them into the king's hand."[104] After Richard had fallen into the emperor's control on his journey home from the East, Eleanor began in February 1193 to exercise direct authority in the kingdom.[105] That she was not invested with formal regency powers is a clear testimony to the undisputable nature of her prestige. She acted as judge, as dispenser of grace and favor, and as supervisor of the realm's defenses.[106] The emotions she felt at Richard's captivity must have been affected by memories of her own imprisonment, and her passionate, wrathful frenzy to secure his release is attested, not only by the enormous sums of money she raised for his ransom,[107] but also by the letters Peter of Blois wrote for her, to stimulate a reluctant pope to intervene. Appealing to him for pity, taunting and deriding him, she called on him and God to come to the aid of Richard, whom she proudly elevated over other mortals by extolling him as "my son, the soldier of Christ, the christ of the Lord, the pilgrim of the crucifix."[108] In these letters Eleanor shamelessly and extravagantly exploited her position as mother and defenseless woman in order to move the pope to do her will.

If Richard was petulantly impatient at the length of his captivity,[109] he must have appreciated Eleanor's efforts on his behalf, for he summoned her to come to him in Germany to preside over his release, which finally occurred on February 4, 1194.[110] Surprising as the idea at first appears, Eleanor may well have advised Richard to do homage to the emperor for the kingdom of England in order to gain his freedom.[111] Her concern for him and for the realm's welfare must have made her anxious to see him speedily released, and John and Philip Augustus were using every effort to try to delay the process. Furthermore, she may have realized that this step would advance the emperor's aim of asserting his power over France, whose king, Philip Augustus, had recently accepted her son John's homage.[112] It would also assure Richard of an ally to help him deal with the threat posed by this alliance. At a deeper level the move can perhaps be viewed as an act of deferred hostility toward Henry II, who had dreamed of seeing himself ruler of the empire and the whole world.[113]

Eleanor returned triumphant to England with her son, and she remained with him constantly until June 1194, when she left the kingdom for the last time. Before this, her eminence was demonstrated at Richard's crown-wearing at Winchester in April 1194, when she, rather than Richard's estranged wife, Berengaria, presided as queen, sitting opposite the king, surrounded by her attendants.[114] And it should not be forgotten that, as the wives of her sons came and went, it was she who received the payment known as queen's gold.[115]

After arranging a reconciliation between Richard and John,[116] Eleanor retired to Fontevrault, the abbey she had often honored with gifts and privileges. If she there performed such decorous acts as granting favors to petitioners,[117] her influence is also reflected in important political decisions implemented by Richard. In 1196 her daughter Joanna, widow of William of Sicily, married Raymond VI of Toulouse, and thus ties of marriage accomplished what armies had been unable to effect. Her hereditary claims to Toulouse were relinquished, but the count of Toulouse promised that he and his heirs would hold certain lands as vassals of the dukes of Aquitaine.[118] In the same year, Eleanor's grandson Otto of Brunswick was invested with the county of Poitou, and in July 1198, through Richard's efforts, he was crowned emperor.[119] Thus a grandson who was ruler of Poitou, the land Eleanor had inherited from her ancestors, became the first Angevin to occupy the throne Henry II had wanted for himself.

The year 1199 found Eleanor in honorable retreat at Fontevrault. The queen had in the last years suffered much. By the beginning of 1199 she had lost all but four of her ten children, and in 1199 she was destined to lose two more. Spring brought the unexpected passing of Richard, who, before dying, summoned his mother to his side, and who was later buried with his father at Fontevrault. Still, the death of "her dearest son" did not defeat her.[120] She proudly led the mercenaries Richard had been commanding north to Anjou, where she devastated the lands of those supporting the claims her grandson Arthur of Brittany was advancing against her son John.[121] Next she conducted a whirlwind tour of her Poitevin and Gascon lands to insure their loyalty.[122] In July 1199 she formally recognized Philip Augustus's overlordship of Poitou, thus emphasizing her own authority in the county. Then she received her son John as her vassal for the land. Stating in the act of transfer that she was making the grant to him as "her legal heir," she clearly suggested that it was he, rather than Arthur, who should properly succeed to the kingdom of England.[123]

In the fall of 1199, Eleanor lost another child, Joanna, wife of Raymond of Toulouse; she too was buried at Fontevrault, among the nuns of the house.[124] Eleanor's vigor was not diminished by this additional blow, and, when a truce was concluded between John and Philip Augustus involving the projected marriage of one of her granddaughters and Philip's own son Louis, Eleanor departed for Castile, where, the chroniclers report, she selected Blanche rather than the elder sister Urraca as Louis's bride.[125]

This was not the last of Eleanor's political activities, for early in 1201 she intervened from her sickbed to preserve for John the loyalty of a powerful Poitevin baron.[126] In the summer of 1202, involved in John's struggle with Philip Augustus and Arthur of Brittany, she found herself besieged by Arthur in the castle of Mirebeau before John came to her rescue.[127] After this triumph, the rest was disappointment and tragedy. In the spring of 1203 she learned of Arthur's death and doubtless heard the rumors that John was responsible for it.[128] A year later came the capitulation of Richard's beloved Château-Gaillard to the French, and within the month Eleanor died, to be buried at Fontevrault, like her daughter Joanna, in the habit of a nun.[129]

Such, then, was Eleanor's life. To its end she remained intoxicated with the exercise of power and political maneuvering, at which she excelled, and the book her funeral effigy shows her reading for eternity must be the book of Kings rather than any gospel, book of hours, or collection of poems. For Eleanor, patronage of the arts and the pursuit of culture were of secondary importance in comparison with the intrigues, political manipulation, and direction of affairs of state into which she channeled her energies.

Eleanor's extraordinary talent for ruling enabled her for sixty-seven years to retain the loyalty of the stormy lands which had come to her from her father when she was only fifteen. Her accomplishments as regent of England before 1163 and as its ruler during much of Richard's reign were impressive. This is not to say, however, that her efforts were always directed toward positive ends. Her dogged, compulsive pursuit of her grandfather's dream of annexing Toulouse was fundamentally misguided and irrational—and in the end unsuccessful. Her passionate pride and jealous dedication to upholding her rights and status led her to undertake and execute vendettas aimed simply at avenging indignities she had suffered. On the other hand, had Eleanor not utilized the determination and tenacity she inherited from her forebears to surmount the challenges her two husbands presented to her, she might not have survived to outlive them both as queen and to triumph in signal fashion over Henry II.

In terms of later events and developments, Eleanor's chief significance can be argued to stem from her role as mother. It was this aspect of her life which affected the attitudes and policies of her sons Richard and John, and through them—particularly through John—the subsequent constitutional development of England. Her children were important to her; but, self-sufficient, self-concerned activist that she was, she tended to view them as instruments of her will, or obstacles blocking its exercise, rather than as individuals to be nurtured and cherished. She never plotted against them as she plotted against her husbands, but the balance and intensity of her loyalties shifted in response to changes in their relative power and usefulness to her.

Both Richard and John possessed traits of character like their mother's, but neither in them nor in any of her other children does there appear the rare combination of qualities which made her the outstanding, able ruler she was. Richard was said to be "spirited and bold in the attack, and determined and pertinacious in executing his plans,"[130] but he lacked his mother's patience and the realistic practicality which marked most of her ventures. The cause of monarchy in England suffered because of this. John inherited Eleanor's determination to tolerate no threat to her authority, but he was even more impatient and injudicious than his brother, and in him the self-confidence and boldness possessed by both Eleanor and Richard were wanting.[131] The paranoia and unprincipled opportunism which were his downfall and England's misfortune are understandable in the light of the rejection and consequent loneliness he must have suffered as a child and the family jealousies he endured as an adolescent; and some, if not most, of the responsibility for this situation is Eleanor's.

But it would be unfortunate to end this assessment of Eleanor's accomplishments on a negative note. Consider, then, her role as grandmother. In choosing Blanche of Castile to be the wife of Louis VIII of France and the future mother of Saint Louis, Eleanor must be credited with providing for France a queen mother very like herself, who was, however, different enough from Eleanor to be able to produce for France a king and a tradition which Eleanor's alliance with the devilish Angevin dismally failed to furnish for England.

NOTES

1. H. G. Richardson, "The Letters and Charters of Eleanor of Aquitaine," *English Historical Review* 74 (1959):193 n.1; cf. idem and G. O. Sayles, *The Governance of Mediaeval England from the Conquest to Magna Carta* (Edinburgh: University Press, 1963), p. 326 n.2.

2. Cf. the comments of Edmond-René Labande, "Pour une image véri-

dique d'Aliénor d'Aquitaine," *Bulletin de la Société des Antiquaires de l'Ouest,* 4th ser. 2(1952):175 n.1.

3. Ibid.; see also Richardson, "Letters."

4. Mary Anne Everett Green, *Lives of the Princesses of England,* 6 vols. (London: H. Colburn, 1849–1855), I, 218.

5. William Stubbs, Introduction to *Memoriale Fratris Walteri de Coventria,* Rolls Series, no. 58, 2 vols. (London, 1872–1873), II, xxviii.

6. Ibid., p. xxx.

7. See F. M. Chambers, "Some Legends concerning Eleanor of Aquitaine," *Speculum* 16(1941):460.

8. Agnes Strickland, *Lives of the Queens of England, from the Norman Conquest,* 6 vols. (London: Bell and Daldy, 1864–1865), I, 169.

9. Richardson and Sayles, *Governance,* p. 326.

10. Alfred Richard, *Histoire des comtes de Poitou 778–1204,* 2 vols. (Paris: A. Picard et fils, 1903), I, 488, esp. n.1.

11. Ibid.; see also II, 53.

12. Alfred Jeanroy, ed., *Les Chansons de Guillaume IX, duc d'Aquitaine (1071–1127)* (Paris: H. Champion, 1913), pp. iii–iv.

13. Régine Pernoud, *Eleanor of Aquitaine,* trans. Peter Wiles (London: A. Michel, 1967), p. 18.

14. Jeanroy, ed., *Les Chansons,* p. iv.

15. See Reto R. Bezzola, *Les Origines et la formation de la littérature courtoise en Occident (500–1200),* vol. 2, *La Société féodale et la transformation de la littérature de cour,* part 2, *Les Grandes Maisons féodales après la chute des Carolingiens et leur influence sur les lettres jusqu'au xii*^{e} *siècle,* Bibliothèque de l'Ecole des Hautes Etudes, Sciences Historiques et Philologiques, no. 313 (Paris: H. Champion, 1960), pp. 262–271.

16. Ibid., pp. 306–311, 314. For the relationships among William IX's grandmother, mother, and father, which may well have influenced his own attitude toward women, see ibid., pp. 259–261.

17. Jeanroy, ed., *Les Chansons,* pp. 7–8.

18. The biography of William IX describes him as "uns dels majors cortes del mon, e dels majors trichadors de dompnas [one of the great courtly men of the world, and one of the great deceivers of women]," and says that he "anet lonc temps per lo mon per enganar las domnas [traveled long throughout the world to deceive women]" (Jeanroy, ed., *Les Chansons,* p. 30). (Translations are mine unless otherwise indicated). Cf. the comments of Bezzola, *Les Origines,* II(2), 306, and of Moshé Lazar, *Amour courtois et Fin'amors dans la littérature du XII*^{e} *siècle,* Bibliothèque Française et Romane, Section C, Etudes Littéraires, no. 8 (Paris: C. Klincksieck, ca. 1964), p. 69. For a probing and stimulating assessment of William's poems, see the summary of the paper presented by Judith Davis at the Eighth Conference on Medieval Studies, April 29–May 2, 1973, at Western Michigan University, Kalamazoo, "Guillaume IX d'Aquitaine, *Homo ludens* and Uncourtly Lover," in "Abstracts of the Papers," mimeographed (Kalamazoo: Western Michigan University, 1973), no. 2, pp. 94–95; see also Pierre Belperron, *La "Joie d'amour," contribution à l'étude des troubadours et de l'amour courtois* (Paris: Plon, 1948), pp. 35–44. For William's deferential attitude to-

ward women, see the classic poem no. IX (Jeanroy, ed., *Les Chansons*, pp. 21–24).

19. Bezzola, *Les Origines*, II(2), 286–287; Richard, *Histoire*, I, 473–474; J. Daoust, "Fontevrault," *Dictionnaire d'histoire et de géographie ecclésiastiques*, ed. A. Baudrillart et al. (Paris, 1909–), XVII, 961–962.

20. Bezzola, *Les Origines*, II(2), 293; cf. Jeanroy, ed., *Les Chansons*, p. ix.

21. Lazar, *Amour courtois*, pp. 37–38, 78–79; Bezzola, *Les Origines*, II(2), 317–318, 320–321; Belperron, *La "Joie d'amour,"* pp. 105–121; Alfred Jeanroy, ed., *Les Poésies de Cercamon* (Paris: Librairie ancienne Honoré Champion, Edouard Champion, 1922), no. IV; pp. iv–vi; J.-M.-L. Dejeanne, ed., *Poésies complètes du troubadour Marcabru*, Bibliothèque Méridionale, ser. 1, no. 12 (Toulouse: E. Privat, 1909), nos. IX, XIX, XXXVII, XL, XLIV; p. 2.

22. *S. Bernardi Vita Secunda*, ed. Jean Mabillon, rev. J.-P. Migne, in *Patrologia latina*, ed. J-P. Migne (Paris, 1844–1864), CLXXXV, cols. 503–506. It is possible that, at some time in Eleanor's childhood, William X may have clashed unsuccessfully with his father over William IX's affair with the *vicomtesse* of Châtellerault; see, however, Richard, *Histoire*, I, 478 n.2, and cf. Bezzola, *Les Origines*, II(2), 271.

23. Richard, *Histoire*, II, 45, 51.

24. See ibid., pp. 18 and 45, for the fact that no act refers to Eleanor's mother or brother after March 1130.

25. Gerald of Wales, *De Principis Instructione Liber*, vol. 8 of *Giraldi Cambrensis Opera*, ed. G. F. Warner, Rolls Series, no. 21 (London, 1891), p. 306.

26. Abbot Suger, *Vie de Louis VI le*

Gros, ed. Henri Waquet (Paris: Société d'Edition "Les Belles Lettres," 1964), p. 280: ". . . antequam iter aggrederetur et etiam in itinere moriens, filiam . . . desponsandam totamque terram suam eidem [the king Louis VI] retinendam et deliberasse et dimisisse [before he set forth and even on his journey, at the moment of death, he delivered and entrusted to him (Louis) his daughter to be married and his lands to be guarded]."

27. See ibid., p. 282, for a description of the coronation of Eleanor *diademate regni* (with the diadem of the kingdom) and the marriage.

28. See Pierre Chaplais, "Le Traité de Paris de 1259 et l'inféodation de la Gascogne allodiale," *Le Moyen Age* 61(1955):121–137. Note, too, that Robert de Torigni attributes Louis VII's anger at Eleanor's marriage to Henry to the fact that "habebat enim duas filias de ea, et ideo nolebat ut ab aliquo illa filios exciperet, unde praedictae filiae suae exheredarentur [he had two daughters by her, and he had no wish that she should have sons by another, for thus his own daughters by her would be disinherited]" (*Chronique de Robert de Torigni*, ed. Léopold-Victor Delisle, 2 vols. [Rouen: A. Le Brument, 1872–1873], I, 260–261). It seems clear that Louis's concern involved Aquitaine's ties with France as well as his daughters' future.

29. Suger, *Vie*, p. 266.

30. Ibid., p. 268; Suger calls him *pulcherrimum* (most handsome).

31. See the passages quoted by Labande, "Pour une image," p. 185 n.45, and p. 190 n.71. See also William of Newburgh, *Historia Rerum Anglicarum*, vol. 1 of *Chronicles of the Reigns of Stephen, Henry II, and*

Richard I, ed. Richard Howlett, Rolls Series, no. 82 (London, 1884), p. 92.

32. Labande, "Pour une image," pp. 178–179.

33. John of Salisbury, *Historia Pontificalis: Memoirs of the Papal Court*, ed. and trans. Marjorie Chibnall (London: Thomas Nelson and Sons, 1956), p. 53: "Erat inter secretarios regis miles eunuchus quem illa semper oderat et consueuerat deridere, fidelis et familiarissimus regi, sicut et patri eius antea fuerat, Terricus scilicet Gualerancius [there was one knight amongst the king's secretaries, called Terricus Gualerancius, a eunuch whom the queen had always hated and mocked, but who was faithful and had the king's ear like his father's before him]" (Chibnall's translation). See also Labande, "Pour une image," p. 185 n.45.

34. Labande, "Pour une image," p. 180 n.25.

35. Ibid., pp. 179–180.

36. See William of Newburgh, *Historia*, p. 92, for the suggestion that Louis encouraged his wife to join the expedition.

37. Virginia G. Berry, "The Second Crusade," in *The First Hundred Years*, ed. Marshall W. Baldwin, vol. 1 of *A History of the Crusades*, ed. K. M. Setton (Madison: University of Wisconsin Press, 1969), pp. 468–469.

38. Labande, "Pour une image," pp. 182–184; Pernoud, *Eleanor*, p. 52.

39. Labande, "Pour une image," pp. 185–186; John of Salisbury, *Historia*, pp. 52–53.

40. Labande, "Pour une image," pp. 187–191; John of Salisbury, *Historia*, pp. 61–62.

41. See Robert de Torigni, *Chronique*, I, 255, for the peace arranged in the late summer at Paris between Geof-frey Plantagenet and his son Henry, on the one hand, and Louis VII, on the other. At that time Henry did homage to Louis for Normandy.

42. Labande, "Pour une image," pp. 191–193; Robert de Torigni, *Chronique*, I, 256.

43. A. L. Poole, *From Domesday Book to Magna Carta 1087–1216*, vol. 3 of *The Oxford History of England*, ed. G. N. Clark (Oxford: Oxford University Press, 1951), p. 161. Cf. the comments of Gervase of Canterbury, quoted in Labande, "Pour une image," p. 198 n.106.

44. For these stories, see Gerald of Wales, *De Principis*, pp. 301, 309; cf. W. L. Warren, *King John* (New York: Norton, 1961), p. 2.

45. Poole, *Domesday Book*, pp. 128–129.

46. Ibid., p. 326 n.6; Geneviève François-Souchal, "Les Emaux de Grandmont au XIIᵉ siècle," *Bulletin Monumental* 121(1963):131, 137.

47. See Labande, "Pour une image," p. 193, for the installation of Eleanor's men in the duchy of Aquitaine in the spring of 1152. For Eleanor's calculation in selecting Henry as her future husband, see William of Newburgh, *Historia*, p. 93. Robert de Torigni, taking a different and more tentative approach, says that Henry married Eleanor "sive repentino sive praemeditato consilio [either impetuously or premeditatedly]" (*Chronique*, I, 260).

48. Labande, "Pour une image," p. 197 n.104; the other aggressive suitor was Thibaud de Blois.

49. See Labande, "Pour une image," pp. 197–198; cf. William of Newburgh, *Historia*, p. 93.

50. See the passage of Gervase of

Canterbury quoted in Labande, "Pour une image," p. 198 n.106.

51. For Louis's anger, see note 28 above.

52. Richardson, "Letters," p. 193.

53. Z. N. Brooke and C. N. L. Brooke, "Henry II, Duke of Normandy and Aquitaine," *English Historical Review* 61(1946):88.

54. Labande, "Pour une image," p. 199; Richard, *Histoire*, II, 115.

55. Poole, *Domesday Book*, p. 166.

56. Ibid., pp. 165–166.

57. Labande, "Pour une image," p. 199.

58. For evidence that it was considered proper in the twelfth century for a noble mother to nurse her children, see *Le Chevalier au Cygne et Godefroid de Bouillon: Poème historique. . .*, ed. Le Baron de Reiffenberg and Adolphe Borgnet, Monuments pour Servir à l'Histoire des Provinces de Namur, de Hainaut et de Luxembourg, vols. 4–6 (Brussels: M. Hayez, 1846–1854), I, 124–126; Jean Renart, *Galeran de Bretagne: Roman du XIIIᵉ siècle*, ed. Lucien Foulet (Paris: E. Champion, 1925), lines 428–591 (esp. 559–591), 1030–1034, 1106–1123; for background see pp. iii–v. See also Elie Berger, *Histoire de Blanche de Castille, reine de France*, Bibliothèque des Ecoles françaises d'Athènes et de Rome, fasc. 70 (Paris: Thorin et fils, 1895), p. 21. However, as John Benton has pointed out in a letter to me dated May 25, 1973, this practice, however admirable, "must have been *very* rare."

59. See Green, *Princesses*, I, 216; cf. Robert de Torigni, *Chronique*, I, 328, 356, 369.

60. Richardson, "Letters," p. 196; cf. Labande, "Pour une image," p. 204.

61. Poole, *Domesday Book*, p. 330;

Richard, *Histoire*, II, 164–165; Friedrich Hardegen, *Imperialpolitik König Heinrichs II. von England*, Heidelberger Abhandlungen zur mittleren und neueren Geschichte, ed. Karl Hampe, Erich Marcks, and Dietrich Schäfer, vol. 12 (Heidelberg: Carl Winter's Universitätsbuchhandlung, 1905), p. 26; William Stubbs, ed., *Gesta Regis Henrici Secundi Benedicti Abbatis*, Rolls Series, no. 49, 2 vols. (London, 1867), I, 36; Claude de Vic and J.-J. Vaissete, *Histoire générale de Languedoc. . .*, ed. A. Molinier et al., 15 vols. (Toulouse, 1872–1893), VI, 53. William, the first son of Eleanor and Henry, had died in 1156 (Pernoud, *Eleanor*, Ch. 10).

62. For the chronology of these events, see Poole, *Domesday Book*, pp. 332–333.

63. See Richardson, "Letters," p. 197, for the fact that all writs issued in Eleanor's name are dated before Michaelmas 1163; however, see below, following note 105, for a comment on the possible insignificance of this circumstance.

64. Labande, "Pour une image," pp. 202–204; cf. Pernoud, *Eleanor*, pp. 135–149.

65. Cf. Bezzola, *Les Origines*, II(2), 287.

66. It is noteworthy that Henry took this step after the death of his mother, which occurred in the fall of 1167 (François-Souchal, "Les Emaux," pp. 131, 137).

67. Richard, *Histoire*, II, 375.

68. See above, at note 4.

69. Poole, *Domesday Book*, pp. 328–329, 331.

70. Richard, *Histoire*, II, 150.

71. Labande, "Pour une image," p. 205; J. C. Robertson, ed., *Materials for the History of Thomas Becket*, Rolls

Series, no. 67, 7 vols. (London, 1875–1885), III, 103.

72. Stubbs, ed., *Gesta Regis Henrici Secundi*, I, 30 n.8.

73. Pernoud, *Eleanor*, p. 152; cf. Labande, "Pour une image," pp. 206–208.

74. Labande, "Pour une image," pp. 213–214, esp. n.202, where the passage from Richard le Poitevin is quoted in full.

75. See Richardson, "Letters," p. 208 n.3, for the story of Eleanor's ewerer, who became enamored of a married woman and was hanged after being charged with felony by the woman's son.

76. Pernoud, *Eleanor*, p. 152; cf. Labande, "Pour une image," p. 207 n.168. For a refreshingly direct and unprejudiced consideration of the problem, see Paul Remy, "Les 'Cours d'amour': Légende et réalité," *Revue de l'Université de Bruxelles*, n.s. 7(1955):179–197.

77. See the study by D. W. Robertson, Jr., "The Subject of the *De Amore* of Andreas Capellanus," *Modern Philology* 50(1953):145–161, esp. 156, 161; cf. Christopher Kertesz, "The *De Arte (Honeste) Amandi* of Andreas Capellanus," *Texas Studies in Literature and Language: A Journal of the Humanities* 13(1971):5–16.

78. Gerald of Wales, *De Principis*, pp. 298–301.

79. Andreas Capellanus, *De Amore Libri Tres*, ed. E. Trojel, 2d ed. (Munich: Eidos Verlag, 1964), pp. 76–77, 273–274, 278–279; trans. John Jay Parry, *The Art of Courtly Love*, Records of Civilization, Sources and Studies, no. 33 (New York: Columbia University Press, 1941), pp. 66, 168–169, 170. Cf. the assessment of John F. Benton, "The

Court of Champagne as a Literary Center," *Speculum* 36(1961):581.

80. When Gerald of Wales first referred to Eleanor in his *De Principis Instructione Liber*, he called her "nobilis"; in the same section of the book Gerald called Henry II "nobilitatis oppressor" (pp. 59–60). In a later portion, Gerald presented rumors and alleged facts concerning Eleanor's ancestry and career (pp. 298–301).

81. As the Trojel edition makes clear, the accuracy of the date which I have given in my text can be questioned (Andreas, *De Amore*, p. 155 n.1). On the other hand, the weight of the manuscript evidence suggests that May 1, 1174, was the date most commonly assigned to the letter. For the kalends of May—a time of new leaves, flowers, and songs of men and birds—see Joseph Linskill, ed., *The Poems of the Troubadour Raimbaut de Vaqueiras* (The Hague: Mouton, 1964), pp. 185–190; Jeanroy, ed., *Les Poésies de Cercamon*, no. IV, p. 11.

82. Andreas, *De Amore*, pp. 152–155; trans. Parry, *The Art*, pp. 105–107; cf. Benton, "The Court of Champagne," pp. 581–582. On the letter and its significance, see Kertesz, "The *De Arte*," pp. 8, 13.

83. Labande, "Pour une image," pp. 210–211. Without considering any other evidence, Parry concluded on the basis of the letter that it was after this, "in the summer of 1174," that "King Henry came to Poitiers, took Queen Eleanor back to England, where she was imprisoned for a time, and sent the other ladies to their homes" (*The Art*, p. 16).

84. For a lengthy and detailed analysis of Henry's importance as a

literary patron, see Ulrich Broich,
"Heinrich II. als Patron der Literatur
seiner Zeit," in *Studien zum literarischen Patronat im England des 12.
Jahrhunderts*, by Walter F. Schirmer
and Ulrich Broich, Arbeitsgemeinschaft
für Forschung des Landes Vordrhein-
Westfalen, Wissenschaftliche
Abhandlungen, vol. 23 (Köln and Op-
laden: Westdeutscher Verlag, 1962),
pp. 27–203. See also Bezzola, *Les Origines*, vol. 3, *La Société courtoise: Littérature de cour et littérature courtoise*,
esp. part 1, *La Cour d'Angleterre
comme centre littéraire sous les rois an-
gevins (1154–1199)*, Bibliothèque de
l'Ecole des Hautes Etudes, Sciences Historiques et Philologiques, no. 319
(Paris: H. Champion, 1963), and, for a
convenient summary of Bezzola's position, vol. 3, part 2, *Les Cours de France,
d'Outre-Mer et de Sicile au xiie siècle*,
Bibliothèque de l'Ecole des Hautes
Etudes, Sciences Historiques et Philologiques, no. 320 (Paris: H. Champion,
1963), p. 314. See also William Stubbs,
"Learning and Literature at the Court
of Henry II," in *Seventeen Lectures on
the Study of Medieval and Modern History and Kindred Subjects*, 3d ed. (Oxford: Clarendon Press, 1900), pp.
115–155 (lectures given in June 1878);
and Charles Homer Haskins, "Henry II
as a Patron of Literature," in *Essays in
Medieval History Presented to Thomas
Frederick Tout* (Manchester, 1925), pp.
71–77.

It is not clear why Richardson believes that Eleanor "was perhaps more
often absent than present" in Poitiers
between 1168 and 1173 ("Letters," p.
198). Travel, in any case, would not
have prevented her from being "the
presiding genius in a society of
troubadours and knights who lived for

chivalry and love, the tournament and
war" (Poole, *Domesday Book*, p. 333),
cf. Richardson's criticism of this passage ("Letters," p. 198).

85. See Stubbs, ed., *Gesta Regis Henrici Secundi*, I, 42.

86. Gerald of Wales, *De Principis*, p.
232; and, for more reliable evidence,
Labande, "Pour une image," pp. 212–
213.

87. Gerald of Wales, *De Principis*, p.
306. In the will which he drew up in
1182, Henry left two thousand silver
marks to Fontevrault (ibid., p. 192).

88. Poole, *Domesday Book*, p. 341.

89. Stubbs, ed., *Gesta Regis Henrici
Secundi*, I, 305; cf. Richardson, "Letters," p. 198 n.6.

90. Stubbs, ed., *Gesta Regis Henrici
Secundi*, I, 313, 333–334.

91. Ibid., pp. 337–338: ". . . pro
certo sciret, quod ipsa regina mater sua
cum exercitu magno devastare vacaret
terram suam."

92. Ibid.

93. Gerald of Wales, *De Principis*, p.
246; de Vic and Vaissete, *Histoire générale*, VI, 131, 133; Poole, *Domesday
Book*, p. 344; Richard, *Histoire*, II,
243–245.

94. Poole, *Domesday Book*, pp.
344–346; cf. Stubbs, ed., *Gesta Regis
Henrici Secundi*, II, 50, and Gerald of
Wales, *De Principis*, p. 295; see also
Roger of Hoveden, *Chronica Magistri
Rogeri de Houedene*, ed. William
Stubbs, Rolls Series, no. 51, 4 vols.
(London, 1868–1871), II, 362–363,
366.

95. Gerald of Wales, *De Principis*, p.
306: "In loco obscuro tantaeque ma-
jestati longe indebito." Gerald considered it an act of divine retribution that
Henry was buried in the house in which
he had wanted to confine Eleanor long

before she herself had died. In 1170 Henry had planned to be buried at Grandmont, "near the exit of the chapter house, at the feet of the master of the house who was buried there." Those who heard him describe his plans were astounded and said that this would be "contra dignitatem regni sui" (Stubbs, ed., *Gesta Regis Henrici Secundi*, I, 7). I have seen no evidence that Henry II selected Fontevrault as his burial place, and the house was probably chosen for reasons of convenience, since Henry died at Colombières, not far from Fontevrault (Poole, *Domesday Book*, p. 346). For Henry's relations with Grandmont, see François-Souchal, "Les Emaux," pp. 43, 135–142, 150.

96. William Marshal, *L'Histoire de Guillaume le Maréchal, comte de Striguil et de Pembroke, Régent d'Angleterre de 1216 à 1219*, ed. Paul Meyer, Société de l'Histoire de France, Publications, nos. 255, 268, 304, 3 vols. (Paris, 1891–1901), I, lines 9503–9510. It is not clear to me why Richardson rejects the idea that Richard ordered his mother's release ("Letters," p. 200).

97. William Stubbs, ed., *Gesta Ricardi Ducis Normanniae*, in vol. 2 of *Gesta Regis Henrici Secundi*, ed. idem, pp. 74–75: ". . . ut a propria persona sua argumentum eliceret captiones molestas esse hominibus, et jocundissimam animae refocillationem ab ipsis emergere [so that in their own person proof might be furnished that imprisonment is grievous to men and that release from prison most delightfully revives the spirits]." Cf. Roger of Hoveden, *Chronica*, III, 4–5. Although the *Gesta Ricardi* suggests that Eleanor issued all her commands in accordance with her son's instructions, Hoveden's chronicle, which parallels this account,

connects Richard's express mandate only with the regulations enumerating the different procedures to be followed in the cases of different categories of prisoners.

98. Stubbs, ed., *Gesta Ricardi*, II, 74–75; Hoveden, *Chronica*, III, 4–5.

99. Richardson, "Letters," p. 200.

100. Stubbs, ed., *Gesta Ricardi*, II, 99; cf. Richardson, "Letters," p. 211 n.2.

101. Richard was not the only one to succumb to Eleanor's considerable ability to bend people to her will. Richard of Devizes wrote of her, in another context, "Et quis esset tam ferus aut ferreus quem in sua uota femina illa non flecteret [And who might have been so beastly or obdurate that that woman might not have bent him to her will]" (*Chronicon Richardi Divisensis de Tempore Regis Richardi Primi: The Chronicle of Richard of Devizes of the Time of King Richard the First*, ed. John T. Appleby [London: Thomas Nelson and Sons, 1963], p. 60; see pp. 13–14 for Eleanor's intercession with Richard on John's behalf).

102. H. G. Richardson, "The Marriage and Coronation of Isabelle of Angoulême," *English Historical Review* 61(1946):311–313. Richardson does not prove conclusively that the stories concerning Henry II's relationship with Alice have no foundation in fact.

It may be purely fortuitous that Berengaria was "puella prudentiore quam pulcra [a girl more sensible than stunning]," while Eleanor could be described as "femina incomparabilis, pulcra et pudica, potens et modesta, humilis et diserta [an incomparable woman, beautiful and virtuous, powerful and forebearing, humble and eloquent of speech]" (Devizes, *Chronicon*, p. 25).

Eleanor may, however, have selected Berengaria for Richard at least partly because she suspected that Berengaria would pose no threat to her own influence over her son. For Richard's engagement to Berengaria, see Labande, "Pour une image," pp. 218–219. It is probably a reflection of Eleanor's interest in the marriage that Berengaria's dower was composed of Gascon lands (Chaplais, "Le Traité," p. 133; cf. Richard, *Histoire*, II, 301).

103. For Alice's final release, see Hoveden, *Chronica*, III, 303.

104. Stubbs, ed., *Gesta Ricardi*, p. 236: ". . . ipsi saisirent in manu regis omnes terras et castella sua." Cf. Labande, "Pour une image," p. 220 n.233. Richardson states ("Letters," p. 201) that at this time Eleanor was simply acting as "mediator" between John and Walter of Coutances, but the passage in the *Gesta Ricardi* suggests that she was playing an active and centrally important role in the government.

105. Richardson, "Letters," p. 201.

106. Ibid., pp. 201–202; see Devizes, *Chronicon*, pp. 59–60, for the help she gave inhabitants of her dower lands in Ely.

107. Labande, "Pour une image," p. 223; Poole, *Domesday Book*, pp. 364–366.

108. Thomas Rymer and Robert Sanderson, *Foedera, Conventiones . . .* , ed. Adam Clarke and Frederick Holbrooke, 4 vols. (London, 1816–1869), I, 58: ". . . filium meum militem Christi, christum Domini, peregrinum Crucifixi." The letters are printed in *Foedera*, pp. 56–59. In them Eleanor refers several times to Richard as the "christ"—or anointed—of the Lord. See p. 58 for the phrases "respice in faciem christi tui [look on the face of your christ]" and

"adversus christum Domini filium meum [against the christ of the lord, my son]." The possible impact of this terminology on contemporaries is obscured by the conventions governing capitalization observed by Rymer. Excerpts from the letters appear in Labande, "Pour une image," pp. 221–222.

For an affectionate letter which Richard sent to Eleanor from Germany, in which he called her "mater carissima" and "mater dulcissima," see "Epistolae Cantuarienses: The Letters of the Prior and Convent of Christ Church, Canterbury; From A.D. 1187 to A.D. 1199," in *Chronicles and Memorials of the Reign of Richard I*, ed. William Stubbs, Rolls Series, no. 38, 2 vols. (London, 1864–1865), II, 362. His other surviving letters to Eleanor are, however, far more formal (Stubbs, ed., *Chronicles and Memorials*, II, 364–365; Hoveden, *Chronica*, III, 208–210).

109. As Hoveden points out, Richard was in captivity with the emperor for one year, six weeks, and three days; he had previously been imprisoned for three months (Hoveden, *Chronica*, III, 234; cf. Philip Henderson, *Richard Coeur de Lion: A Biography* [London: R. Hale, 1958], p. 199). Whether the poem complaining about the length of his imprisonment which has been attributed to Richard is actually his is impossible to establish; thus, the song may or may not reflect Richard's own feelings about his captivity (Henderson, *Richard*, p. 199; see p. 233 for the other poem which Richard may have written).

110. Richardson, "Letters," p. 202; Labande, "Pour une image," p. 223, esp. n.249.

111. The interpolated passage in which Roger of Hoveden deals with Richard's homage to the emperor for

England is curious, occurring as it does in advance of the section in which Roger discusses the arrangements for Richard's ransom and release; the interpolated passage is never alluded to in the latter section. The emperor's proposal to grant Richard control over Provence—an award which was to include the homage of the king of Aragon and the count of Toulouse—would have appealed to both Richard and Eleanor, and it is not impossible that the coronation planned in connection with the transfer of Provence might have become confused in observers' eyes with a hypothesized infeudation of England (Hoveden, *Chronica*, III, 202, 227; cf. de Vic and Vaissete, *Histoire générale*, VI, 149). There is, however, no reference to any coronation ceremony in connection with the actual release of Richard into his mother's hands, although Hoveden explicitly notes that Richard promised annuities to many imperial subjects "pro homagiis et fidelitatibus, et auxiliis eorum contra regem Franciae [for acts of homage and fealty, and their support against the king of France]" (*Chronica*, III, 234).

As Hoveden shows, Richard's position immediately before his release was precarious, for John and Philip Augustus were busily engaged in negotiations to persuade the emperor to keep Richard in captivity (*Chronica*, III, 229–232). Under these circumstances, Richard might well have agreed to do homage, particularly since, then as later, Richard—and Eleanor as well—must have been aware that it was in their best interest to take any and every step to reduce the likelihood of a Franco-Imperial alliance (Hoveden, *Chronica*, III, 301). It is possible that the emperor was relying on a vassalic bond in 1195, when he encouraged Richard to invade

France, sending him a "coronam magnam auream, et valde pretiosam, in mutuae dilectionis signum [a great gold crown, exceedingly precious, in token of mutual affection]," and when he subsequently asserted his right to approve any peace concluded between Richard and Philip Augustus (Hoveden, *Chronica*, III, 300–302). The problem, however, is far from being resolved, and additional investigation is needed.

112. Labande, "Pour une image," p. 223. See also Poole, *Domesday Book*, p. 366, esp. n.6; Warren, *King John*, pp. 44–45; Geoffrey Barraclough, *The Origins of Modern Germany*, 2d. ed. (Oxford: Basil Blackwell, 1947), p. 199, esp. n.1.

113. See Gerald of Wales (*De Principis*, p. 157), whose statement is supported by the facts assembled by Hardegen in *Imperialpolitik König Heinrichs II*.

114. Richardson and Sayles, *Governance*, p. 153; cf. Richardson, "Letters," p. 203 n.7; Labande, "Pour une image," p. 224.

115. Richardson, "Letters," p. 210, esp. n.4; and see pp. 209–211 for a discussion of the portion of reliefs due to the king which was customarily paid to the queen.

116. Ibid., p. 204. Richardson's difficulties with Eleanor's itinerary can be resolved if the queen is assumed to have been in England rather than on the Continent when the reconciliation was effected. Note that William Marshal does not refer to Eleanor when he discusses the peace (*L'Histoire*, I, lines 10341–10348) and that Roger of Hoveden simply says that the ties between the two brothers were renewed, "mediante Alienor regina matre eorum [through the mediation of their mother,

Eleanor the queen]" (*Chronica*, III, 251–252.

117. Richardson, "Letters," p. 205, esp. n.2.

118. Labande, "Pour une image," p. 224; Green, *Princesses*, I, 360–361; de Vic and Vaissete, *Histoire générale*, VI, 173–174.

119. Poole, *Domesday Book*, pp. 376–377; Barraclough, *Origins*, pp. 209–210; Richard, *Histoire*, II, 299ff., esp. pp. 313–314.

120. Ralph of Coggeshall, *Chronicon Anglicanum*, ed. J. Stevenson, Rolls Series, no. 66 (London, 1875), p. 96; Antoine Perrier, "De nouvelles précisions sur la mort de Richard Coeur de Lion," *Bulletin de la Société Archéologique et Historique du Limousin*, 113th year, 87(1958):37–50, esp. 49–50 for Eleanor's donation to the abbey of Turpenay, made on April 21, 1199, ten days after Richard's funeral, to provide for his salvation. See also Warren, *King John*, p. 48; and Pernoud, *Eleanor*, pp. 245–246; but note that Eleanor did not reserve the expression *carissimum* for Richard, as Pernoud asserts. When Eleanor gave Poitou to John in 1199, she addressed him as "karissimo filio nostro" (Thomas Duffus Hardy, ed., *Rotuli Chartarum in Turri Londoniensi Asservati* [London: G. Eyre and A. Spottiswoode, 1837], I, 30b).

121. Hoveden, *Chronica*, IV, 88; cf. Warren, *King John*, p. 50.

122. Labande, "Pour une image," p. 221; cf. Perrier, "De nouvelles précisions," p. 44.

123. Hardy, ed., *Rotuli Chartarum*, I, 30b: ". . . sicut recto heredi nostro"; cf. Pernoud, *Eleanor*, p. 251; Richardson, "Letters," p. 205. As sovereign ruler of Aquitaine, Eleanor did not do homage for the duchy: see Chaplais, "Le Traité," pp. 121–137.

124. Green, *Princesses*, I, 366–367; Hoveden, *Chronica*, IV, 96. Joanna's son Raymond VII of Toulouse was later buried with his mother and grandmother in Fontevrault (Daoust, "Fontevrault," p. 963).

125. Labande, "Pour une image," pp. 229–230; Pernoud, *Eleanor*, pp. 259–260.

126. Labande, "Pour une image," p. 231; Poole, *Domesday Book*, pp. 380–381; Richardson and Sayles, *Governance*, pp. 323–325.

127. Labande, "Pour une image," p. 232; Poole, *Domesday Book*, pp. 381–382; Pernoud, *Eleanor*, pp. 263–264.

128. Labande, "Pour une image," pp. 232–233.

129. Ibid., pp. 233–234.

130. Gerald of Wales, *De Principis*, p. 246: "Sicut enim animosus erat et audax ad aggrediendum, sic pertinax quoque et perseverans ad perficiendum."

131. For a perceptive, convincing analysis of John's character, see Warren, *King John*, pp. 256–259.

2. Cupid, the Lady, and the Poet: Modes of Love at Eleanor of Aquitaine's Court

MOSHÉ LAZAR

The central and predominant theme in religious and secular literature of the Middle Ages, after the end of the eleventh century, is that of love. Whereas in religious literature the principal character is the Virgin Mary—the heavenly lady—in secular literature it is generally a married woman—the earthly lady, the lady of the troubadours and storytellers and, later still, to some extent, the lady of Dante and Petrarch. This literature is in clear opposition to that of the preceding century, which revolves around the masculine world of Jesus and the feudal warrior. Indeed, epic poetry gives but scant importance to female characters and to the theme of love. In passing from the eleventh to the twelfth century we witness a veritable transformation of society and its manners, a metamorphosis of the collective mentality, a rearrangement of the moral, literary, and esthetic values, a qualitative change in the appreciation of life and its earthly pleasures. Man's destiny is no longer exclusively to serve God and the emperor on the battlefield and in the Crusades. He is henceforth subordinated to a new code of manners, a different mode of loyalty and service, and finds pleasure and reward in courting a noble lady of his choice. Feudal service, warrior virtues, and soldierly language are now succeeded by *service d'amour*, courtly virtues, and poetic expression. "We shall yet talk of this day in ladies' chambers," said the count of Soissons, at the Battle of Al-Mansurah. [1] The historian Marc Bloch quite rightly deduces from this statement that "this remark, the equivalent of which it would be impossible to find in the *chansons de geste*, . . . is characteristic of a society in which sophistication has made its appearance and, with it, the influence of women." [2] This profound change in feudal society came about through the combined influence of various factors—economic, political, and cultural. By the early twelfth century,

social life had begun to be organized outside church circles and sometimes in open opposition to their ascetic trends. After having caught a
glimpse of the richness of the East through Spain and Sicily, which had
already benefited from oriental civilization, the crusaders had discovered
the marvels from across the seas with their own eyes. A new world, bright
and colored, had revealed itself to them: a civilization that was not
Christian, that gave considerable importance to life on earth, that prefer-
red happiness and love to suffering and penitence. Negation of earthly
life was therefore to be replaced by an affirmation of life in this world;
and, whereas the former had resulted in a rich body of literary and
artistic works centered around an *ars moriendi* (art of dying), the latter
would give rise to a mainstream in medieval civilization inspired by an
ars amandi (art of loving). The development of commercial relations with
the East was a predominant factor in the evolution of thought and the
change in manners. Imported goods created new needs, and the taste for
a life of luxury encouraged the formation, outside the church, of an
aristocratic society, indifferent to the ascetic and reformist ideology of
Cluny and other religious orders. Writers and poets soon satisfied the
needs of the new social classes and came to occupy an important place in
the court life which had sprung up around the lords. The aristocracy
needed a social and ethical ideal that would correspond to the change in
manners, and that ideal was to be provided by a close collaboration
between the ladies and the troubadours.

The south of France, indeed, acted as a catalyst and disseminator in
this evolution of the code of sentimental and social behavior among
noble men and women. There the church had always been more lax and
less active than in the north.[3] The clergy's hold on the landowning classes
was almost nonexistent and the latter were able to freely develop an
ideology of love, a code of secular ethics, a joy of living that are first
reflected in the lyric poetry of the troubadours and are later found in
many of the lais and romances of northern France. The influence of
oriental civilization on manners is illustrated by the testimony of the
moralists of the time, who did not fail to note and decry the changes.
Geoffrey of Vigeois, for example, said: "Time was when the Bishop of
Limoges and the Viscount of Comborn were content to go clad in sheep
and fox skins. But today [i.e., in the days of Queen Eleanor] the humblest
would blush to be seen in such poor things. Now they have clothes
fashioned of rich and precious stuffs, in colors to suit their humor. They
snip out the cloth in rings and longish slashes to show the lining through,
so they look like the devils that we see in paintings . . . Youths affect long
hair and shoes with pointed toes. . . . As for women, you might think

them adders, if you judged by the tails they drag after them."[4] Denouncing the moral corruption of the society in the south at the end of the twelfth century, Orderic Vital wrote: "These effeminate men, these dirty libertines who deserve to burn in hell-fire, shed their warrior costumes and laugh at the exhortations of the priests. They spend their nights at banquets of debauchery and drunkenness, in futile talk, playing dice and other games of chance . . . They take pains to please the women with all kinds of lasciviousness . . . Instead of covering their heads with caps they wear ribbons, and their external appearance is the sad reflection of their souls."[5]

The church preached the sacred and indissoluble character of marriage but was incapable of imposing its authority on the aristocracy. Lords and nobles sought their pleasure outside conjugal life, with their concubines.[6] On the whole, marriage for them was merely an economic and political venture: its goals were the expansion of the fief and continuation of their lineage.[7] The women, wealthy heiresses of large fortunes, lived in idleness, unable to find consolation in their beauty or intelligence. Marriage, which had alienated them from their frequently absent husbands—away at crusades, tournaments, or battles—had not brought them love or happiness. It is not without reason, perhaps, that the *mal-mariée* came to play such an important role in the love literature of that time and that the *chanson de mal-mariée* became an important poetical genre. "We should not assume," writes J. F. Benton, "that a literature of loose morals was something which medieval women imposed on their men."[8] Nevertheless, there is reason to believe that the *mal-mariée* sought and found in the love poetry a compensation for her disappointments, a kind of literary revenge. We should always distinguish between extraconjugal love documented by real facts and adulterous love as a literary mode encouraged and inspired by the twelfth-century lady in southern France. "Any idealization of sexual love, in a society where marriage is purely utilitarian, must begin by being an idealization of adultery," writes C. S. Lewis.[9] This idealization inspired certain basic elements of the *service d'amour* of the Provençal troubadours. Many of the social and terminological aspects of this *service d'amour* were modeled on feudal service: by calling his lady *mi dons* (my lord), the troubadour acknowledged her authority as a vassal acknowledges that of his feudal lord. The troubadour thus became, in the realm of poetry and fiction at least, his lady's servant and lover.

It is in this historical, social, and psychological context that one must situate Eleanor of Aquitaine's personal life and her contribution to the shaping and diffusion of the various modes of love which are too often vaguely and confusingly assembled under the rubric *courtly love*. By her origins, her life style, and her activities, Eleanor became a source of inspiration for many poets and writers, a catalyzer of concepts and fashions suited to the new aristocratic society, a mediator between different worlds and cultures, the Herald of Cupid, and the Lady among Ladies.

Numerous essays and articles, many of which resort to mere fantasy or gossip, have for more than a century been devoted to Eleanor of Aquitaine but have failed to convey a truthful portrayal of her personality and her role in twelfth-century political, social, and cultural life.[10] Amy Kelly's historical essay, although dealing more with the political events and intricacies of the queen's lifetime than with her personality, offers nevertheless the most provocative and important reappraisal of Eleanor, whose figure dominated several decades of a cultural renaissance.[11] Kelly's work has been supplemented, and frequently corrected, by two studies deeply anchored in historical and literary source material, namely those by Edmond-René Labande and Rita Lejeune.[12] These scholarly essays present us with a more precise image of Eleanor as both a product and a shaping spirit of her time.[13]

Born in 1122, among the first generation of the troubadours, Eleanor inherited a rich cultural background in which many great figures of her family had played a leading role. Her forebear William the Great, duke of Aquitaine and count of Poitou (993–1030), was the patron of a most important literary center.[14] Her grandfather William IX (1071–1127), the first known troubadour, illustrated in his poetry the basic principles of the new and revolutionary mode of love, that of *fin'amors*, and his own life was a perfect illustration of both his political and his religious independence.[15] Eleanor's father, William X (who died in 1137), if not exactly comparable to these predecessors, patronized nevertheless an illustrious court in which the most important troubadours of the second generation gathered and at which perhaps appeared those storytellers who first brought the "Matter of Britain" to the continent.[16] Under his auspices such works as *La Canso d'Antiocha*, the *Historia Karoli Magni* (by the pseudo-Turpin), and *Le Guide du pèlerin* were composed and gained wide exposure. Eleanor, thus, inherited from her forebears a rich literary tradition and, at the same time, a spirit of liberality and intellectual freedom. In the words of Amy Kelly, "Altogether the mind of the young duchess had been freely exposed to a great variety of ideas and made hospitable to novelty."[17] In this lineage of illustrious and history-shaping men, Eleanor of Aquitaine was soon to become the first woman to orient the spirit and the ideals of a new society in which love songs and romances of love progressively superseded warriors' epics, crusaders' and pilgrims' chronicles. Her own life reflects most of the important changes which characterized the renaissance of the twelfth century and reveals a great lust for life in the midst of a civilization which made death and afterlife the haven of its longings. Southern France, Paris, Antioch, England, and Poitiers are the main locales in Eleanor's life, an intricate life full of personal experiences and actions influential to her society.

While she was married to Louis VII, Eleanor's life in Paris was not suited to her temperament and expectations and had the taste of exile. The epics in *langue d'oïl* and the sermons of Saint Bernard or Suger could not replace the lyrics in *langue d'oc* and the joyous court she had known in the south.[18] Bernard's opinion of her—he considered her to be the evil genius behind some of the king's more unsavory actions—and of women in general certainly did not alleviate her feelings of being a *mal-mariée*. Was she afforded some comfort by jongleurs and troubadours who had followed her to Paris? Some scholars tend to believe so and even assert that there she knew Jaufré Rudel, and that Eleanor is the figure behind the *princesse lointaine* of his songs.[19] These facts are not documented, and we have no reason to accept them. Her intimate circle probably included speakers of *langue d'oc*, and she never ceased to cultivate the literature and songs of her native country. In any case, she would be surrounded by ladies and troubadours when she enthusiastically joined her husband in the Second Crusade, which she did because of her deep desire to escape the boredom of her life, and not because of any real religious motivation. "The bull of Vézelay," writes Kelly, "expressly forbade falcons, hounds, and rich habiliments, and it proscribed concubines, troubadours, and other camp followers. Nevertheless a good many luxuries got across the Rhine . . . Though she doubtless had her chaplain and said her prayers, her entourage was on the whole distinctly secular." Kelly adds that Eleanor had included in her ranks many barons of her provinces, many "friends and kinsmen of Raymond of Antioch, all dreaming of glorious and profitable careers in the Orient . . . with whom Eleanor could express herself in her native dialect . . . There were troubadours among them who, singing of love and beauty, accustomed the queen to moods of grandeur and elation."[20] The events of this long journey to Jerusalem (Eleanor's close relationship with her uncle Raymond of Antioch, her unhappiness with the king, her decision to divorce) and the gossip and legends which followed are well known.[21] But of special interest to us, in this journey, is Eleanor's personal discovery of the Orient, of which she had already had some glimpses through the Hispano-Arabic civilization. She was twenty-five years old; life in Antioch was paradise compared to that in Paris and even to that in her own provinces, and to help her forget the ten years spent in a monkish and ascetic surrounding she discovered a city in which Moslem culture rivaled with Greek and Roman remnants of the past. It is against the background of this journey's experiences that we can understand fully Eleanor's second marriage, to Henry II Plantagenet, the founding of her own literary court, the changes in her life style, the type of works which were dedicated to her or which she sponsored after her return from Antioch,[22] the kind of poetry and romances she inspired, and the modes of love in whose formulation and dissemination she was particularly interested.[23]

Eleanor's role, and that of her family, in the promotion and diffusion of the troubadours' ideology of *cortezia* and *fin'amors* is well known.[24] Apart from Bernart de Ventadorn, who mentions her in four songs, many troubadours gathered now and then at her court; among them, Cercamon, Marcabru, Alegret, Marcoat, Peire de Valeria, Peire Rogier, Bernart Marti, Peire d'Auvergne, and Rigaut de Barbézieux.[25] It was at her court that themes and topics from Ovid's poetry made their way into the troubadours' songs and into the early romances predating those of Chrétien de Troyes.[26] During the formative years of the French courtly romance, Eleanor's court was a melting pot for various folkloric and narrative traditions and a fertile ground for the confrontation or the synthesis of different concepts of love. From Poitiers (1152–1154), through Normandy, Maine, and Anjou (1154, 1158, 1159–1162), England (1154–1156, 1157–1158, 1163–1164), and back to Poitou and Aquitaine (1166–1173), Eleanor's court carried out one of the most enriching cultural exchanges in history. This cross-fertilization has been clearly elucidated by several scholars, among them Jean Frappier[27] and Rita Lejeune. Lejeune writes: "Circumstances had determined that this protector of the arts had a personal court and that this court was very itinerant from 1154 to 1156. Political, economic, and sentimental reasons carried this court (often far from that of the King) in numerous vessels from England, to Anjou, Normandy, and Aquitaine. What could be more natural, therefore, than that her entourage would collect hither and yon, the accounts of the Breton *conteurs*, and even the *conteurs* themselves?"[28] But Eleanor's role and, later, that of her daughter Marie de Champagne did not consist only in being cultural intermediaries or passive patrons of literary works. They were passionately interested in certain modes of love, which we will try to elucidate, and were strongly opposed or at least resistant to others. There is no doubt that the poetry of the troubadours, the *Lais* of Marie de France,[29] the *Tristan* by Thomas,[30] the *Lancelot* by Chrétien de Troyes, and other similar works corresponded more to their taste than *Erec* and *Cligés* by Chrétien, or *Eracle* and *Ille et Galeran* by Gautier d'Arras.

The various modes of love illustrated in medieval literature, from the twelfth to the fourteenth century, have often been described by a single concept: *amour courtois* (courtly love). This term, never employed by the medieval writers, was coined by Gaston Paris in his essay on *Lancelot* [31] and has since then served most medievalists to characterize a variety of contradictory modes of love. When one looks at studies on the love literature of the Middle Ages, one is struck by the great confusion which reigns in the use of such ill-defined terms as *courtoisie* (courtliness) and *amour courtois*. They are used as though it were possible to lump together all the periods of the Middle Ages and to interchange the order of authors and works. This confusion has also led to a monolithic evaluation of the nature and meaning of love in medieval poetry and romance, as though the troubadours' ideology of love were identical, for example, to that of the Italian poets of the *dolce stil novo*. [32] The confusion becomes even greater when we find medievalists interchanging the concepts of courtliness and courtly love, as does J. Wettstein when he states: "As is customary, we have used *courtliness* and *courtly love* interchangeably." [33] Without going into a detailed discussion here, let us say that courtliness is the ethical and social ideal of chivalry, a code of good manners, and is not an *ars amandi*, that is, an art or a mode of love. One can be courtly, according to twelfth-century texts, without loving, but one cannot love without being courtly. Must this love which integrates the courtly virtues be labeled therefore *courtly love*? I think not; for, thus defined, the concept of courtly love is not the correct one to qualify the arts of love illustrated in a wide variety of literary works of the twelfth century in France and later in Italy, Spain, Germany, and England. "One of the great disadvantages," writes W. T. H. Jackson, "of a term like *courtly love* is the ease with which it can be stretched to cover many different types and genres." [34] The term in question, no doubt, is too vague and loose. Does it mean love described in "courtly" style by a "court" writer? A passion between lovers who are guided by a code of "courtly" behavior? Love inside the limits of the married couple, or outside of marriage? Love between "young" people (*jovens*) who live in court circles? Although an inadequate concept to circumscribe the various modes of love in medieval literature, should it be considered only as a "modern" invention of a critic? Is it only a "myth" of pseudo-romantic scholarship? [35] I think not. But many scholars in recent years have felt uneasy in using the term *courtly love*, some even qualifying it "an impediment to our understanding of medieval texts," [36] and it has also become fashionable among some medievalists, who follow D. W. Robertson's misleading interpretations, to see courtly-love literature as being conceived and expressed in an *ironic* mode. "I have sought to show," writes Robertson, "that works presumably illustrative of 'courtly love' like the *De Amore* of Andreas Capellanus, or the *Lancelot* of Chrétien de Troyes, or the *Roman de la Rose*, are, in fact, ironic and humorous."[37] It seems rather obvious that, if there is any irony or humor in these texts, it has to do mainly with details in the treatment of certain topics or stylistic devices and not with the constitutive elements of courtliness or with the mode of courtly love. Robertson himself, in an afterthought or rather in an *a parte*, is obliged to concede that "what is being satirized in the works in question is not 'courtly love' at all, but idolatrous passion." Robertson's statements were made at a conference dedicated to clarifying "the meaning of courtly love,"[38] but it seems that some of its participants have not only added to the already existing confusion, while trying to proscribe the concept of courtly love, but have projected into twelfth-century texts characteristic elements from works composed at the last phase of a declining mode and at a time when its topics had reached their ultimate petrification. This phenomenon of "ironization" of literary themes and stylistic devices occurs also in Ariosto's *Orlando Furioso* or Cervantes's *Don Quixote*, but it would be absurd to infer from these texts that the *Song of Roland* or the *Amadis de Gaule* was "ironic and humorous." Anachronistic readings of medieval texts will be of no avail in seeking to comprehend their specific meanings.[39]

Thus, if the concept of courtly love is inadequate to describe the various modes of love existing within medieval love literature, it is because of the inherent false assumption that Lancelot's love should be considered the model of all kinds of courtly love illustrated in a great variety of differentiated literary texts. If the love in *Lancelot* is courtly love, then the kinds of love exemplified in the *Tristan* romance, or in *Erec*, *Cligés*, and *Yvain* of Chrétien, should be excluded from the concept. Even for the twelfth-century love literature in France alone, it seems absolutely imperative to make a clear distinction between *three modes of love* that cannot be reduced to a single common denominator:

1. *Fin'amors*: a new mode of love and the central theme of the Provençal troubadours' poetry, also illustrated in Chrétien de Troyes's *Lancelot* and integrated into Thomas's *Tristan* and the *Lais* of Marie de France.
2. *Passionate love* or *Tristan-love*: a mode of tragic love illustrated by the *Tristan* romance of Thomas, by most of the lais of Marie de France, and including the characteristic and constitutive elements of *fin'amors*.
3. *Conjugal courtly love*: a mode of anti–*fin'amors* and anti–tragic love (or anti–Tristan-love), refusing the adulterous relationship illustrated in the texts of the first and second modes and the idolatrous passion

which binds the lovers. This *reaction* to the first two modes is exemplified in all of Chrétien's romances except *Lancelot* and proclaims a mode of love which, dominated by the rules of reason and the code of courtliness, should lead to marriage and exist only inside marriage.

These three modes of love could also be described, according to their sociohistorical and psychological-cultural contexts, as the *aristocratic mode*, the *mythical mode*, and the *bourgeois mode*.

The aristocratic mode of *fin'amors*, extolled by all the troubadours for over a century, was, from the very start, a doctrine of love that fell outside Christian teaching and was the exact opposite of the traditional view on marriage. It asserts the excellence and superiority of love outside marriage. The poet's invocations, in Provençal songs, are always addressed to a married woman. The latter's husband merely earns the epithets *ugly, jealous, old, dull*, and a few less agreeable ones. For the troubadours, the opposition between *fin'amors* and conjugal love is absolute and irreducible. When they speak of this extramarital love they generally use the terms *fin'amors* (noble or refined love), *amor veraia* or *verai'amors* (true love), and *bon'amors* (excellent love). According to them, this particular love, the only noble and true one, cannot exist between husband and wife. Conjugal relations are contractual relations, not love relations. Love between husband and wife is a question of a social and political contract that makes man the master and woman an asset to be obtained once and for all. At best they can be friends (*amis*), never lovers. On the other hand, *fin'amors* essentially involves anxiety, longing, separations, distance, suffering, unfulfilled desires; the joys it provides are always temporary and threatened. Cupid has struck the fire in the poet's innocent heart, *fin'amors* is a desirable and delectable hell, and the *joy d'amors*, which the lady could grant, is as difficult to reach as paradise. But, as we shall see, this paradise did not always remain a utopian ideal or a Platonic wish.

In order to deserve the married lady's love and favors, the lover must live in complete submission, do what pleases her, accept pain with joy and patience, worship her as an idol, and fear her as a lord. On the other hand, relations between the lady and her lover were not conceived in a spiritual and Platonic context (as has too often been claimed by many scholars), but in an erotic and often carnal framework. Obviously, the troubadour does not always express his carnal desires aloud and openly, but hides behind poetic formulas and behind metaphors elaborated in a hermetic style. In the final analysis,[40] *fin'amors* is a kind of sublimation of extramarital love, a poetic exaltation of adultery.[41] Whether *fin'amors* represented a social reality or only a poetic reality, whether it exalted real experiences or was only a "play" [42]—compensating for frustrations—between the lady and the poet, does not alter its fundamental meaning in the Provençal love songs. Considered immoral and a sin by the church, *fin'amors*, for the troubadours, is the only true and moral love. When they invoke God and the saints it is never in order to confess their sins or express remorse; it is always to ask for help in winning their lady's favors. As a general rule one can say that, in the love literature of the twelfth century, God is always on the side of the adulterous lovers and never on that of the deceived husband. Some troubadours state very clearly that the lady is their earthly paradise and that they would not exchange her for any heavenly kingdom, that God created her to inspire love and be loved, that if her husband ill-treats her she should find ways to avenge herself through a new love. Even in *Aucassin et Nicolette*, the early thirteenth-century *chantefable*, where *fin'amors* is not the mode of love (Nicolette not being a married lady), heavenly paradise is ridiculed as compared to true earthly love. The viscount of Beaucaire, Nicolette's adoptive father, queries Aucassin: "What do you think you would have gained if you had made her your mistress or taken her to your bed? Precious little, for your soul would sojourn in hell for it till the end of time, for you'd never enter heaven." To which Aucassin replies:

What would I do in heaven? I have no wish to enter there, unless I have Nicolette, my own sweet love, whom I love so dearly. For to heaven go only such people as I'll tell you of: all those doddering priests and the halt and one-armed dotards who grovel all day and all night in front of the altars and in fusty crypts, and the folk garbed in rags and tatters and old, worn cloaks, who go barefoot and bare-buttocked and who die of hunger and thirst and cold and wretchedness. These are the ones who go to heaven, and I want nothing to do with them. Nay, I would go to hell; for to hell go the pretty clerks and the fine knights killed in tournaments and splendid wars, good soldiers and all free and noble men. I want to go along with these. And there too go the lovely ladies, gently bred and mannered, those who have had two lovers or three besides their lords, and there go gold and silver, and silk and sable, and harpers and minstrels and all the kings of this world. I want to go along with these, provided I have Nicolette, my own sweet love, with me. [43]

Contrary to the troubadours' *fin'amors*, which is oriented toward the eventual triumph of the lovers and the ultimate joy of love, the romance of *Tristan* of Thomas and the verse narratives of Marie de France illustrate a mode of love that finds its inspiration in Celtic mythology and is dominated by the idea of fate and death. But, like the poems of *fin'amors*, they extol love outside marriage as the only valid and true love, though they always emphasize its passionate nature and the "irrational madness" that binds the lovers. Fate has brought the lovers face to face, and henceforth nothing can separate them; even in death they are united in the same tomb. This love is never the result of free choice. Unlike *fin'amors*, the mode of passionate or tragic love takes no note of concepts of will and reason, joy and measure. The setting of the Tristan story in the framework of destiny, the inevitable course of events which precipitates the lovers to their tragic end, the use of the potion which binds the lovers "against their will," and other characteristics of the lovers' behavior have induced some medievalists to affirm that, contrary to what has been said by others, Béroul's version of the story is the *courtly* one and that of Thomas the anticourtly work. This view, as expressed by Pierre Jonin,[44] for example, is only partly true. The version of Thomas does not pretend to be representative of the mode of courtly love but, on the contrary, is a synthesis of *fin'amors* and tragic love. Bartina Wind's statement that there is something in the lovers' behavior that does not correspond to the rules of courtliness can be accepted without restriction,[45] provided that we bear in mind that the romance of Thomas nevertheless remains in the tradition of *fin'amors*. Indeed, we find in the love songs of certain troubadours, in those of Bernart de Ventadorn for example, a combination of *cortezia, mezura, passion*, and *fin'amors*. Stefan Hofer's assumption that the use of the potion was a device allowing the introduction of an adulterous love into the story[46] must be considered with serious reserve.

The Tristan story, having absorbed in its Celtic framework the main principles of *fin'amors*, must have been known already on the Continent before its literary elaborations by Thomas and Béroul. It appears now that the version of the romance by Thomas, after having matured gradually at Eleanor's court,[47] could have been composed between 1150 and 1160 and was probably commissioned by the queen,[48] while that by Béroul could have been written in an archaic style either between 1165 and 1170 or in the last decades of the twelfth century.[49] Ernest Hoepffner's assumption that the version of Thomas was composed after Chrétien's *Cligés*[50] is absolutely arbitrary, given the violence with which Chrétien opposes the mode of tragic love, which had gained notoriety and public attention only after its elaboration in Thomas's successful romance. Even before appearing in the form of a romance (unless such a verse narrative existed before 1150 and was lost), the story of the tragic lovers Tristan and Isolde was mentioned by several troubadours who were related to Eleanor's or even to her father's court. These mentions by Cercamon, Bernart de Ventadorn, and Raimbaut d'Orange can be dated between 1150 and 1160. Lejeune infers from these facts that there might have existed a Provençal version of the Tristan story before 1150, not only in oral tradition but also in written form.[51] This is an assumption, among others in her study, which would be interesting if more seriously documented. As for the interpretation of the meaning of tragic love in *Tristan*, it seems unacceptable to us to lump all the versions of the legend together (twelfth- and thirteenth-century elaborations) as if they were composed by a single author, which several scholars do, or to explain the story and its components in the light of Wagner's opera and the doctrine of the Cathars, as do Denis de Rougemont[52] and his followers. The meaning of tragic love in the versions of Thomas, Béroul, and Gottfried von Strasbourg has to be studied in the particular framework of each text, with attention to their common source and constitutive elements, in the way we would proceed in studying the meanings of the different dramatic versions of Oedipus, Faust, or Don Juan composed by individual playwrights in various sociohistorical and cultural contexts.[53]

These two views of love, that of *fin'amors* and that of passionate love, shared the favors of the aristocracy in the twelfth century and enjoyed tremendous success. Their influence in the second half of that century affirmed itself clearly in the aristocratic courts of northern France. Educated women, such as Eleanor of Aquitaine and Marie de Champagne, played a determining role in the dissemination of these ideas. However, outside the aristocracy of the north there must have been readers—especially among a certain bourgeoisie that was then gaining ground—who could not accept the sublimation of adultery as ethical. The writer who best understood the nature and meaning of the fashionable views of love and who was to put them in a framework—the better to combat and denounce them—was Chrétien de Troyes. In a series of romances which are not far from being *romans à thèse*, he puts forward for the courtly men and women of his time a conception of love which, while borrowing certain elements from the preceding doctrines, condemns adultery and extols love within marriage. It is therefore correct to speak here of a *conjugal courtly love*.

The harmonious relationship between courtly love and chivalric adventures, the reconciliation of love and marriage—these are the problems that Chrétien de Troyes illustrates in most of his romances. There is only one that does not follow this pattern, *Lancelot*.[54] This romance, which was commissioned by the countess of Champagne, is a perfect illustration of the troubadours' *fin'amors*. Another romance, *Cligés*, is a controversial work that criticizes and unequivocally denounces the idea of passionate love represented by the tragic couple, Tristan and Isolde.[55] Opposite them Chrétien de Troyes places the happy couple, Cligés and Fénice, who find within the framework of marriage a love based on will and reason, a love that crowns the chivalric adventures and triumphs over the torments of passion. In a marriage of love, as conceived by Chrétien de Troyes, husband and wife rigidly observe all the principles of *courtoisie*, the woman becoming the *lady* and the husband her *knight*, and condemn love outside marriage as unlawful and immoral. This view is, therefore, the complete opposite of that presented by the troubadours.

Fin'amors, with its carnal, erotic, and adulterous nature, is a view common to all troubadours without exception. How could this doctrine arise and develop within a society that had been Christianized for centuries? Since it was irreconcilable with the teaching of the church, should one not assume that the love extolled by the troubadours ought to be interpreted, not literally, but, on the contrary, in an allegorical sense? In other words, is it not a spiritual and mystical love? If this were so, this love would be Platonic, and the troubadours' lady, like Dante's Beatrice two centuries later, would be a mediator between man and God. And from there to affirming that the Virgin Mary was the model for the poetic creation of the lady is but a step. The *mater mediatrix* would be the prototype for the *mulier mediatrix*. Finally, if this were truly so, the Middle Ages would again be completely spiritual, purely symbolic.

Allegorical and esoteric commentaries of this kind have been put forward by many medievalists in an attempt to reconcile *fin'amors* with Christian theology. Thus, to quote but a few of the great medievalists, one finds Carl Appel affirming: "There is no doubt here about what *fin'amors* means. . . . It is no longer an earthly love. *Fin'amors* is elevated to the heavens. It is love that addresses itself to God and becomes united with Him."[56] Dimitri Scheludko, speaking of Marcabru's conception of love, writes that he has "identified *fin'amors* directly with divine love."[57] Eduard Wechssler identifies courtly love and the *caritas* of Christian mysticism when he says: "The spiritual ground on which this civilization fed was the Church and Christianity. . . . The troubadours' courtly love borrowed the crown of *caritas*, the cardinal Christian virtue."[58] J. Wilcox, in his article entitled "Defining Courtly Love," writes, "The worship of woman may have been suggested by the worship of Mary."[59] This "Christianization" of the secular love songs of the troubadours and the interpretation of them as religious allegorical poetry dominate particularly the studies by Mario Casella[60] and Diego Zorzi.[61] It seems as if these scholars seek to explain the troubadours' poetry, as theologians did the *Song of Songs*, in a mystical sense.

Medievalists who have upheld the thesis of Christian spirituality and of mystical Platonism in *fin'amors* seem to find the best proof to demonstrate their point in the poetry of Jaufré Rudel, the poet of the *amor de lonh* (distant love).[62] The theme of love for a lady whom the poet has never seen, or has seen only in his dreams, is already found in the first troubadour,

William IX of Poitiers, and before him in universal poetry from earliest times. In principle, therefore, the theme of "distant love" bears no relation to mystical love for the heavenly lady. Will it be objected that in Jaufré Rudel that theme is spiritualized and Christianized? We will now see that this is not so. The only "Christianization" one can speak of is to be found in the esoteric interpretations of the scholars mentioned above.

The three or four poems in which the theme of "distant love" appears clearly show that the poet's declarations of love are addressed to a real woman, not to an imaginary or supernatural being. In one the poet exclaims:

Amors de terra lonhdana   *Love from a distant land*,
Per vos totz lo cors mi dol.   *For you my whole heart aches*.
                                        (poem II, lines 8–9)

The lady is in a foreign land, in another region of France. Why would it be the Holy Land, as one critic has claimed? The poet asks the lady to receive him

. . . d'amor doussana   *. . . with a gentle love*,
Dinz vergier o sotz cortina.   *In the garden or alcove*.
                                        (poem II, lines 12–13)

Let us note immediately that the words *garden* and *alcove*, which are found in every troubadour's work, are always employed in an erotic and carnal context, expressing the secret intimacy to which the lovers aspire.[63]

In another song, Jaufré Rudel clearly indicates the nature and object of his love:

Las pimpas sian als pastors   Let the shepherds keep their pipes
Et als enfans burdenz petitz,   And the children their toys,
E mias sian tals amors   And may I have such loves
Don ieu sia jauzens jauzitz!   In whom I find and to whom I bring
                                     enjoyment!
                                        (poem III, lines 9–12)

But, if the poet is sad, it is because he is separated from his lady, who is afar. Is it an imaginary woman or a supernatural being? The rest of the poem leaves no doubt on this score: the lady is married, her husband is with her, and her lover cannot join her:

Luenh es lo castelhs e la tors   Distant are the castle and tower
On elha jay e sos maritz.   In which she lies with her husband.
                                        (poem III, lines 17–18)

We therefore find here, as in the previous poem, the idea of distance in space, distance caused also by the fact that the husband is with the lady. One must bear this in mind in order to grasp the true nature of "distant love." In addition, if the lady does not grant the lover her favors, if she is haughty and distant with him, is it not a distant love? Could not the true meaning of *amor de lonh* be, in fact, *impossible, unfulfilled love*? The rest of the poem throws light on this point: whereas the lady lies with her husband, the lover lies awake, obsessed by the lady's body:

Et en dormen sotz cobertors	And while sleeping under the sheets,
Es lai ab lieis mos esperitz.	My mind is over there with her [in the desire for her body].

(poem III, lines 35–36)

What he desires is to hold his lady in a "secluded spot" (*luecs aisitz*).[64] In another poem the poet tells us of his joy at being free of a dangerous love, the cause of a nocturnal misfortune, and at having found a new love. In this it has been easy for some scholars to interpret "dangerous love" as "earthly love" and "new love" as "divine love" and to conclude that a sinner has been converted. But, to reach this conclusion, it is necessary to explain all the concrete and realistic details of the poem symbolically. Indeed, what is Jaufré Rudel speaking of? Let us listen to him:

Mielhs mi fora jazer vestitz	T'were better I had slept clothed
Que despolhatz sotz cobertor,	Than unclothed under the sheets,
E puesc vos en traire auctor	And I can cite as evidence
La nueyt quant ieu fuy assalhitz.	That night I was set upon.
Totz temps n'aurai mon cor dolen,	My heart will ever grieve,
Quar aissi·s n'aneron rizen,	For they departed laughing,
Qu'enquer en sospir e·n pantays.	And I am still sighing and distressed.

(poem IV, lines 36–42)

This, therefore, is the very realistic story of a misfortune in love: the lover was surprised one night with his lady, when he was sleeping unclothed under the sheets. The poet's new joy can be explained by this unfortunate love: he has found another woman whom he can love without exposing himself to danger. The rest of the poem even seems to hint that it is a young girl, not a married woman. It mentions a brother whose sister bestows her love upon the poet. In the esoteric exegesis of certain scholars this "brother" and "sister" have become allegorical representations of carnal love and mystical love, Adam and Eve, Jesus and Mary, etc. It is easy to see where such interpretations lead us.

In yet another poem, in which the theme of distant love predominates, we find these lines:

Mas per un ben que me'n eschay
N'ai dos mals, quar tan m'es de lonh.
. . . .
Mas non sai quoras la veyrai,
Car trop son nostras terras lonh.
. . . .
Ja mais d'amor no·m jauziray
Si no·m jau d'est'amor de lonh,
Que gensor ni melhor no·n sai
Ves nulha part, ni pres ni lonh.
. . . .
Qu'ieu veya sest'amor de lonh,
Verayamen, en tals aizis,
Que la cambra e·l jardis
Mi resembles tos temps palatz!

For one good I received from her
I am suffering two ills, so distant is she
   being toward me
. . . .
I do not know when I will see her,
For our lands are too far apart.
. . . .
I will never enjoy any love
If I do not enjoy this distant love,
For I know no nobler or better lady
Anywhere, either near or afar.
. . . .
I long to see this distant love,
Truly, in some secluded spot,
As the alcove and garden
Always seem like a palace to me!
(poem V, lines 10–11, 24–25, 29–32,
39–42)

Grace Frank thinks that "distant love is Jerusalem reconquered rather than an earthly lady"; [65] Jeanroy thinks it is "divine love"; Carl Appel feels it is the Virgin Mary; and so forth. The concrete terms are symbolically interpreted, real characters become allegorical figures, and realistic episodes are not commented upon. Thus, for Appel, the "desired company of the lady is the gathering of blessed souls in paradise or even an earthly community devoted to serving Mary." [66] The terms *garden* and *alcove* are transformed into "cloister cell" and "cloister gardens," etc. But, after all, *amor de lonh* is only a more refined and hermetic expression of *fin'amors*: secret love, love outside marriage. The Virgin Mary and Christian mysticism have no place in this mode of love.

Etienne Gilson, an outstanding authority on the religious thought and mysticism of the Middle Ages, has taken a clear stand against those scholars who have sought to establish an identity between the troubadours' view of love and that of the mystics. He states, quite rightly: "There will always be as many sophisms available as one wishes to justify such a thesis, but it will remain a sophism and for a very good reason—mystical love being the denial of carnal love, one cannot borrow the description of one to describe the other; it is not enough to say that their object is not the same, one must add that they cannot have the same nature precisely because they do not have the same object." [67] And elsewhere he notes: "Discussions of courtly love are sometimes conducted in a most questionable manner. It would appear that from the first troubadour to Dante, authors and works are interchangeable. They are not." [68] Another theologian, Father A. J. Denomy, in his study on the troubadours' *fin'amors* writes: "There is absolutely no need to seek the origins of courtly love among elements as alien to it as the worship of the Virgin Mary. At the time of the first troubadours worship and veneration of the Virgin had not yet reached the peaks of popularity they were to attain later under the influence of Saint Bernard. . . . And even then devotion to and veneration of the Virgin are enough to explain people's worshipping her but not worshipping women in general, nor, in particular, those women who were the object of the troubadours' adulterous love." [69]

Let us now examine one last point: the decline of the troubadours' ideology of love. After having dominated thought for over a century and having influenced the views of courtly love and passionate love, the doctrine of *fin'amors* suddenly became involved, in the late twelfth and early thirteenth centuries, in a violent struggle between the church and a heresy then in vogue, the Catharist heresy, and also in a political struggle between northern and southern France. The Albigensian crusade directed against the heretical communities of the Cathars swept away with it a profane poetry that was already becoming decadent and destroyed southern civilization. The increasing delving of the church into public affairs and the arts, with concomitant threats and condemnations, ended by converting certain poets into religious troubadours. And, as the worship of the Virgin spread, antifeminist works multiplied. One could no longer extol sensual and sexual love for the lady; it was necessary to extol Our Lady. In Malfré Ermengaud's doctrinal poem *Lo Breviari d'Amor*, we read: "Satan, desiring to make men suffer, inspired in them an idolatrous love of women. Instead of adoring their Creator as they ought, with all their heart and all their mind, they had a guilty passion for women whom they made into idols. Therefore, be assured that whoever adores them certainly adores Satan and makes a god of the most disloyal demon Belial." [70] Such a statement would have been inconceivable in the twelfth-century literature at Eleanor's court. It was the fruit of the Albigensian crusade. I even believe that, if the Virgin Mary became the central figure in the religious poetry of the thirteenth and fourteenth centuries, it was because in the twelfth the troubadours had given women a place and attributes that they had not previously had in European civilization. The worship of the lady, without a doubt, influenced the terminology of that of Our Lady. Without the troubadours' lady there would have been no spiritualized and mystical lady of Dante. [71] The ideal of love that the troubadours introduced into a society which had been Christianized for centuries, its adulterous nature, and its ethic were irreconcilable with the teachings of the church. But, for the troubadours, adulterous love such as they conceived it was not to be condemned and was not a mortal sin. Quite the contrary; and that is what counts. One must look at it from their viewpoint, not from that of the church. One must not seek to reconcile the troubadours' *fin'amors*, their way of life, and their manner of expressing themselves with the Christian religion and ethics under which they lived. This divorce between religious and social life, between faith and love ideology is a reality that one must accept as it is. The fundamental contradiction between *amor mundi* and *amor Dei*, of which Saint Augustine speaks, created no conflict in the minds of the twelfth-century aristocracy and in those of the troubadours. This way of viewing the coexistence of two opposed truths (*due contrarie veritates*) can be explained really only in the light of the philosophy of Avicenna and his disciples, as developed later by Averroes and his Latin followers. The troubadours must have borrowed, from this tradition foreign to Christianity, certain ideas of their "art of loving" which were more idealistic and more refined than the concepts of Ovid's *Ars Amatoria* and more suited to the courtly society of their times. The question, for them, is not *amor dei* or *amor mundi*, "sacred love" or "secular love," but one *and* the other. This coexistence of both truths, which survived in various forms until the Renaissance, as the historian Lucien Febvre has so ably illustrated,[72] is an objective medieval reality. The troubadours' doctrine of love is a tangible and convincing testimony of this social and cultural reality.

"The society of the *clercs*, under Eleanor, had like William of Aquitaine, the first troubadour, and like Eleanor herself, two faces," writes Lejeune, rightly.[73] Brought up in a family tradition of liberality and spiritual independence, Eleanor contributed greatly to the assertion of the validity of earthly life and pleasures and to the promotion of their literary expression. Courtliness (*cortezia*) and *fin'amors* constituted a well-established tradition in Eleanor's family before she herself became involved in inspiring new generations of poets and in helping to disseminate their new concepts of love. It was also her court which became the catalyzing factor in the integration of Celtic myths and folk tales into the fabric of Continental literature. Out of the three modes of love, which we have briefly outlined in this study, Eleanor of Aquitaine was inclined by her nature and spirit to encourage those of *fin'amors* and tragic love exclusively. Her daughter Marie de Champagne followed essentially the same path by giving Chrétien de Troyes the "subject matter and its meaning" (*matiere et san*) of his *Lancelot*, a story whose content and moral implications were contrary to the writer's personal taste and *credo*. She was also behind the composition of the two first parts of Andreas Capellanus's *De Amore*, where *fin'amors* is extolled.[74] The third part, where this mode of love is condemned, was not inspired by her: "The chaplain's discourse is so full of the conflict between pagan naturalism and

Christian restraint that the reader perceives through his mind's eye the shadow of Marie at his elbow, correcting, refining, interpolating, and deleting. . . . It is therefore not surprising to find that André at some time added to his work a final section, *De Remedio*, in which he repudiates the essential philosophy of the major portion."[75] between the new *ars amatoria* (art of loving) and a Christianized version of the *remedia amoris* (remedy for love), Eleanor of Aquitaine, like her grandfather William IX and her daughter Marie, opted for the mode of *fin'amors*, a highly refined expression of an erotic and adulterous love, but conceived as *verai'amors*, the only possible mode of real, true love.

NOTES

1. Quoted by Marc Bloch, *Feudal Society*, trans. L. A. Manyon (Chicago: University of Chicago Press, 1961), p. 307.

2. Ibid. From the strictly literary point of view, at least, we must reject J. F. Benton's affirmations: "Courtesy was created by men for their own satisfaction, and it emphasized a woman's role as an object, sexual or otherwise. . . . When men ignored chivalry, women were better off"; "The second feudal age, like the first, remained a man's world" ("Clio and Venus: An Historical View of Medieval Love," in *The Meaning of Courtly Love*, ed. F. X. Newman [Albany: State University of New York Press, 1968], pp. 35, 36).

3. Cf. Reto R. Bezzola, "Guillaume IX et les origines de l'amour courtois," *Romania* 66(1940–1941):160: "A la civilisation cléricale et érudite du Nord, bornée, en dehors du monde de l'Eglise, sans doute à des milieux très restreints, le Sud opposait une civilisation toute profane, dont la mollesse et les extravagances choquèrent toujours le Nord, depuis Louis le Pieux, dont l'Astronome vante l'aversion pour les moeurs détestables d'Aquitaine [in opposition to the

learned, clerical society of the North, undoubtedly extremely limited outside the orbit of the Church, the South set up a wholly worldly civilization, the slackness and extravagance of which had always shocked the North since the reign of Louis the Pious, whose Astronomer prided himself on his aversion for the detestable mores of Aquitaine]." (Translations are mine or the editor's unless otherwise indicated.)

4. Geoffroy de Vigeois, *Recueil des historiens de la France*, cited by Amy Kelly, *Eleanor of Aquitaine and the Four Kings* (Cambridge: Harvard University Press, 1963), p. 165 (Kelly's translation).

5. Ordericus Vitalis, *Histoire ecclésiastique*, cited by Alfred Jeanroy, *La Poésie lyrique des troubadours* (Paris: H. Didier, 1934), p. 84.

6. J. F. Benton's information on marriage and adultery, as described by canonistic writers and court cases ("Clio and Venus," pp. 24–25), is certainly of interest, but he concedes "that if a man were sufficiently powerful he could easily put himself above both law and private vengeance and seduce the wives of his neighbors or subjects with impunity

. . . and William IX of Aquitaine felt free to boast humorously about his conquests." See also the following note.

7. Cf. C. S. Lewis, *The Allegory of Love* (New York: Oxford University Press, 1960), p. 13: "Marriages had nothing to do with love, and no 'nonsense' about marriage was tolerated. All matches were matches of interest, and worse still, of an interest that was continually changing."

8. Benton, "Clio and Venus," p. 28.

9. Lewis, *The Allegory of Love*, p. 13.

10. For a detailed bibliography, see Edmond-René Labande, "Pour une image véridique d'Aliénor d'Aquitaine," *Bulletin de la Société des Antiquaires de l'Ouest*, 4th ser. 2(1952):175–234.

11. Kelly, *Eleanor of Aquitaine*. In many instances various parts of this work come very close to fiction and romance and rest on fragile literary and historical evidence, particularly the chapters dedicated to Eleanor and Bernart de Ventadorn and to the "courts of love."

12. Labande, "Pour une image"; Rita Lejeune, "Rôle littéraire d'Aliénor d'Aquitaine et de sa famille," *Cultura Neolatina* 14(1954):5–57; idem, "Rôle littéraire de la famille d'Aliénor d'Aquitaine," *Cahiers de Civilisation Médiévale* 1, no. 3(1958):303–320.

13. Interesting historical remarks are also to be found in H. G. Richardson, "The Letters and Charters of Eleanor of Aquitaine," *English Historical Review* 74(1959):193–213.

14. See Bezzola, "Guillaume IX," pp. 160–164; R. Louis, *Girart, Comte de Vienne, dans les chansons de geste* (Auxerre: Aux Bureaux de l'Imprimerie moderne, 1947), I, 337–340; Kelly, *Eleanor of Aquitaine*, p. 5: "In the midst of heavy campaigns, [William] gave his nights to reading. Alone throughout long evenings he conned the treasury of books he had acquired by exchange with other potentates, or by loan from the great monastic libraries of Limoges and Cluny."

15. Bezzola, "Guillaume IX"; Alfred Jeanroy, ed., *Les Chansons de Guillaume IX, duc d'Aquitaine*, Classiques Français du Moyen Age (Paris: H. Champion, 1947). For the interpretation of the concept of *fin'amors* and William's poetry, see my study, *Amour courtois et Fin'amors dans la littérature du XIIe siècle* (Paris: C. Klincksieck, 1964).

16. Louis, *Girart*, pp. 348–354; Jean Frappier, *Le Roman breton: Des origines à Chrétien de Troyes* (Paris: Centre de Documentation Universitaire, 1954); Lejeune, "Rôle littéraire d'Aliénor," pp. 7–8.

17. Kelly, *Eleanor of Aquitaine*, p. 5. "The family had founded Cluny . . . and they had seated popes in Rome; but more often the dukes were found supporting antipopes, scourging their local bishops, and abetting the schisms that sprang up abundantly on the soil of Aquitaine" (ibid.).

18. Cf. ibid., p. 31: "Paris offered no proper arena for women, for duchesses, for queens. She was bored with dialectic, bored with universals, with discourse upon the unfathomable nature of the Trinity, bored with bishops and with abbés and the ecclesiastical conclaves over which they presided, bored with dedications and with pious pilgrimages. She was not a little bored by her overlord."

19. E. Monaci, "Ancora di Jaufré Rudel," *Rendiconti Reale Accademia dei Lincei*, 5th ser. 2(1893):930–931. Monaci's opinion is accepted by S. San-

tangelo, "L'amore lontano di Jaufré Rudel," *Sicolorum Gymnasium* 6(1953):1–23, and by Lejeune, "Rôle littéraire d'Aliénor," p. 9 n. 17. On Rudel's concept of "distant love" and its various interpretations, see Lazar, *Amour courtois*, pp. 86–102.

20. Kelly, *Eleanor of Aquitaine*, pp. 38, 39.

21. See Labande, "Pour une image," pp. 181 ff.; Kelly, *Eleanor of Aquitaine*, pp. 56–59. Both agree that the stories are all suspect "in view of their Frankish source," but "they became, in spite of efforts to stifle them, a stock in trade, revived from time to time, of scandal-mongers and balladeers, and so pursued the Duchess of Aquitaine to the end of her days and farther down the corridors of history" (Kelly, p. 63).

22. Works composed in her entourage in order to please her: *Chanson de Girart de Roussillon*; *Pèlerinage de Charlemagne*; *Prise d'Orange*; *Roman de Rou*, by Wace; *Tristan*, by Thomas; and others. See Lejeune, "Rôle littéraire d'Aliénor," pp. 10–11, 16–17, 24; but it is very doubtful whether all the works this scholar attributes to Eleanor's entourage were really composed in her circle. That the *Brut* by Wace was dedicated to her around 1155 is also not seriously documented.

23. Lejeune, "Rôle littéraire de la famille," pp. 319–337; J. F. Benton, "The Court of Champagne as a Literary Center," *Speculum* 36(1961):551–591.

24. See István Frank, "Du rôle des troubadours dans la poésie lyrique moderne," in *Mélanges de linguistique et de littérature romanes offerts à Mario Roques*, 4 vols. (Paris: Didier, 1950), I, 77: "Le succès de la poésie courtoise nous apparaît en quelque sorte comme l'affaire de la famille ducale d'Aquitaine

[the success of courtly poetry appears to be, in a way, the affair of the ducal family of Aquitaine]." Alfred Jeanroy, who did not think much of Eleanor, wrote the following unacceptable statement: "La frivole et vaniteuse Eléonore ne pouvait avoir que des regards complaisants pour ces distributeurs de gloire qu'étaient les troubadours [the frivolous and vain Eleanor could only look with complaisance on those distributors of glory, the troubadours]" (*La Poésie lyrique*, p. 151).

25. Lejeune, "Rôle littéraire d'Aliénor," p. 19. Lejeune's statement that these troubadours constituted a special group, a "definite school" of poetry, does not correspond to any documented reality and cannot be deduced from the content of their songs. See Lazar, *Amour courtois*, pp. 47–55.

26. See, among others, E. Faral, *Recherches sur les sources latines des contes et romans courtois du Moyen Age* (Paris: Champion, 1913); Cornelis de Boer, *La Normandie et la Renaissance classique dans la littérature française du XIIe siècle* (Gröningen: M. de Waal, 1912); M. Wilmotte, *Origines du roman en France* (Paris: Boivin, 1941); Lejeune, "Rôle littéraire d'Aliénor," pp. 21–24.

27. Frappier, *Le Roman breton*, p. 54.

28. Lejeune, "Rôle littéraire d'Aliénor," p. 38.

29. On Marie de France and her relationship to King Henry's family, see J. C. Fox, "Marie de France," *English Historical Review* 25(1910):303–306; 26(1911):317–326.

30. This Thomas has been identified as Thomas of Kent (author of the *Roman de toute chevalerie*) by M. Dominica Legge, *Anglo-Norman in the Cloisters* (Edinburgh: University Press, 1950), pp. 38–43. Lejeune, in "Rôle lit-

téraire d'Aliénor," p. 24, accepts Legge's thesis, which has been refuted quite convincingly by Bartina H. Wind, "Faut-il identifier Thomas, auteur de Tristan, avec Thomas de Kent?" in *Saggi e ricerche in memoria de Ettore Li Gotti*, nos. 6–8 of *Bollettino, Centro di Studi Filologici e Linguistici Siciliani* (Palermo, 1962), no. 8, pp. 479–490.

31. Gaston Paris, "Etudes sur les romans de la Table Ronde: Lancelot du Lac. II. Le *Conte de la Charrette*," *Romania* 12(1883):459–534.

32. On the imperative necessity of distinguishing the various concepts (*courtliness, courtly love, fin'amors*, etc.), see Jean Frappier, "Vues sur les conceptions courtoises dans les littératures d'oc et d'oï au XIIᵉ siècle," *Cahiers de Civilisation Médiévale* 2, no. 2(1959):133–155, based on my thesis presented at the Sorbonne in 1957 and published in 1964 (Lazar, *Amour courtois*).

33. J. Wettstein, "Mezura—l'idéal des troubadours: Son essence et ses aspects" (Thesis, University of Zurich, 1945), p. 10 n. 1.

34. W. T. H. Jackson, "Faith Unfaithful: The German Reaction to Courtly Love," in *The Meaning of Courtly Love*, ed. Newman, p. 74; see also p. 93: Love was not "the same in Chrétien as in Bernart de Ventadorn, nor even the same in Heinrich von Morungen as in his contemporary Walther von der Vogelweide."

35. See E. Talbot Donaldson, "The Myth of Courtly Love," *Ventures* 5(1965):16–23.

36. D. W. Robertson, "The Concept of Courtly Love as an Impediment to the Understanding of Medieval Texts," in *The Meaning of Courtly Love*, ed. Newman, p. 17: "The study of courtly love, if it belongs anywhere, should be conducted only as the subject is an aspect of nineteenth and twentieth century cultural history. The subject has nothing to do with the Middle Ages"; J. F. Benton, "Clio and Venus," p. 37: "As currently employed, 'courtly love' has no useful meaning, and it is not worth saving by redefinition."

37. Robertson, "The Concept of Courtly Love," p. 3. Basing his interpretations on late thirteenth- and fourteenth-century texts, in particular Chaucer's works, Robertson extrapolates conclusions that are then applied to the literature of the twelfth century. W. T. H. Jackson remarks: "Now, by the 14th century, the time of Chaucer, such views were things of the past, historical and archaic. They were being reevaluated as a historical phenomenon, not as something which had just evolved and was still eminently discussable as a living thing" (in "Discussion," in *The Meaning of Courtly Love*, ed. Newman, p. 93).

38. The lectures and discussions of that conference, published in *The Meaning of Courtly Love*, ed. Newman, have been sharply criticized by Jean Frappier, "Sur un procès fait à l'amour courtois," *Romania* 93(1972):145–193. I cannot but agree totally with his strong critical remarks.

39. Cf. Charles S. Singleton, in "Discussion," in *The Meaning of Courtly Love*, ed. Newman, p. 94: "History misused is a very great impediment to the understanding of *any* literary text."

40. For a detailed analysis of the themes and the meaning of *fin'amors*, see Lazar, *Amour courtois*, pp. 55–148.

41. Confusing courtliness and courtly love (or, more correctly, *fin'amors*), Benton writes: "In terms of the conventional standards of the court of Champagne,

Chrétien's Lancelot was not more of a hero for loving Guinivere, but a felon" ("Clio and Venus," p. 28). According to the principles of *fin'amors*, Lancelot's "adulterous" love and his unconditional loyalty to Guinivere have nothing to do with the "conventional standards" prevailing in the framework of daily reality.

42. Charles S. Singleton ("Dante: Within Courtly Love and Beyond," in *The Meaning of Courtly Love*, ed. Newman, pp. 47–48), following J. Huizinga's concept of *homo ludens*, conceives the troubadour or the "courtly lover" as a kind of *Christianus ludens*: "All poetry is play, all art-forms are play"; the troubadours "did play at courtly love"; there is no contradiction between play with Venus and love for God. Furthermore, in accordance with Dante's terminology (see *De Vulgari Eloquentia*, II, ii, 6–8, in *Le Opere di Dante: Testo critico della Società Dantesca Italiana*, ed. M. Barbi, et. al. [Florence: R. Bemporad & Figlio, 1921]), Singleton distinguishes between *amoris accensio* (fire of love) and *directio voluntatis* (direction of the will), the first representing the "courtly-love" tradition, the mode in which Dante too wrote in his youth, the second a spiritualized love surpassing that tradition.

43. Pauline Matarasso, trans., *Aucassin and Nicolette and Other Tales* (Baltimore, Md.: Penguin Books, 1971), pp. 28–29.

44. Pierre Jonin, *Les Personnages féminins dans les romans français de Tristan au XIIe siècle*, Annales de la Faculté des Lettres d'Aix-Marseille, no. 22 (Aix-en-Provence: Editions Ophrys, 1958), esp. p. 334: "Si le fond de la vie sentimentale des deux amants chez Thomas est souvent en opposition irréductible avec la doctrine courtoise, son

expression n'en est pas aussi proche qu'on veut bien le dire [if the substance of the lovers' feelings in Thomas's version is often totally incompatible with the courtly doctrine, the expression of those feelings is not as close to the doctrine as is said, either]."

45. Bartina H. Wind, "Eléments courtois dans Béroul et Thomas," *Romance Philology* 14, no. 1(1960):1–13. She writes: "L'oeuvre de Thomas n'est courtoise que dans la conception des personnages secondaires, dans l'ambiance où baigne le drame, qui par lui-même échappe à l'influence courtoise. Tristan et Iseut unis dans l'amour ont une grandeur qui manque à la poésie courtoise. [Thomas's work is courtly only in the treatment of secondary characters, in the ambiance surrounding the conflict, which of itself escapes courtly influence. Tristan and Isolde united in love have a grandeur lacking in courtly poetry.]" (p. 7)

46. Stefan Hofer, "Streitfragen zur altfranzösischen Literatur," *Zeitschrift für romanische Philologie* 65(1949):285–286.

47. See R. S. Loomis, *The Romance of Tristram and Ysolt* (New York: Columbia University Press, 1931), p. xi.

48. Bartina H. Wind, *Les Fragments de Tristan de Thomas* (Leiden: E. J. Brill, 1950), pp. 13–16, proposed the date 1180–1190, but in the second edition (Geneva: Droz, 1960), p. 17, she admitted that the romance was probably composed between 1150 and 1160; Maurice Delbouille, "A propos de la patrie et de la date de Floire et Blanchefleur (version aristocratique)," in *Mélanges . . . offerts à Mario Roques*, IV, 83, proposed the date of 1165; Lejeune's assumption ("Rôle littéraire d'Aliénor," pp. 33–35) that Thomas's *Tristan* was composed be-

tween 1154 and 1158 can be accepted.

49. Ernest Muret and L. M. Defourques [pseud. of Lucien Foulet and Mario Roques], *Béroul: Le Roman de Tristan* (Paris: H. Champion, 1947), proposed 1165–1170, a date which I am willing to accept, contrary to Lejeune's proposition postponing its composition until the end of the twelfth century.

50. Ernest Hoepffner, "Chrétien de Troyes et Thomas d'Angleterre," *Romania* 55(1929):1–16.

51. Lejeune, "Rôle littéraire d'Aliénor," p. 32: "Le personnage de Tristan s'est donc répandu dans la littérature occitane d'abord. Et pourquoi n'y aurait-il pas eu un poème de Tristan, écrit en langue d'oc, qui se serait perdu comme d'autres en langue d'oïl? La supposition n'a rien d'invraisemblable. Toutefois, même si le thème de Tristan et Iseut n'a été connu des troubadours que par la voie orale, il reste que la belle légende amoureuse, quand elle a passé sur le continent, l'a fait par la cour de Poitiers. [The character Tristan thus spread first into Provençal literature. And why could there not have been a Tristan poem, written in Provençal, which would have been lost like its northern counterparts? The supposition is not at all unlikely. Nonetheless, even if the Tristan and Isolde theme was known by the troubadours only in an oral form, the fact remains that this beautiful love legend, when it crossed over to the Continent, did so through the court at Poitiers.]"

52. Denis de Rougemont, *L'Amour et l'Occident* (Paris: Plon, 1939).

53. Unfortunately, the tendency to do away with history, chronology, and philological-textual analysis is a widespread fashion in literary criticism.

54. See Lazar, *Amour courtois*, pp. 233–243; idem, "Lancelot et la 'mulier

mediatrix,'" *L'Esprit Créateur* 9, no. 4(1969):243–256.

55. Jean Frappier, *Chrétien de Troyes* (Paris: Hatier, 1968), p. 106, defines *Cligés* as "a revised and corrected version of *Tristan*"; see also Lazar, *Amour courtois*, pp. 213–232.

56. Carl Appel, "Zu Marcabru," *Zeitschrift für romanische Philologie* 43(1923):454.

57. Dimitri Scheludko, "Über die Theorien der Liebe bei den Trobadors," *Zeitschrift für romanische Philologie* 60(1940):234.

58. Eduard Wechssler, *Das Kulturproblem des Minnesangs*, vol. 1, *Minnesang und Christentum* (Halle: Niemeyer, 1909), p. 216; see also Guido Errante, *Sulla lirica romanza delle origini* (New York: Vanni, 1943), p. 377.

59. J. Wilcox, "Defining Courtly Love," in *Papers of the Michigan Academy* 12(1930):313.

60. Mario Casella, "Poesia e storia" [on William IX and Jaufré Rudel], *Archivo storico italiano* 96(1938):3–63, 153–199.

61. Diego Zorzi, *Valori religiosi nella letteratura provenzale*, Publ. Univ. Cattolica del S. Cuore, n.s., vol. 44 (Milan: Vita e Pensiero, 1954).

62. Alfred Jeanroy, ed., *Les Chansons de Jaufré Rudel*, Classiques Français du Moyen Age, vol. 15 (Paris: H. Champion, 1915). All quotations from Rudel's poetry are from this edition; the translations are mine.

63. See Lazar, *Amour courtois*, Ch. 5, "L'Imagerie érotique," esp. pp. 123–124.

64. In this instance the expression *secluded spot* replaces *garden* and *alcove*.

65. Grace Frank, "The Distant Love of J. Rudel," *Modern Language Notes* 57(1942):532.

66. Carl Appel, "Wiederum zu Jaufré Rudel," *Archiv* 107(1901):343.

67. Etienne Gilson, *La Théologie mystique de Saint Bernard*, Etudes de Philosophie Médiévale, no. 20 (Paris: J. Vrin, 1934), p. 201

68. Ibid., p. 193.

69. A. J. Denomy, "An Inquiry to the Origins of Courtly Love," *Medieval Studies* 6(1944): 193 n. 32.

70. Malfré Ermengaud, *Lo Breviari d'Amor*, ed. G. Azaïs, vol. 2 (Paris-Beziers, 1881), lines 27456–27468.

71. Cf. Lewis, *The Allegory of Love*, p. 8: "There is no evidence that the quasi-religious tone of medieval love poetry has been transferred from the worship of the Blessed Virgin; it is just as likely—it is even more likely—that the colouring of certain hymns to the Virgin has been borrowed from the love poetry."

72. Lucien Febvre, *Le Problème de l'incroyance au XVIᵉ siècle: La Religion de Rabelais* (Paris: A. Michel, 1942); idem, *Autour de l'Heptaméron: Amour sacré, amour profane* (Paris: Gallimard, 1944).

73. Lejeune, "Rôle littéraire d'Aliénor," p. 28.

74. See Lazar, *Amour courtois*, pp. 268–278.

75. Kelly, *Eleanor of Aquitaine*, p. 163.

3. Music in the Life and Times of Eleanor of Aquitaine

REBECCA A. BALTZER

It is safe to say that, had Eleanor of Aquitaine not made a significant mark on twelfth-century politics and culture, the history of music in the Middle Ages would be very different from what it is. Both directly and indirectly, Eleanor and her family and their descendants, who eventually married into just about every royal house in Europe, profoundly affected the development of medieval music. They did this both as patrons and as practitioners of the art.

It is hardly necessary to mention that Eleanor's grandfather William, the ninth duke of Aquitaine and seventh count of Poitou (1071–1127), is the earliest known troubadour whose Old Provençal lyrics and music survive.[1] His son William X evidently passed on to the young Eleanor a love of poetry and music, though she was no more than fifteen at the time of his death in 1137. Eleanor herself over a period of twenty-one years produced ten children; though she outlived all but two of them, their musical legacies extended even into the fourteenth century. Her two daughters by Louis VII of France, Marie, countess of Champagne, and Alix, countess of Blois, were extremely important patrons of lyric poetry and romance, particularly Marie; they learned the arts of courtly love at Eleanor's court during the third quarter of the twelfth century and later carried on the traditions in establishments of their own.

That such traditions continued to bear fruit is clear from the fact that Marie's grandson—Eleanor's great-grandson—was the most celebrated trouvère in the thirteenth century, Thibaud IV of Champagne (1201–1253). His extant songs outnumber those of every other medieval musician, and he occupies a very large place in the great *chansonnier* collections of the thirteenth century.[2]

Two of the sons of Eleanor and Henry II of England are known to have had musicopoetic interests: Richard the Lionhearted is the author of two songs, one in Old French that survives with music and the other in Poitevin dialect,[3] and Geoffrey of Brittany is one of the partners (along with the trouvère Gace Brulé) in a *jeu-parti*, which musically debates a question of courtly love.[4]

Among Eleanor's other children, the most important from a musical standpoint is her daughter Eleanor, who was married at the tender age of nine to Alfonso VIII of Castile. Their court became something of a center of musical patronage on the Iberian peninsula, and this heritage affected their offspring for several generations. Alfonso himself was the founder of the Cistercian monastery of Las Huelgas at Burgos in 1180; he is thus ultimately though indirectly responsible for a large and important musical manuscript compiled at the monastery in the early fourteenth century.[5] It contains a wide variety of Mass pieces, motets, and conductus, including a monophonic lament upon Alfonso's death in the year 1214—*Rex obiit, et labitur Castelle gloria* ("The King is dead, and the glory of Castile collapses").[6]

Of the nearly one dozen children born to the younger Eleanor and Alfonso VIII, two became the mothers of saints as well as of musician-poets. Blanche of Castile, whose grandmother Eleanor of Aquitaine personally chose her to be the bride of Louis VIII of France, may herself have been the author of a religious trouvère song which in its unique source is simply attributed to *la röine Blanche*; but whether Blanche of Castile is the *röine* in question has been disputed.[7] In any case, she was certainly the mother of Louis IX of France (Saint Louis); and her youngest son, Charles d'Anjou, the great-grandson of Eleanor of Aquitaine, is the author of several surviving trouvère songs,[8] though he was evidently too busy with politics to rival the creations of Thibaud of Champagne. Charles became king of Sicily in 1265, and his court was known for its patronage of both trouvères and troubadours,[9] including the trouvère Adam de la Halle, one of the few known to have written polyphonic music as well as monophonic songs.[10]

Another daughter of the younger Eleanor and Alfonso VIII, Berengaria, became the mother of Ferdinand III of Castile (Saint Ferdinand) and the grandmother of Alfonso X of Castile and León, known as Alfonso el Sabio (1221–1284). The latter was thus the great-great-grandson of Eleanor of Aquitaine and Henry II. It was at the court of Alfonso el Sabio, sometime after 1252, that the largest extant collection of Galician-Portuguese lyrics from this period, the Cantigas de Santa Maria, was compiled, and a number of them may have been composed by Alfonso himself.[11]

But enough of family trees and royal relations. Before we can properly understand the full effect of Eleanor of Aquitaine and her family upon medieval music, we must first see exactly what types of music flourished in the twelfth century and how these types have come down to us. First of all, no instrumental music has been preserved from the twelfth century, though there is abundant evidence that it enjoyed a healthy existence. The preserved twelfth-century repertory thus divides into music with Latin text, most of which is at least sacred if not directly liturgical, and music with vernacular text, nearly all of which is secular, whatever the language used. Just as in the case of instrumental music, almost no music with vernacular text was written down during the twelfth century. For instance, the earliest extant collections of troubadour and trouvère songs that include the melodies along with the poems date from the mid-thirteenth century, though they are full of the works of twelfth-century poet-musicians.[12] Such a situation strongly implies that, during the twelfth century and much of the thirteenth, the melodies of vernacular songs were transmitted primarily by oral tradition; a similar tradition must have been used for instrumental music as well.[13]

Thus the manuscript sources that actually date from the twelfth century almost without exception contain only sacred music with Latin text. They may be purely liturgical chantbooks, or they may be collections of liturgical dramas, tropes, sequences or proses, and strophic poems called either versus or conductus. Several manuscripts also contain these same sorts of works—particularly tropes, versus, and conductus—set in two-part polyphony as a means of increasing the musical elaborateness of a particular ceremonial or liturgical occasion. The important point for our purposes is that these manuscripts and their style of polyphony are products of the Angevin Empire in Eleanor's time, and this is music with which she was undoubtedly acquainted. (In fact, musicologists now tend to refer to this repertory as Aquitanian polyphony.)

Three manuscripts containing this polyphonic repertory are known to have been in the possession of the Abbey of Saint Martial at Limoges in the early thirteenth century;[14] a fourth and somewhat later source dating from the early thirteenth century contains many of the same works but originated probably near the Spanish border.[15] Further spread of the Aquitanian style can be seen in the more than twenty polyphonic pieces in the well-known Codex Calixtinus, containing, in part, music for the Office of Saint James (Santiago) in Compostela.[16] The codex, which seems to have been compiled over a period of some thirty years in the mid-twelfth century, originated not in Spain but somewhere in the middle of France, to judge from its more northern style of notation.[17] Finally, we find a similar kind of polyphony in some musical flyleaves now in Cambridge University Library; they date from the very end of the twelfth century and come from the North of France.[18] The style which originated in Eleanor's homeland shows every evidence of having traveled throughout the Angevin realms, even across the English Channel.

But during the course of the twelfth century, just as we witness the change from Romanesque to Gothic in the visual arts, we can see a shift in musical leadership beginning in the third quarter of the century. It is a shift from the Romanesque South and West to the Gothic North, from the Angevin Empire to the royal domain of the French kings in the Ile de France. It was in the second half of the twelfth century that the trouvères and the language of Old French rose to challenge the supremacy of the Old Provençal troubadours, a development in which Eleanor's court figured significantly. And as the fortunes of the Capetian kings and the intellectual attractions of Paris began to increase, in the second half of the century Parisian composers of polyphony began to take the lead over their southern and western counterparts.

Music from the Parisian school—the so-called Notre Dame school—is preserved in a number of manuscripts which, like the vernacular chansonniers, are no earlier than the mid-thirteenth century, even though some of their repertory goes back as far as the 1160's. For our purposes, the two most important of these manuscripts are a mid-thirteenth-century Parisian source now in the Biblioteca Laurenziana in Florence[19] and a slightly younger manuscript copied somewhere across the English Channel, now in the ducal library of Wolfenbüttel.[20] These two sources contain a number of what we might call "occasional" pieces of music that bear direct relation to events in the lives of Eleanor and her family. The pieces are conductus, Latin compositions for either one or two voices; and their strophic texts comment upon great events, such as crusades, coronations, or royal deaths.[21] For the most part, they are the work of anonymous clerics, unlike the vernacular songs, whose authors are much more likely to be known to us by name. These Latin conductus required trained musicians—clerics, like their composers—for their performance; theirs is a written and composed tradition, not an oral and improvised one.[22]

The oldest piece of music bearing some demonstrable relation to Eleanor of Aquitaine is a troubadour song by Marcabru, *Pax! in nomine Domini*, that dates from the year 1137.[23] It laments the event that precipitated Eleanor's entry into political affairs, namely, the death of her father, William X of Aquitaine. William had set out on an Easter pilgrimage to Santiago de Compostela, accompanied part way by Eleanor. Having fallen ill en route, he lived only long enough to reach Compostela and died before the main altar of the cathedral, where he was subsequently buried. Marcabru's song has eight strophes, and in the first lines he announces his authorship of both poem and music. Sounding the twin themes of pilgrimage and crusade, he both extols Compostela as a washing place and site of holy cleansing and rails against the pagans who have not been driven out of Spain. The last stanza reads:

Desnaturat son li Frances,	Degenerate are the French
Si de l'afar Dieu dizon no	If they refuse to support God,
Qu'ie·us ai comes.	For I have warned them.
Antiocha, pretz e valor	Antioch, Guyenne, and Poitou
Sai plora Guiana e Peitaus.	Weep for worthiness and valor.
Dieus, seigner, al tieu lavador	Lord God, in your washing place
L'arma del comte met en paus;	Give peace to the count's soul;
E sai gart Peitieus e Niort	And may the Lord who rose from the
Lo seigner qui ressors del vas.	tomb
	Keep safe Poitiers and Niort.[24]

Less than three months later, Eleanor, who had quite suddenly become a political trophy, was married in Bordeaux to Louis VII of France.

When Bernard of Clairvaux issued the call for the Second Crusade at Easter of 1146 in Vézelay, Eleanor's daughter Marie was less than two years old, but that did not stop the queen from taking the cross along with her husband, Louis. They departed at Pentecost of 1147.[25] An anonymous Old French poet has left us an exhortation to crusade, *Chevalier, mult estes guariz*, composed sometime between the spring of 1146 and that of 1147; it is thus the oldest datable trouvère song, and the unique source of poem and melody is an Erfurt manuscript.[26] Each of the seven stanzas concludes with the same refrain, mentioning Eleanor's husband, who was known for his monkish piety:

Ki ore irat od Loovis	He who goes with Louis
Ja mar d'enfern avrat pouur,	Will never have fear of Hell,
Char s'alme en iert en parëis	For his soul will go to Paradise
Od les angles nostre Segnor.	With the angels of our Lord.[27]

The third stanza in particular cites the king's good example in taking the cross:

Pernez essample a Lodevis,	Follow the example of Louis,
Ki plus ad que vus nen avez:	Who is far richer than you:
Riches est e poestëiz,	Wealthier and more powerful
Sur tuz altres reis curunez:	Than all other crowned kings.
Deguerpit ad e vair e gris,	He has left behind costly furs,
Chastels e viles e citez:	Castles, towns, and cities:
Il est turnez a icelui	He has turned toward Him
Ki pur nus fut en croiz penez.	Who suffered for us on the cross.[28]

After two and a half years of crusading, and growing marital differences, Eleanor and Louis had their marriage dissolved on grounds of consanguinity on March 21, 1152. Less than two months later, to the shock of the Parisian court and clergy, Eleanor married her equally close relation Henry Plantagenet, Count of Anjou, in Poitiers. On Sunday, December 19, 1154, Henry and Eleanor were crowned king and queen of England at Westminster in London. While the chroniclers mentioned the many bishops present and reported that the occasion was a joyous one,[29] a more detailed account of such goings-on appeared the following year in the *Roman de Brut* of Robert Wace, written under the aegis of the royal couple. Musicologist Yvonne Rokseth suggested some thirty-five years ago that Wace's description of the coronation of the legendary King Arthur is probably a reasonable facsimile of Henry and Eleanor's coronation the year before.[30] Wace mentions a procession of bishops and other clergy to the king's palace, the presence of knights and vassals, and the actual crowning; then he tell us that

Quant la messe fu comenciee,	When the Mass had commenced,
Ke le jur fu mult exalciee,	Which was of exceptional proportions,
Mult oïssiez orgues suner	The sound of the organ was heard by
E clers chanter e orgener,	many,
Voiz abaissier e voiz lever,	And clerics chanted in polyphony, [31]
Chanz avaler e chanz munter.	With voices subsiding and lifting,
	Song falling and rising.[32]

It is likely that such polyphony was of the type found in the contemporary Codex Calixtinus and the Saint Martial sources mentioned earlier, since they contain the style which flourished in Angevin realms. Although we cannot be sure whether he is referring to Aquitanian or to Parisian organum, John of Salisbury gives us an even more colorful description of the performance of liturgical polyphony in his *Policraticus*, which he brought forth in 1159:

Before the face of the Lord, in the very recesses of the sanctuary, showing off in a riot of wanton sound, they [the singers] strive through effeminate mannerisms, through the breaking up of notes and phrases, to astound and to weaken simple souls. Were you to hear these caressing melodies, starting, chiming in, resounding, falling away, intertwining, and twittering, you would think it to be the harmony not of men, but of sirens. You would marvel at the facility of the voices, unrivaled by that of the nightingale, or the parrot, or any other more melodious. This facility is displayed in long ascents and descents, in the dividing or doubling of notes, in the repetition of phrases, and the piling of these one upon the other. The high or even the highest notes are so tempered by the lower and the lowest that the ear loses its power to distinguish, and the mind, soothed by such sweet-ness, is unable to judge of that which it has heard.[33]

Such a description is a performance in itself.

From 1155 to 1174, a period of not quite twenty years, Eleanor was most active as a patron of the literary and musical arts. Her itinerary shows her temporarily in England for the birth of several of her children, but mostly on the Continent. While she moved about through her and Henry's Continental territories, holding her elaborate Christmas court in a different location every year, she returned most often to Poitiers for extended stays.[34] It was during this time that the famous courts of love were held, when poets of the South and the North met and mingled, when Arthurian romances came into full flower, and when Eleanor, her daughters, and her daughters-in-law established doctrines of chivalry which had a profound effect on courtly life and ideals. The troubadour songs of Bernart de Ventadorn[35] are eloquent testimony to these ideals, as are the early trouvère songs and the romances of Chrétien de Troyes.[36]

We may turn again to contemporary romances for depictions of special courtly occasions, giving us a better idea of music's part in the scheme. In Wace's *Roman de Brut* of 1155, immediately after the coronation cere-mony and Mass for King Arthur already described, we find an account of the courtly entertainment which followed:

Quant li reis leva del mangier,	When the King rose from table,
Alez sunt tuit esbanier;	All went out from the city to take
De la cité es chans eissirent,	Their pleasure in the fields;
A plusurs gieus se deportirent;	They amused themselves with several games.

. . . .

Les dames sur les murs muntoent	The ladies climbed upon the walls
Pur esgarder cels ki juoent;	To watch those who were at sport;
Ki ami aveit en la place	She who had a love on the field
Tost li turnot l'oil e la face.	Turned her eye to him at once.
Mult out a la curt jugleürs,	At the court were many jugglers,
Chanteürs, estrumenteürs;	Singers and instrumentalists;
Mult peüssiez oïr chançuns,	There one could hear many songs,
Rotruenges e novels suns,	Rotrouenges, and new tunes,
Vïeleüres, lais de notes,	Vielle-players, noted lais,
Lais de vïeles, lais de rotes,	Lais for vielle, lais for rote,
Lais de harpes, lais de frestels,	Lais for harp, lais for pipes,
Lires, tympes e chalemels,	Lyras, cymbals, and shawms,
Symphonies, psalteriuns,	Hurdy-gurdies, psalteries,
Monacordes, timbes, coruns.	Monochords, timbrels, bagpipes.

Assez i out tresgeteürs,	There were also magicians,
Joeresses e jugleürs;	Performers, and jugglers;
Li un dient contes e fables,	Some tell tales and fables,
Alquant demandent dez e tables.	Others ask for dice and backgammon.[37]

Quite similar descriptions appear in the romance *Erec et Enide* by Chrétien de Troyes, whose patron was Eleanor's Capetian daughter Marie de Champagne. *Erec*, the first of Chrétien's romances, dates from around 1165–1170. Whenever a royal wedding, coronation, or other joyous occasion is described, music takes an important part in the proceedings. For instance, we find that after the wedding of Erec and Enide,

Quant la corz fu tote asanblee,	When the court was all assembled,
n'ot menestrel an la contree	there was not a minstrel in the countryside
qui rien seüst de nul deduit,	
qui a la cort ne fussent tuit.	with pleasing accomplishment
An la sale molt grant joie ot;	that did not come to the court.
chascuns servi de ce qu'il sot;	In the great hall there was much joy,
cil saut, cil tunbe, cil anchante,	each one contributing what he could:
li uns sifle, li autres chante,	one jumps, one tumbles, one does magic;
cil flaüte, cil chalemele,	one whistles, another sings,
cil gigue, li autres vïele;	one plays the flute, one the shawm,
puceles querolent et dancent;	one the gigue, another the vielle.
trestuit de joie fere tancent.	Maidens sing and dance,
Riens n'est qui joie puisse fere	and outdo each other in merrymaking.
ne cuer d'ome a leesce trere,	Nothing which can give joy
qui as noces ne fust le jor.	and incline the heart to gladness
Sonent tinbre, sonent tabor,	was left undone at the wedding that day.
muses, estives et freteles,	There is playing of timbrel, tabor, bagpipes, panpipes,
et buisines et chalemeles.	buisines, and shawms.[38]

On another joyous occasion at court it is mentioned that

Harpes, vïeles, i resonent,	Harps, vielles, gigues, psaltery,
gigues, sautier et sinphonies,	and organistrums resound,
et trestotes les armonies	and all the other hurdy-gurdies
qu'an porroit dire ne nomer.	that one could name.[39]

If one needs a testimonial for twelfth-century instrumental music, one has it abundantly in the romances.[40]

While Eleanor and her court enjoyed such diversions on the Continent, Henry was engaged in more somber events. A monophonic Latin conductus written sometime between 1165 and 1170, *In rama sonat gemitus*, comments sympathetically about the exile of Thomas Becket to the Continent. Its unique source is the thirteenth-century Wolfenbüttel manuscript that was copied somewhere in England, though its repertory is largely Parisian. The cleric who wrote this piece was no friend of Henry's, for the allegorical text reads:

In Rama sonat gemitus	In Rama a cry goes up
plorante Rachel Anglie.	from the wailing Rachel of England.
Herodis namque genitus	For a descendant of Herod
dat ipsum ignominie:	gives that same woman to ignominy:
en eius primogenitus	behold, her first-born
et Ioseph Cantuarie	and the Joseph of Canterbury
exulat si sit venditus	is in exile as if he were sold
Egyptum colit Gallie.	and he lives in the Egypt of France.[41]

As Denis Stevens interprets it, Rama represents Canterbury; the wailing Rachel of England is the church; the descendant of Herod, who was known for his infanticide, is of course King Henry; and Becket himself is Joseph, the first-born of Canterbury (that is, the first archbishop born in England), who is forced to go abroad as if sold into Egypt.[42] It is a song that would not have pleased Queen Eleanor.[43]

Saint Thomas of Canterbury is the subject of three more pieces composed probably during Eleanor's lifetime, though they cannot be more precisely dated than "after 1170."[44] All three appear primarily in Parisian sources. *Christi miles*, a conductus for two voices, speaks of the martyred archbishop as a soldier of Christ,[45] and the three-voice conductus *Novus miles sequitur* takes up a similar theme.[46] The third piece, also for three voices, is strictly liturgical—a Parisian setting of the responsory *Jacet granum* to be sung as part of the Office of Saint Thomas.[47]

Because of her role in encouraging her sons to rebel against their father, Eleanor was sequestered by King Henry in either Winchester or Salisbury beginning in 1174. For some ten years her movements were quite restricted, but during the last five years of Henry's life she was able to travel back and forth to the Continent.[48] Even if Eleanor herself was not a direct participant, the doings of her family continued to inspire "occasional" works of music.

One such event was the coronation of Philip Augustus of France, which took place at Reims on All Saints' Day, November 1, 1179. Philip of course did not accede to the throne until his father's death the following year, but the Capetians had discovered the wisdom of crowning their successors in advance. Since Henry II was technically a vassal of the Capetian king, it was necessary for him to be represented at the coronation, and his own heir-apparent, the Young King Henry, was chosen for this obligation. Contemporary chroniclers tell us that the Young King Henry bore Philip's crown in procession to the coronation.[49] The occasion was commemorated in a two-voice conductus, *Ver pacis aperit*, with text by Gautier de Châtillon, who was a friend of the presiding archbishop, Philip's uncle.[50] Though the poem's five strophes are rather abstract and obscure, Leo Schrade has suggested that *Ver pacis* may have had a role in the coronation ceremony itself rather than at the ensuing festival banquet, pointing out that various ideas in the text metaphorically parallel the themes of the coronation liturgy.[51]

In the year 1181, Henry the Liberal, count of Champagne and husband of Eleanor's daughter Marie, died, and his passing is commemorated in a monophonic Latin planctus, *Omnis in lacrimas*.[52] Its seven strophes, organized in paired musical stanzas like those of a sequence or prose, speak with a good bit of feeling about the loss to all segments of society in the count's realm. Only two years later Eleanor's oldest son, the Young King Henry, while feuding with his brothers and his father, fell ill of a fever and died in the Limousin at the age of twenty-eight in June of 1183. The troubadour Bertran de Born, whose political *sirventes* had helped to fan the flames of rebellion among Eleanor's sons, composed not one but two *planhs* on the Young King's death, though neither has music extant.[53]

It was evidently during the early 1180's that the young trouvère Gace Brulé was a member of the circle around another of Eleanor's sons, Geoffrey of Brittany.[54] At the end of the song *Li plusour ont d'Amours chanté* (Raynaud 413), in fact, Gace speaks of some advice given him by the count of Brittany.[55] *Gace, par droit me respondés* (Raynaud 948), the *jeu-parti* mentioned earlier in which Geoffrey and Gace were partners, is the earliest Old French example of the genre known.[56] The debate deals with the question of whether the count ought to continue to love a lady who has betrayed and abandoned him; Gace's answer is that he should.

In the summer of 1186, Geoffrey was in Paris visiting Philip Augustus, who had hopes of driving further wedges between the Angevin father and sons. Geoffrey was accidentally trampled by a horse in a tournament; and, although Philip is said to have summoned the best doctors in Paris, Geoffrey died on August 19. Like his older brother, the Young King, he was only twenty-eight when he died. Philip Augustus seems to have been more grieved by the event than anyone else; he saw to it that the count of Brittany was buried with a good deal of ceremony before the high altar of Notre Dame de Paris, consecrated only four years earlier.[57] Geoffrey's untimely end is the subject of a *planh* by Bertran de Born[58] and not one but two Latin laments, the monophonic *Anglia, planctus itera* and the two-voice *Eclypsim patitur*, both unique to the Florence manuscript of Parisian origin.[59] The latter two works must have been composed by clerics close to Philip Augustus, for the almost subjective outpourings of grief are rare in the usually more impersonal Latin poetry. Geoffrey is referred to as "the flower of Brittany," and Paris is said to suffer as much as his native land from his eclipse.[60] The end of *Eclypsim patitur* even cites the circumstance of Geoffrey's fatal injury, with the line "equa non novit parcere [the mare did not know to stop]." The beginning of *Anglia, planctus itera* seems to refer indirectly to the death of the Young King Henry three years before, for the text opens with the words, "O England, renew your lamentations and return to mourning; consider the double loss, now that the two-fold star has set."[61]

The unrelieved grief of these poems is in evident contrast to the mood of the two-voice conductus composed upon the death of Henry II three years later in 1189. *In occasu sideris*, found in both the Florence and Wolfenbüttel manuscripts, has a poem of three strophes all sung to the same music.[62] The first strophe offers England consolation after the royal death, but it also notes already the rising of a new star which will bring a prosperous day; the second and third strophes continue the compliment and tribute to *Richardus Pictaviae, Rex futurus Angliae*—Richard of Poitou, the future king of England. It was in early July of 1189 that Henry died, and Richard the Lionhearted was crowned at Westminster on the third of September. His mother Eleanor, now released from capitivity, took charge of preparations for his coronation in the interim before he crossed from the Continent. Richard's accession is commemorated in a two-voice conductus, *Redit aetas aurea*, found in the Florence and Wolfenbüttel manuscripts.[63] Of the four strophes of this attractive piece, the first and third are set musically in a through-composed fashion, with long melismas on the penultimate syllable of each; the second and fourth strophes are to be sung to the music of the first and third, respectively. The poem strikes a jubilant tone, rejoicing in the power of king and country:

Redit aetas aurea	The golden age returns;
Mundus renovatur.	The world is renewed.
Dives nunc deprimitur,	The rich man is now cast down;
Pauper exaltatur,	The poor is lifted up.
Omnis suo principi	Every citizen wishes
Plebs congratulatur,	Joy to his prince.
Nec est locus sceleri,	Nor is the place defiled;
Scelus datur funeri,	The wicked one is given to death;
Scandala fugantur.	The stumbling blocks flee.

Deus regem contulit	God chose the king
Nobis praeoptatum,	Preferred by us;
Terra cornu protulit	The earth brought forth
Copiae ditatum,	The fruitful horn of plenty.
Murmur omne populi	The unrest of all the people
Prorsus est sedatum,	Has subsided absolutely;
Plebs sub pace regia	Citizens under royal peace
Gaudet, pax, iustitia	Rejoice; peace and justice
Sese osculantur.	Embrace one another.
Pius, potens, humilis	Pious, powerful, humble,
Dives et maturus	Rich and mature in age,
Aetate, sed docilis	But docile and secure
Et rerum securus	In his circumstances,
Suarum, preficitur	He is put in charge
Angliae, daturus	Of England; he shall give
Rapinis interitum,	Death to the plunderers,
Clero iuris aditum,	Access to the clerk of the law,
Locum veritatis.	And a position to truth.
Gaudeat Pictavia,	Let Poitou rejoice,
Iam rege ditata,	Now that it is enriched with a king;
Tumescat Normannia	Let Normandy swell with pride,
Auro coronata,	Now that it is crowned in gold;
Vasco, Scotus, Britones	Navarre, Scotland, and Brittany
Obtinent optata,	Obtain their desires;
Sine dolo Cambria	Without guile Wales
Servit et Hibernia	Is in bondage, and Ireland
Nostrae potestati.	Does service to our power.[64]

At the time of Richard's accession in 1189, the Third Crusade to the Holy Land was a matter of central concern, and nearly all the "occasional" pieces of music from the 1190's are a result of that concern, whether they are subjective and personal vernacular lyrics[65] or the more objective and philosophical Latin conductus. Philip Augustus and Richard the Lionhearted both took the cross, but their forces did not succeed in retaking Jerusalem. A monophonic Latin conductus dating from the early 1190's, *Sede Syon, in pulvere*, laments the fall of Jerusalem in the year 1187 and looks specifically to Eleanor's grandson Henry of Champagne, son of Marie de Champagne and nephew of both Richard and Philip, to recapture it. The fifth of its six strophes reads:

Divinae nutu gratiae	By the will of divine grace,
Solus comes Campaniae	The Count of Champagne alone
Spei favillam suscitat,	Stirs the spark of hope;

Fidelis Sion filius	The faithful son of Syon,
Velut alter Heraclius	As if another Heraclius,
Fide ferroque militat.[66]	Fights with faith and sword.[66]

Richard the Lionhearted's famous song of captivity, *Ja nus hons pris*, was written to his half-sister Marie de Champagne while he was imprisoned on the Danube by Leopold of Austria in 1193–1194. The poem comprises six strophes followed by a double *envoi*, all set to a single musical stanza with *aab* form. Provoked by the slow response to ransom demands, Richard notes with frustration in Strophe Four that

N'est pas merveille, se j'ai le cuer dolent,	What marvel that my heart is sad and sore
Quant mes sires tient ma terre en torment.	When my own lord torments my helpless lands!
S'or il membroit de nostre serement,	Well do I know that, if he held his hands,
Que nos fëismes andui communaument,	Remembering the common oath we swore,
Bien sai de voir que cëans longuement,	I should not here imprisoned with my song
Ne seroie pas pris.	Remain a prisoner long.[67]

This complaint refers to Philip Augustus, who had returned home from the crusade a full year before and taken advantage of Richard's absence. The double *envoi* appeals directly to his "Contesse suer" Marie for aid, and mentions also the "dame de Chartres," his other half-sister, Alix.

Having vigorously worked for and finally secured Richard's release from captivity, Eleanor seems to have enjoyed several years of relative peace in the mid-1190's, but her sorrows were not yet done. From the year 1198 is preserved a monophonic Latin planctus, *Jerusalem, Jerusalem, quae occidis et lapidas*.[68] Its four strophes lament the death of Eleanor's grandson Henry of Champagne in the Holy Land in September 1197 and mention also the death of his grief-stricken mother, Marie de Champagne, six months later in March 1198. In 1199, tragedy struck again, when the heirless King Richard was fatally wounded in a minor siege. The moving lament on his death by the troubadour Gaucelm Faidit, *Fortz chausa es*, mourns the loss through six strophes and compares Richard to Alexander the Great, Charlemagne, and King Arthur; the closing *tornada* petitions the Lord to show mercy upon the king's soul.[69]

To steady the hand of her last and least capable son, John Lackland, Eleanor was once more forced to return to political matters. In the summer of 1199 she spent nearly a week in Tours on the banks of the Loire, where she did homage to Philip Augustus for Poitou.[70] There is extant a two-voice conductus in praise of the city of Tours, *In ripa Ligeris*, that stylistically could well date from about this time;[71] if the piece was in fact prompted by this occasion, it more likely stems from the retinue of Philip Augustus than from that of Eleanor, to whom this meeting was undoubtedly rather unpleasant. *In ripa Ligeris* is the sort of piece that would have delighted the twelfth-century equivalent of a chamber of commerce, for it praises the city's fine climate, beautiful surroundings, and happy citizens. It concludes by saying that the French, the Spanish, the Italians, and the Greeks with great vigor do envy the natives of Tours.[72] As part of the bargain with Philip Augustus, Eleanor agreed to select one of her granddaughters as the bride for his son, the future Louis VIII; at the age of nearly eighty in 1200 she traveled across the Pyrenees and chose Blanche of Castile to become a Capetian queen. History confirmed the wisdom of her choice.

In the last four years of her life, after 1200, Eleanor seems to have gradually retired from the world, and her death and burial at Fontevrault in the spring of 1204 seem to have caused little stir. If there were magnificent laments composed upon *her* passing, as there were for her sons and grandsons who preceded her, they have escaped us. But the absence of such musical testimonials in no way diminishes the importance of her effect upon the music of the twelfth and thirteenth centuries. No other medieval monarch inspired so much music as did Eleanor and her family; her court and her realms were fertile soil for a significant flowering of music in the high Middle Ages. Without her, the course of history *and* the course of music would be entirely different.

NOTES

Note: When this article was presented as part of the symposium, a number of the musical compositions discussed were performed by members of the University of Texas Collegium Musicum under the direction of Gilbert L. Blount.

1. Although twelve poems by William IX are extant, only one, *Pos de chantar m'es pres talens*, survives with a portion of melody. The extant repertory of troubadour melodies is transcribed by Friedrich Gennrich, *Der musikalische Nachlass der Troubadours*, vols. III and IV of his *Summa musicae medii aevi* (Darmstadt, 1958, 1960). For William's song, see III, 25, and IV, 23.

2. Since he became King of Navarre in 1234, Thibaud is often identified in the musical manuscripts simply as *le roi de Navarre*. See Friedrich Gennrich, "Thibaut IV," in *Die Musik in Geschichte und Gegenwart*, ed. Friedrich Blume, vol. XIII (Kassel: Barenreiter, 1966), cols. 335–337, esp. 336; see also the list under Thibaud's name in Hans Spanke's revised edition of *G*.

*Raynauds Bibliographie des altfran-
zösischen Liedes, neu bearbeitet und
ergänzt, erster Teil* (Leiden: Brill,
1955), p. 32; hereafter cited as
Raynaud. No complete musical edition
is available, though a number of songs
have been transcribed in various publications of trouvère music by Gennrich
and others. Trouvère songs will be identified by their Raynaud number.

3. *Ja nus hons pris* (Raynaud 1891)
and *Dalfin, je'us voill deresnier*
(Raynaud 1274a); see also the listing in
Alfred Pillet and Henry Carstens, *Bibliographie der Troubadours* (Halle:
Niemeyer, 1933), pp. 379–380; hereafter cited as Pillet-Carstens. Both songs
date from the 1190's.

4. *Gace, par droit me respondés*
(Raynaud 948).

5. Burgos, Monastery of Las Huelgas, manuscript without shelf number.
See the facsimile, transcription, and
commentary published by Higini Anglès, *El Còdex musical de las Huelgas*, 3
vols. (Barcelona: Institut d'Estudis
Catalans, 1931).

6. Anglès, *El Còdex*, II, folios
161v–162; transcription, III, no. 169.
See Anglès's comments in I, 354.

7. See the composition, *Amours, ou
trop tart me sui pris* (Raynaud 1604a),
and the discussion by Jean Maillard,
*Roi-trouvère du XIIIᵉ siècle: Charles
d'Anjou* ([Dallas]: American Institute
of Musicology, 1967), pp. 66–68.

8. Edited by Maillard, *Roi-trouvère*,
pp. 37–63.

9. Ibid., pp. 27–32.

10. The old Coussemaker edition of
Adam's compositions has been super-
seded by Nigel Wilkins, *The Lyric
Works of Adam de la Halle* ([Rome]:
American Institute of Musicology,
1967).

11. Musical edition by Higini Anglès,
*La música de las Cantigas de Santa
María del rey Alfonso el Sabio* (Barcelona: Diputación Provincial de Barcelona, Biblioteca Central, 1943).

12. The earliest collection of any size
is that in Paris, Bibliothèque Nationale
(Bibl. Nat.), *français 20050*, which
dates from the middle of the thirteenth
century; see the facsimile by Paul Meyer
and Gaston Raynaud, *Le Chansonnier
français de Saint-Germain-des-Prés*
(Paris, 1892).

13. See the discussion of written and
oral traditions in chanson transmission
by Hendrik van der Werf, *The Chansons of the Troubadours and Trouvères: A Study of the Melodies and
Their Relation to the Poems* (Utrecht:
A. Oosthoek, 1972), pp. 26–34.

14. Paris, Bibl. Nat., *latin 1139*,
latin 3549, and *latin 3719*. Descriptions, bibliography, and inventories
appear in Gilbert Reaney's *Manuscripts of Polyphonic Music, 11th–
Early 14th Century*, Répertoire International des Sources Musicales, B IV¹
(Munich-Duisberg: G. Henle, 1966),
pp. 402–409.

15. British Museum, Additional
36881. See Reaney, *Manuscripts*, pp.
519–521.

16. Santiago de Compostela, Biblioteca de la Catedral, Codex Calixtinus. A facsimile edition that is today
almost inaccessible was issued by
W. M. Whitehill and German Prado as
Liber Sancti Jacobi: Codex Calixtinus,
3 vols. (Santiago de Compostela: Con-
sejo Superior de Investigaciones Cien-
tíficas, Instituto P. Sarmiento de Es-
tudios Gallegos, 1944). A diplomatic
facsimile by Peter Wagner which appeared in 1931 is more widely available: *Die Gesänge der Jakobusliturgie*

zu Santiago de Compostela (Fribourg, Switz.: Kommissionsverlag, Universitäts-Buchhandlung, Gebr. Hess Co., 1931).

17. See Reaney, *Manuscripts*, pp. 238–239, and, more recently, Max Lütolf, *Die mehrstimmigen Ordinarium Missae-Sätze vom ausgehenden 11. bis zur Wende des 13. zum 14. Jahrhundert*, 2 vols. (Bern: Paul Haupt, 1970), I, 78–95, esp. 88–89.

18. Cambridge, University Library, Ff.1.17, inventoried by Reaney, *Manuscripts*, pp. 485–486. See also Lütolf, *Die mehrstimmigen Ordinarium*, I, 46–57.

19. Florence, Biblioteca Laurenziana, MS Pluteus 29, 1. Published by Luther Dittmer, *Firenze, Biblioteca Mediceo-Laurenziana, Pluteo 29, 1: Facsimile Reproduction of the Manuscript*, Publications of Mediaeval Musical Manuscripts, nos. 10–11 (Brooklyn: Institute of Mediaeval Music, 1966–1967); hereafter cited as *F*.

20. Wolfenbüttel, Herzog August Bibliothek 677 (olim Helmstedt 628). Facsimile by J. H. Baxter, *An Old St. Andrews Music Book (Cod. Helmst. 628)*, St. Andrews University Publications, no. 30 (London: Humphrey Milford, 1931); hereafter cited as *W1*.

21. Most of the texts are edited in vols. XX and XXI of *Analecta hymnica medii aevi*, ed. Clemens Blume and Guido M. Dreves, 55 vols. (Leipzig, 1886–1922); hereafter cited as *Analecta hymnica*. For additional comment on the "occasional" texts in the Florence manuscript, see Léopold Delisle's report dealing with *F* in the *Annuaire-Bulletin de la Société de l'Histoire de France* 22(1885):100–139.

22. The quality of these "occasional" Latin texts is generally below that of the best Latin poetry of the period, which fact suggests that they may well have been produced by court clerics whose main duties lay elsewhere but whose Latin was good enough for versification, when necessary. The quality of the music, however, is characteristic of the conductus repertory as a whole—some mediocre, some quite excellent.

23. Pillet-Carstens 293.35. The only copy with music is in Paris, Bibl. Nat., *français* 844, folio 194v; see the facsimile edition by Jean and Louise Beck, *Le Manuscrit du roi: Fonds français no. 844 de la Bibliothèque Nationale*, Corpus cantilenarum medii aevi, 1st ser., no. 2 (Philadelphia: University of Pennsylvania Press, 1938), vol. 1. Friedrich Gennrich has published several transcriptions of this piece, including those in *Lo gai saber: 50 ausgewählte Troubadourlieder* (Darmstadt, 1959), pp. 4–5; in *Troubadours, Trouvères, Minne- und Meistergesang*, vol. II of *Das Musikwerk* (Cologne: Arno Volk, 1951), p. 12; and in *Der musikalische Nachlass der Troubadours*, III, 28.

24. Text from Gennrich, *Lo gai saber*, p. 5; my translation.

25. See the itinerary for Eleanor published by Rita Lejeune as an appendix to her article, "Rôle littéraire d'Aliénor d'Aquitaine et de sa famille," *Cultura Neolatina* 14(1954):5–57; the itinerary begins on p. 50. Additional information on Eleanor's movements appears in H. G. Richardson's "The Letters and Charters of Eleanor of Aquitaine," *The English Historical Review* 74(1959):193–213.

26. Raynaud 1548a; Erfurt, Wissenschaftliche Bibliothek der Stadt Erfurt, Bibliothek Amploniana, 8° 32,

folio 88. The best facsimile is in Pierre Aubry's *Les Plus Anciens Monuments de la musique française* (Paris: H. Welter, 1905), pl. 3. Both a facsimile and a transcription are included in Friedrich Gennrich's *Exempla altfranzösischer Lyrik: 40 altfranzösische Lieder* (Darmstadt, 1958), pp. vi–vii, 1–2; a transcription alone is in Gennrich's *Troubadours, Trouvères, Minne-und Meistergesang*, p. 42.

27. Text from Gennrich, *Exempla altfranzösischer Lyrik*, p. 1; my translation.

28. Ibid.

29. See, for instance, R. W. Eyton, *Court, Household, and Itinerary of King Henry II* (London, 1878), pp. 1–2.

30. Yvonne Rokseth, *Polyphonies du XIIIᵉ siècle: Le Manuscrit H 196 de la Faculté de Médecine de Montpellier*, 4 vols. (Paris: Editions de l'Oiseau-Lyre, 1935–1939), IV, 40.

31. *Organer* here means to sing organum, i.e., polyphony.

32. Wace, *Le Roman de Brut de Wace*, ed. Ivor Arnold, 2 vols. (Paris: Société des Anciens Textes Français, 1940), II, 546–547, lines 10419–10424; my translation.

33. John of Salisbury, *Joannis Saresberiensis Episcopi Carnotensis Policratici*, ed. Clement Webb, 2 vols. (Oxford: Oxford University Press, 1909), I, 41–42 (Book I, Ch. 6). The translation is adapted from those of H. E. Wooldridge, *Oxford History of Music*, 2d ed. (London: Oxford University Press, 1929), I, 290; Joseph Pike, *Frivolities of Courtiers and Footprints of Philosophers* (Minneapolis: University of Minnesota Press, 1938), p. 32; and Janet Knapp, Introduction to *The Polyphonic Conductus: The Florence*

Repertory (New Haven: Yale University Press, forthcoming), with special thanks to Knapp.

34. Lejeune, "Rôle littéraire d'Aliénor," pp. 53–55.

35. Critical edition of the poetry (with French translations, introduction, notes, and glossary) by Moshé Lazar, *Bernard de Ventadour, Troubadour du XIIᵉ siècle: Chansons d'amour* (Paris: C. Klincksieck, 1966); English translations by Stephen G. Nichols, Jr., John A. Galm, et al., in *The Songs of Bernart de Ventadorn*, North Carolina Studies in the Romance Languages and Literatures, no. 39 (Chapel Hill: University of North Carolina Press, 1962). The eighteen extant melodies are available in diplomatic facsimile by Carl Appel, "Die Singweisen Bernarts von Ventadorn," *Zeitschrift für romanische Philologie*, Beiheft 81(Halle, 1934), and in rhythmic transcription by Friedrich Gennrich, *Der musikalische Nachlass der Troubadours*.

36. Raynaud, p. 22, lists five songs by Chrétien; their debt to Bernart's poetry is generally acknowledged.

37. Wace, *Roman de Brut*, ed. Arnold, II, 552–553, lines 10521–10524, 10539–10556; my translation. The rotrouenge, like the lai, is an Old French poetic form. For information on musical instruments, see Sibyl Marcuse, *Musical Instruments: A Comprehensive Dictionary* (New York: Doubleday, 1964).

38. Chrétien de Troyes, *Erec et Enide*, ed. Mario Roques, *Les Romans de Chrétien de Troyes*, vol. I; Classiques Français du Moyen Age, no. 80 (Paris: H. Champion, 1953), p. 61, lines 1983–2000; translation adapted from that of W. W. Comfort, *Chrétien de Troyes: Arthurian Romances* (London:

Dent, Everyman's Library, 1914), p. 27.

39. Chrétien de Troyes, *Erec et Enide*, ed. Roques, lines 6330–6333; my translation (cf. Comfort's translation, *Chrétien de Troyes*, p. 82).

40. Werner Bachmann also cites twelfth- and thirteenth-century testimony about the instrumental capabilities expected of minstrels in *The Origins of Bowing and the Development of Bowed String Instruments up to the Thirteenth Century*, trans. Norma Deane (London: Oxford University Press, 1969), pp. 118–119.

41. *W1*, folio 185v (new 168v) (see note 20 above); translation by Denis Stevens, "Music in Honor of St. Thomas of Canterbury," *The Musical Quarterly* 56(1970):317.

42. Stevens, "Music," pp. 317–318.

43. A recent transcription by Alexander Blachly is included as the first piece in *Music in Honour of St. Thomas of Canterbury*, ed. Denis Stevens, Alexander Blachly, Joan Long, and Cornelia Weininger (London: Novello, 1970); an older transcription by Leonard Ellinwood appeared in *The Musical Quarterly* 27(1941):194. The melody has an over-all form of *aab* (2 + 2 + 4 lines), one which came to be a favorite in vernacular lyrics, particularly those of the Northern French trouvères.

44. Denis Stevens makes a case, however, for the dating of the second of these works in early 1173 because of political allusions in the text; see "Music," pp. 338–340.

45. The sole musical source is *F*, folios 373v–375 (see note 19 above); a transcription by Joan Long is included in *Music in Honour of St. Thomas of Canterbury*, ed. Stevens et al., pp. 4–9.

46. The piece is found for two voice-parts in Madrid, Biblioteca Nacional, 20486, folios 139–139v (facsimile by Luther Dittmer), and in the Las Huelgas Codex, folio 101v (see note 5 above); it appears for three voices in *F*, folios 230–230v. If in fact the work dates from 1173, it is unlikely that the third voice was added before the end of the century, even though the three-part version appears in the earliest manuscript source. Published transcriptions are available by Janet Knapp, *Thirty-five Conductus for Two and Three Voices*, Yale Collegium Musicum No. 6 (New Haven: Department of Music, Graduate School, Yale University, 1965), pp. 40–41; Denis Stevens, *Music in Honour of St. Thomas of Canterbury*, ed. Stevens et al., pp. 10–11; and Higini Anglès, *El Còdex musical de las Huelgas*, III, 187, no. 102.

47. Unique to *F*, folios 19v–20v; transcription by Heinrich Husmann, *Die drei- und vierstimmigen Notre-Dame-Organa*, Publikationen älterer Musik, no. 11 (Leipzig: Breitkopf und Härtel, 1940), pp. 43–45.

48. See Lejeune's itinerary, "Rôle littéraire d'Aliénor," p. 55; Richardson, "Letters," pp. 198–200.

49. See, for instance, the accounts of Rigord, Benedict of Peterborough (actually Roger of Hoveden), Ralph of Diceto, and Roger of Hoveden, in *Recueil des historiens des Gaules et de la France*, vol. XVII, ed. Léopold Delisle and M. J. J. Brial (Paris, 1878), pp. 5, 438, 617.

50. The music appears in *F*, folio 355, and St. Gall, Stiftsbibliothek, 383, p. 173; the text alone appears in several other sources. The poem is edited by Karl Strecker in *Die Lieder Walters von Chatillon in der Handschrift 351 von St. Omer* (Berlin: Weidmannsche Ver-

lagsbuchhandlung, 1964), pp. 55–58. I am grateful to Janet Knapp for the loan of her transcriptions of *Ver pacis aperit* and the other polyphonic conductus mentioned subsequently in this discussion.

51. Leo Schrade, "Political Compositions in French Music of the 12th and 13th Centuries," in *Leo Schrade: De Scientia Musicae Studia atque Orationes*, ed. Ernst Lichtenhahn (Bern: Paul Haupt, 1967), pp. 160–168, 180–181; Schrade's essay first appeared in *Annales musicologiques* 1(1953):9–63. Since the lower voice-part of *Ver pacis aperit* appears in a chansonnier with the Old French text *Ma joie me semont* by Blondel de Nesle (Raynaud 1924), the question of which version came first has been a subject of much debate; see Schrade, "Political Compositions," p. 161.

52. F, folio 415v; text edited in *Analecta hymnica*, XXI, 180.

53. *Mon chan fenisc ab dol et ab mal traire* (Pillet-Carstens 80.26) and *Si tuit le dol e·lh plor e·lh marrimen* (Pillet-Carstens 80.41), though there are conflicting attributions of the latter to two other poets. The texts are edited by Albert Stimming, *Bertran von Born*, 2d ed. (Halle: Niemeyer, 1913), pp. 74–78, and Carl Appel, *Die Lieder Bertrans von Born*, Sammlung romanischer Übungstexte, nos. 19–20 (Halle: Niemeyer, 1932), pp. 39–42, 98–99.

54. See Friedrich Gennrich, "Gace Brulé," in *Die Musik in Geschichte und Gegenwart*, ed. Blume, vol. IV (1955), cols. 1215–1223. After Geoffrey's death, Gace was associated with the court of Marie de Champagne.

55. Ibid., cols. 1217–1218. Texts of this and other poems by Gace are edited by Gédéon Huet, *Chansons de Gace Brulé* (Paris: Didot, 1902); no complete musical edition is available.

56. See Arthur Långfors, A. Jeanroy, and L. Brandin, eds., *Recueil général des jeux-partis français*, 2 vols. (Paris: Société des Anciens Textes Français, 1926), I, 7–10, xiv–xvii.

57. See the account of events given by Ralph of Diceto in his *Imaginibus historiarum*, in *Recueil des historiens des Gaules et de la France*, vol. XVII, ed. Delisle and Brial, p. 628.

58. *A totz dic que ja mais no volh* (Pillet-Carstens 80.6a), preserved in a single source without music; the text is edited by Appel, *Die Lieder Bertrans von Born*, pp. 63–65.

59. *Anglia, planctus itera* appears in F on folios 421v–422, where it is one of the more melismatic of the monophonic pieces in fascicle 10; the text is edited in *Analecta hymnica*, XXI, 177, with the comment "nur ein Bruchstück des Ganzen [only a fragment of the whole]." *Eclypsim patitur* is on folios 322v–323 in F, and its text is edited in *Analecta hymnica*, XXI, 179.

60. Though it is a commonplace to compare the death of a noble personage with an eclipse of the sun (as happens in both of these poems), it is interesting that Ralph of Diceto's chronicle mentions eclipses of both the sun and the moon in the late spring of 1186, only a few months before Geoffrey's death (*Recueil des historiens des Gaules et de la France*, vol. XVII, ed. Delisle and Brial, p. 627).

61. Anglia, planctus itera / Et ad luctum revertere, / Duplex dampnum considera / Duplici merso sidere.

62. F, folios 350v–351; W1, folio 117 (new 108); text edited in *Analecta hymnica*, XXI, 178.

63. F, folios 318v–319; W1, folio 110v (new 101v).

64. Cf. *Analecta hymnica*, XXI,

177–178. I wish to thank James H. Cook for assistance with the translation.

65. Some examples are given by Joseph Bédier and Pierre Aubry, *Les Chansons de croisade avec leurs mélodies* (Paris, 1909).

66. *F*, folios 419v–420; strophes 1, 3, and 5 are written out with music, while strophes 2, 4, and 6 are to be sung to the immediately prior melody. The complete poem is in *Analecta hymnica*, XXI, 164; my translation. Heraclius was the patriarch of Jerusalem who in 1185 had journeyed to the West to seek aid from Henry II and Philip Augustus.

67. Raynaud 1891; Pillet-Carstens 420.2; text and translation from Henry Adams, *Mont-Saint-Michel and Chartres* (Boston: Houghton Mifflin, 1913), p. 222. Gennrich includes a musical transcription in *Exempla altfran-*

zösischer Lyrik, pp. 6–7 (see note 26 above).

68. *F*, folios 434–435; text in *Analecta hymnica*, XXI, 181.

69. Pillet-Carstens 167.22. Two readily accessible musical transcriptions by Gennrich can be found in *Troubadours, Trouvères, Minne- und Meistergesang*, pp. 17–18, and *Lo gai saber*, pp. 49–50.

70. See Lejeune's itinerary, "Rôle littéraire d'Aliénor," p. 57; Richardson, "Letters," pp. 198–200.

71. *F*, folios 339v–340v; text in *Analecta hymnica*, XXI, 182.

72. Gallus, Hispanus, Apulus / et Greculus / invident Turonensibus / cum viribus / profunde.

4. Eleanor, Abbot Suger, and Saint-Denis

ELEANOR S. GREENHILL

Following the arrival of the new queen, Eleanor of Aquitaine, in the late summer of 1137,[1] an unprecedented flowering of the arts, centered in the royal abbey of Saint-Denis, took place in the Frankish kingdom. At the abbey church, begun in the 1130's and dedicated in 1144, Gothic architecture, Gothic sculpture, and Gothic stained glass came into being,[2] as if by magic, in a region which did not at the time even possess an architectural school of its own and had been, in terms of the monumental arts, almost totally dormant since the Carolingian period.[3] Even today the consternation of art historians, this phenomenon has been attributed by them almost without exception to the initiative and personality of Abbot Suger of Saint-Denis (1122–1151),[4] a view supported by the existence of certain treatises written by the abbot—or by somebody using his name—which place him at the center of building activity there. Widely known in the edition and translation of Erwin Panofsky, these texts are the *Ordinatio*, enacted at the Abbey in 1140/1141, the *De Consecratione*, written between 1144 and 1146/1147, and the *De Administratione*, composed after the completion of the *De Consecratione* but by 1148/1149.[5] Quite understandably Suger's treatises have been seized upon by art historians for the way in which they let us look into the mind of the great abbot, whom certain scholars have regarded not only as the patron and builder of the new church, but also as the responsible architect who, with no more than a master mason to aid him, created the design and directed the construction.[6] Panofsky, however, has left the question open whether Suger was "responsible or co-responsible for the design of his structures."[7]

The historian who challenges Suger's rule as "creative masterbuilder [*schöpferische Baumeister*]"[8] cannot produce in support of his arguments any sources which carry the weight of Suger's treatises. But it is universally recognized that we do not possess full documentation for the reign of Louis VII[9] or for the abbacy of Suger. All the abbot's letters written before 1145 have been lost or destroyed;[10] they might have thrown much light on the question of royal patronage and on the possible sources of the design. It is only logical and consonant with what we know of medieval practice that the king and queen of the Franks should have substantially supported the reconstruction of the royal abbey,[11] which had been for centuries closely associated with the ruling dynasty. There a long series of Frankish sovereigns lay buried, there the royal insignia were kept in custody, and there the Martyr Denis, Patron of the Franks, was venerated as *dux et protector* of the realm. In 1124, when the kingdom was threatened by invasion, Louis VI had declared himself to be the vassal of the Blessed Denis.[12] The realm had been saved. His son and successor, therefore, both as king and as vassal of the patron, owed the abbey his loyalty and support. It is unthinkable that the pious Louis VII would not have honored these filial and feudal ties by generous subventions, once the abbot had made the decision to rebuild. Failure to do so would have been *lèse-majesté* of the grossest sort and contrary to all we know of medieval practice. [13] The support of all the churches established in his realm, Louis considered the proper function of the king.[14]

Yet Suger nowhere makes explicit reference to royal subsidies, although he frequently alludes to gifts without identifying the donor; and no one has suggested that these gifts might have come from the royal house or been accompanied by royal initiative in the choice of workmen and, therefore, of style. Eleanor's name appears only twice in the treatises, once in connection with the dedication ceremony on June 11, 1144,[15] and once in connection with the crystal vase, which she gave to Louis and "he to the Abbey." [16] This surely cannot be interpreted to mean, however, that Eleanor and Louis bore no part of the expense. While Robert Fawtier questions whether the revenues of Aquitaine added much to the royal household,[17] Eleanor certainly had access to them. There must have been, moreover, in those early years an assumption on Eleanor's part that she would bear Louis a son, that Aquitaine would then be incorporated into the Capetian realm,[18] and that she and her children would, like other Frankish sovereigns, be entombed at Saint-Denis, pantheon of the Frankish house. If wealthy patronage is the basis on which the arts flourish, then the Capetians were, after 1137, in a position to foster the arts as never before.

In the search for the generative forces behind this artistic flowering, one cannot of course fail to reckon with the personality of Suger, his international connections, his preoccupation with Dionysian light metaphysics, and his overriding passion for the aggrandizement of the Capetian dynasty. It has been suggested by Otto von Simson and others that Suger even made the rebuilding of Saint-Denis the instrument of this political goal.[19] The energetic and competitive spirit, moreover, which inspired Suger with the desire to make his church the equal of any in Christendom, as well as his many journeys on behalf of Louis VI, must have played a part in the creation of the new church.[20] So, undoubtedly, did that ideological *renovatio imperii Karoli Magni* (revival of the empire of Charlemagne) which, according to Percy Ernst Schramm, animated both Suger and the Capetian kings. The steps by means of which Louis VI and Louis VII were made to appear the legitimate heirs of the great emperor have been set forth by Schramm and others.[21] It must be said, however, that these steps remained in the realm of the ceremonial, the symbolic, or the literary until, with the construction of the new church, they took on more concrete form. It has been insufficiently stressed that the very design proclaims in the great westwork with flanking towers its Carolingian inspiration.[22] Charlemagne together with his court had indeed been present when the old church, possessing one of the earliest of all westworks, was dedicated in 775. And there were other historic links between the emperor and the abbey.[23]

But the Charles whom this *renovatio* invoked was, as Schramm has pointed out, not so much the historical figure as the Charlemagne of the *Song of Roland*.[24] Committed to writing about the year 1100, the *Roland* envisions Charles as a ruler of a universal Christian kingdom, and places his field of activities far more in south France and Spain than in Aachen. It ascribes to the emperor such apocryphal deeds as the conquest of the Iberian peninsula as far as Cordoba, heart of the Saracen realm (lines 70–71). At least three quarters of a century earlier than the *Roland*, this belief, spread abroad by the jongleurs, appeared in written form in a chronicle (written in 1028–1031) devoted to the counts and history of Aquitaine, by Adhemar de Chabannes.[25]

The actual reconquest of Spain, carried out in the heroic eleventh century by French knights in a series of veritable crusades, was an attempt to make historical reality correspond to the songs of the jongleurs and Adhemar's chronicle. Among the forces which, in the course of that century, achieved this goal were the powerful dukes of Aquitaine. At the time of Eleanor's marriage, they had been engaged for a hundred years and more in the struggle against the Moors, together with their cousins of the House of Burgundy, with the Order of Cluny, which Duke William I of Aquitaine had founded, and with their in-laws, the Spanish monarchs.[26] On numerous occasions they had crossed the Pyrenees as commanders of large contingents of Provençaux, Aquitanians, and Normans.[27] William VIII of Aquitaine, the most powerful seigneur of his

time, had been commander in chief of the "first Spanish crusade" of
1063, mounted at the call of the pope;[28] William's daughter Agnes,
through the intermediary of Cluny, became the first wife of Alfonso VI of
Castile.[29] Another daughter married Pedro I of Navarre and Aragon.[30]
Bernard of Sedirac, chosen by Alfonso VI to be Archbishop of Toledo in
1086, was Cluny-trained and also an Aquitanian.[31] Primate of Spain
after 1088, Bernard introduced into Galacia-Asturias and Castile-León a
veritable Carolingian reform, replacing Mozarabic liturgy with Franco-
Roman and the Visigothic script with Carolingian minuscule.[32] William
IX of Aquitaine, the troubadour and Eleanor's grandfather, married the
widow of the king of Aragon, Philippa of Toulouse. A frequent visitor to
Santiago de Compostela, William had been present at the head of a great
army when, in 1118, the fortress of Cutanda fell to Alfonso Batallador.[33]
One of William's daughters married Ramiro of Aragon.[34] William's son,
Eleanor's father, was that French potentate of the twelfth century who
most venerated the Apostle of Galicia (Saint James), going on annual
visits to his shrine at Compostela.[35] All this makes it clear why William
was buried so prestigiously at the foot of the altar of Saint James when he
died in Compostela on Holy Thursday of 1137[36]—a burial that otherwise might seem surprising in view of Saint Bernard's low opinion of the
schismatic duke and his house.[37] Diego Gelmirez, Cluny-trained archbishop of Santiago,[38] would have been fully aware of the services
which William's ancestors had rendered the shrine and the pilgrimage
centered there.

For William X himself that shrine was undoubtedly rendered venerable
by the memory of his ducal forebears, who had fought so prodigiously in
Spain. Perhaps William knew the dry historical facts of Charlemagne's
ill-starred Spanish adventure as told in Einhard's *Life of Charlemagne*,
written soon after the emperor's death,[39] but he would have had ample
occasion to absorb what pilgrims of lesser rank heard from the jongleurs
and the clerks on the pilgrimage routes. William may well have believed
that Charles had blazed a trail to Santiago from the Port de Cize, at the
southwestern limits of his own territory,[40] and that the emperor had
been, so to speak, the first pilgrim.[41] Like others of his day, he probably
assumed that the emperor and his men had conquered all of Spain.
Ramón Menéndez Pidal has collected the evidence that this belief existed
in the monasteries along the pilgrimage routes in Spain in the late eleventh century. [42] Indeed, so widespread had that belief become that a Spanish chronicler around 1103–1110 found it necessary to attack "these
French boastings [*ces vanteries françaises*]" in a scorching indictment
of Frankish avarice.[43] Aside from legend, William would have known

that Alfonso VI of Castile, his uncle by marriage, had, in imitation of the great Charles, assumed the title of *imperator* after the capture of Toledo in 1085.[44] And since he always maintained close relations with his distant kinsman, Alfonso VII of Castile-León, he may well have been present when the latter assumed the same title at a great Easter court in 1135.[45] William, then, was not the man to resist the pressure of legend, which, as students of the *chansons de geste* assure us, had, by the late eleventh century, become so potent a force that they had made of Santiago as much a Carolingian as a Jacobean shrine.[46]

With the great vaulted basilica, begun over the relics of the Apostle of Galicia in 1077, William was clearly well acquainted. Its nine towers and its ample scale may well have been the concrete visual expression of that sense of victory which inspired both papal and Cluniac building in the late eleventh century.[47] Architectural historians, independently of students of the *chansons de geste*, have pointed to features in the design which, without precedent in Spain,[48] are typical of Carolingian imperial foundations as well as more recent structures built in the old Carolingian lands.[49] Interrupted in 1088 by political controversy, construction at Santiago resumed in 1100 under the auspices of the new bishop, Diego Gelmirez, and under the influence of the enormous pilgrimage shrine of Saint-Sernin in Toulouse, which had been under way from around 1080.[50] Reflected back to France, this design was repeated with local variations in a series of pilgrimage churches which form a group with Saint-Sernin and Santiago: Saint-Martial at Limoges (begun ca. 1080), Sainte-Foy at Conques (ca. 1100), and Saint-Martin at Tours as rebuilt after 1100.[51] In that late-blooming Carolingian Renaissance initiated in Spain by Bernard of Sedirac under the patronage of Cluny, Alfonso VI, and the pope, the shrine of Saint James was the culminating achievement.

Those two sentiments, then, which, according to von Simson, Schramm, and others, inspired Suger and the Capetians—"the idea of Crusade intermingled with the memory of Charlemagne"[52]—had long since been the ruling passion of the Aquitanian dukes. If, as von Simson asserts, the abbey church of Saint-Denis was to become like Santiago de Compostela a great pilgrimage center, Eleanor would have understood such an aim at once. Had not the message which linked her personal destiny to that of the Capetians come directly from Santiago? Did not her father lie buried at the foot of the saint's altar there?[53] Descended from a long line of valorous dukes, who had fought incessantly in Spain against the Moors, Eleanor was surely not the person to stand idly by while the royal abbey was transformed into a pilgrimage center on the order of Santiago. Her influence on affairs in the capital was instantaneous,[54] her presence there the visible sign that the Frankish domain, for the first time since the Carolingian age, stretched southwestward to the flanks of the Pyrenees. Nor did Eleanor, in 1147, take the position of onlooker when the Second Crusade got under way, an enterprise far more daring and costly than the rebuilding of the abbey church.[55]

Those aims which, according to von Simson, inspired the Capetians to rebuild the abbey church were as much a part of Eleanor's heritage as her husband's—and even more so. The Capetians knew nothing of Spain; they had never fought the infidel there, had never gone on pilgrimage to Santiago.[56] Nor indeed had their closest adviser Suger. If the Capetians needed a consultant on affairs in the peninsula and on the latest achievements of Jacobean architectural design when they rebuilt the royal abbey at Saint-Denis, they had one at court—Eleanor herself, which is to say some Poitevin of mature years in her entourage.

Arthur Kingsley Porter long ago asserted that the "Ile-de-France owes much to Santiago."[57] It is the thesis of this study that the new church at Saint-Denis was in truth built "in the likeness of the church of Saint James [ad similitudinem scilicet ecclesie beati Jacobi],"[58] in the sense that it adopted the essential elements of the Jacobean shrine: the ample basilical ground plan, the pilgrimage choir, characterized by ambulatory and radiating chapels, the great westwork with flanking towers, the fireproof construction.[59] To be sure, Suger did not envision for his church a salient transept, which characterizes the Jacobean shrine (because of the dimensions of the pre-existing church), but the outer aisles of the projected nave were so planned as to link up with the ambulatory around the sanctuary, thus providing, in the manner of the pilgrimage shrine, complete and easy circulation from the west entrances to the radiating chapels and back again. Had the projected five-aisled nave been carried out, it would have had thirteen bays,[60] while the narthex provided shelter for hordes of waiting pilgrims. Churches of such amplitude combined with westwork and pilgrimage choir and antedating Saint-Denis are found only in the third church at Cluny, at Santiago, at Saint-Sernin in Toulouse, and at Saint-Martin in Tours—all examples of the grandly scaled pilgrimage shrine. It goes without saying, of course, that Suger's choir was restated in a new and diaphanous formal system which we now call Gothic. But the disposition of that choir on two levels, the lower one being a massive crypt, repeats the arrangement of the chevet of Saint-Martin at Tours,[61] a church Suger knew personally.[62] Moreover, according to the *Pilgrim's Guide*, written in the late 1130's, Saint-Martin was built as a copy of Santiago, and this view has recently been reasserted by a modern scholar.[63] The ultimate Jacobean inspiration of Suger's church seems undeniable. At least we may say that the synthesis which took place at Saint-Denis to produce the first Gothic church had been in part prepared by one which had already produced the pilgrimage shrine. Indeed, architectural historians concede that the ground plan of the great classical Gothic cathedrals, Chartres, Rheims, and Amiens, is based on that of the pilgrimage shrine.[64] That plan, it should not be forgotten, was transmitted to them via Saint-Denis. In addition, the insertion of figural sculpture into the portal of a façade (instead of within a porch or scattered over the entire front), which we find at Saint-Denis, may have antecedents in northern Spain. To be sure, such a figured portal, with carved tympanum and lintel and carried on carved consoles, appeared late in the eleventh century at Charlieu in Burgundy and a short time thereafter in a more elaborate version at Cluny III, but by 1137 both these ensembles had been obscured by the addition of a deep porch or narthex.[65] Such figured tympana appeared late in the eleventh century on the exterior portals of Jaca and San Isidoro in León (the latter now incorporated into a twelfth-century portal),[66] and shortly thereafter on the Puerta de las Platerías at Santiago,[67] where the original disposition has been altered by later additions. Before 1118 the incorporation of figural sculpture into the structure of an exterior portal, which we find at Santiago, appears at the Porte Miègeville on the south flank of Saint-Sernin in Toulouse. As we shall see, that portal was influential in the creation of the royal portals of northern France.[68]

In 1137, when Eleanor arrived in Paris, the old Carolingian wooden-roofed structure was still standing at Saint-Denis, proclaiming the backwardness of this region, at least in terms of architecture. Impossibly antiquated, the abbey church had a narrow western entrance, possibly then already dismantled, and a claustrophobic crypt, where the crush on feast days was intolerable.[69] Suger had in 1125 taken certain preliminary steps to restore the crumbling conventual buildings.[70] Sometime thereafter, he had also patched up the moldering old walls of the nave, as he states in Chapter 24 of *De Administratione*: "The first work on this church which we began under the inspiration of God [was this]: because of the age of the old walls and their impending ruin in some places, we summoned the best painters I could find from different regions, and reverently caused these [walls] to be repaired and becomingly painted with gold and precious colors."[71] These measures suggest that Suger did not originally have in mind a fully developed plan for the reconstruction. On the contrary, he approached the task only slowly and piecemeal. Moreover, to judge from the above passage, he seems to have been delighted with the aesthetic effects conveyed by the flat, painted surfaces, effects by then quite out of date in the progressive schools of French architecture—the Norman, the Burgundian, the Languedocian—where the walls of the fully vaulted churches had by 1130 been opened up by galleries and given a markedly sculptural relief through the use of colonnettes and ascending wall shafts.[72] Suger's aesthetics were archaic, closer to either Byzantine or contemporary Roman than current French taste.

Even while this refurbishing was being completed, Suger decided to enlarge the body of the church and treble the entrance doors.[73] At the same time, he rebuilt the monks' refectory and dormitory. These latter he mentioned as completed, the enlargement of the church as in process, in his testament of June 17, 1137, recorded on the eve of his departure for Bordeaux to witness the nuptials of Louis VII and Eleanor.[74] It is impossible to determine with precision just how far this work of amplification had progressed by that date. We know from Sumner McK. Crosby's excavations that Suger extended the nave westward by some thirty feet before beginning the great westwork, which took up another sixty feet.[75] But the extension of the nave, since it demanded columns, was delayed, as Suger tells us, "for many years," while he studied how to obtain them.[76] He considered bringing ancient marble ones from Rome by water but abandoned that as too risky. Nothing in Suger's testament suggests that he had found a supply of columns or the stone necessary to their manufacture when he went south to Bordeaux, a journey which kept him away from his abbey for the duration of the summer.[77] In the testament, which takes up eight pages in the printed edition, the abbot devotes only one line to the "augmentation" of the new church, and the wording suggests that this measure was only a part of a general campaign to modernize the old monastic buildings, since it is mentioned in the same sentence with the building of a hospice and the repair and renovation of the monks' dormitory and refectory.[78]

The moment when the renovation of the church became Suger's chief preoccupation can be pinpointed in the treatises, although not associated with a specific date: the "unexpected [*inopinata*]" gift of a quarry provided—something unheard of in those parts—stone of a hardness necessary to the manufacture of columns, thus solving Suger's long-standing problem.[79] Subsequently, Suger tells us, a veritable horde of skilled workmen—masons, sculptors, mortarers, stonecutters, and the like— arrived.[80] Nor does Suger say that he called them in; they simply "followed [*succedebat*]." We cannot be sure when these workmen—clearly a whole workshop—arrived, but the very suddenness of that event, as well as its association with the unexpected gift of a quarry, makes it impossible to agree with Crosby and Marcel Aubert that work at Saint-Denis speeded up because Suger had by careful administration gradually acquired the necessary resources and trained the required workers.[81] The speed with which the new workmen proceeded suggests that they were a team already well trained and accustomed to collaboration elsewhere. Their appearance in Paris must have followed very shortly the arrival there of Eleanor herself. But before trying to decide whether there was a causal relationship between these two events, let us follow the course of reconstruction at the abbey.

After the dedication of the western extension, but before carrying the western towers up to their full height, Suger tells us that in July 1140 he "hurried to begin the chamber of divine atonement in the upper choir,"[82] that is, the chevet, celebrated for its glass and precocious ribbed vaults. Following its dedication in June 1144, Suger raised and enlarged the transept wings (*De Administratione*, Ch. 28) and then, abandoning work on the towers a second time, turned his attention to the renewal and enlargement of the "central body of the church which is called the nave."[83] Projected to replace the one painted in gold and precious colors only a few years earlier, that nave was never carried above the foundations,[84] although work continued at a snail's pace throughout the twelfth century.

Saint-Denis, it has been said, surpassed most bishoprics in political significance and territorial wealth; yet Suger's church remained for eighty years a torso while magnificent cathedrals, based upon its design, arose in the royal sees and great bishoprics of northern France.[85] Peculiar circumstances must have prevailed at the royal abbey which did not exist in the bishoprics of the rising cities. What were they?

Since the existing rayonnant nave of Saint-Denis was carried out only in the 1230's with the help of Blanche of Castile,[86] the suspicion arises that the abbey, even at the time of Suger, and in spite of his careful householding, was itself financially inadequate to the task of rebuilding and in all probability dependent even then on royal subsidies.

On the subject of the abbey's financial strength we have no other guide than Suger's own treatises. In them the abbot reports numerous gifts and other "fortunate circumstances," by means of which the campaign was carried forward, as due to the intervention of Divine Providence. It seems justified to see in these gifts and miracles not merely a pious manner of speaking but actual donations. From them, the historian can obtain some insight into the total amount expended on the new church and the proportion of that expense borne by the abbey. In the *De Consecratione*, especially instructive in this regard, Suger represents the entire church and its consecration as a divine gift (Ch. 1). He mentions explicitly the following donations: the gift of the quarry, mentioned above, which "produced very fine and excellent columns" and was exploited to complete not only the nave but the westwork (Ch. 2); the "miracle of the carts," which aided in extricating some of the columns from the quarry (Ch. 3); the miracle of the timbers, found in the valley of the Chevreuse on one of the abbey's own possessions (Ch. 3); the transformation of a golden but "modest" altar panel into something "glorious" by the intervention of the holy martyrs themselves, who handed Suger such a "wealth of gold and most precious gems—unexpected and hardly to be found among Kings"—that they seemed to say "we want it of the best" (Ch. 5); the purchase "by the Grace of God" of a quantity of pearls and gems made possible by a gift of four hundred pounds (Ch. 5); the "memorable event" of the Premonstratensian gift of mutton (Ch. 5).[87]

Undoubtedly the most princely of all these miraculous gifts was that of the quarry. Suger gives an account of it at the very beginning of the *De Consecratione*:

Since in the front part. . .the narrow hall was squeezed in on either side by twin towers neither high nor very sturdy but threatening ruin, we began. . .strenuously to work on this part, having laid very strong material foundations for a straight nave and twin towers. . . . We proceeded with this so great and so sumptuous work to such an extent that, while at first expending little, we lacked much, afterwards accomplishing much, we lacked nothing at all and even confessed in our abundance: Our sufficiency is of God (II Cor. III, 5). Through a gift of God a new quarry, yielding very strong stone, was discovered such as in quality and quantity had never been found in these regions. There arrived a skillful crowd of masons, stonecutters, sculptors, and other workmen, so that—thus and otherwise—Divinity relieved us of our fears and favored us with Its good will by comforting us and by providing us with unexpected [resources].[88]

The wording of this passage makes clear that Suger's insufficient resources were greatly augmented by a sudden turn of fortune. Whence came this unexpected largesse?

On the walls of the narthex and the foundations of the choir, the workmen left their stonemasons' marks, which Crosby has identified as Norman.[89] But Normandy had no tradition of stone figural sculpture.[90] Yet the jambs, tympana, and archivolts of the three western portals were, as all the world knows, adorned with a rich cycle of monumental stone carvings, among them the first true column-statues known to the history of art.[91] If among the *sculptores* mentioned by Suger we may count those who did these carvings, we may plausibly determine their origin, for the statues are in a very distinctive style, the home of which we know. Wilhelm Voege in the last century first pointed out[92] and Willibald Sauerländer has recently maintained that their style "shows signs of evident and strong inspiration from southwest France."[93] The immediate sources have been narrowed even further, to Toulouse and Moissac, those two great generative centers of romanesque sculpture on the pilgrimage roads to Santiago.[94] Since Suger, as far as we know, had never visited those sites,[95] we must ask how this link between the royal abbey and Toulouse/Moissac came about.

Several possible explanations suggest themselves. It is possible that the renown of Toulousan artists had reached Suger, for their sphere of influence extended not only as far as Santiago and back again, but also along the pilgrimage routes into Italy. At Ferrara around 1135, the sculptor Niccolò carved a portal which, like those at Saint-Denis, reveals the inspiration of Saint-Etienne in Toulouse, begun about 1125 or 1130.[96] But the renown of Toulousan sculptors may also have been known to Eleanor. It is also possible, therefore, that another factor may have been at work in their selection at Saint-Denis, namely royal initiative.

As Kelly has pointed out, the first acts taken by Louis as king were in vindication of his new titles as duke of Aquitaine and count of Poitou, an enterprise in which Suger assisted. Among these acts was the reassertion of Eleanor's claim to the County of Toulouse, to which the queen never ceased to regard herself as the rightful heir by virtue of her descent from Philippa of Toulouse, first wife of the Troubadour.[97] Had not Eleanor's own father, had not her uncle Raymond of Antioch been born in the ancestral castle of those counts in the city of Toulouse? Supporting her claim, Louis marched south in the winter of 1137 at the head of an army; and, although a settlement did not take place until 1141,[98] Eleanor or agents acting for her could have, at the very moment of her marriage, commissioned sculptors from the ancient capital of the counts of Toulouse to work at Saint-Denis as evidence of her claim—and now that of her husband, Louis VII—to suzerainty there.

There are still other links—iconographic as well as formal—between the sculptures at Saint-Denis and those of churches in the Saintonge, Eleanor's native region. The theme of the wise and foolish virgins, which appears at Saint-Denis on the piedroits of the main portal, frequently occurs in the West, as Emile Mâle long ago pointed out.[99] Moreover, the carving of figures to follow the curve of the archivolt appeared as a formal innovation in the Saintonge in the 1130's and has long been regarded as a precedent for the similar disposition of figures on the archivolts at Saint-Denis.[100] The deeply splayed and shafted portals at Saint-Denis and Chartres, which reveal the full thickness of the wall, may have been suggested, in the view of Adolf Katzenellenbogen, by the doorways of churches from the same region of western France.[101] The combination of statue and cylindrical pier formerly to be seen in the cloisters at Saint-Denis (and duly reported by Bernard de Montfaucon) is based, according to Sauerländer, on prototypes in southwestern France and northern Spain;[102] that is to say, these sculptures also looked westward—to the pilgrimage routes, to sites never seen by Suger or the Capetians. The placement of the sculptures on the exterior wall, moreover, and their concentration around the portals (rather than being scattered over the facade or placed within a porch) may betray, as indicated above, the influence of Santiago itself, whether directly or indirectly.[103] And, although the problem of the origin of the column-statue is one of the thorniest in all medieval art and still a matter for debate, it has been suggested that prototypes of the column-statues at Saint-Denis may be found on the Puerta de las Platerías at Santiago de Compostela.[104]

At Santiago three marble columns flanking the double entrance of the Puerta de las Platerías, begun about 1103, exhibit surfaces carved in very low relief with registers of small saintly figures standing under arcades; thus they do not emerge from the cylindrical shape.[105] The monumental column-statues at Saint-Denis, executed some thirty-five years later, although carved from the same block as the column, have emerged from the surface to occupy three dimensional space; they create, therefore, a very different impression. Yet the debt to the romanesque relief is still apparent at Saint-Denis, where the figures do not yet respond to the "axial structure of the column."[106] We now know, moreover, that the inspiration for lining the jambs of a deeply splayed portal with monumental figures did not come from Saint-Etienne in Toulouse, for the series of apostles associated with that church, although they provide the source of the *style* at Saint-Denis, were set up, not flanking a portal, but on the interior of the chapter house.[107] The Ferrara portal by Niccolò, although it may have been known to the workmen at Saint-Denis, does not incorporate the small figures on the jambs into columns.[108] George Zarnecki's suggestion of possible influence from the Puerta de las Platerías is, then, most appealing. If, moreover, the west façade visible at Santiago in the 1130's had been preserved (it is described in the *Pilgrim's Guide*), it might well provide in the development of the column-statue a phase intermediate between the older Puerta de las Platerías and Saint-Denis.[109] While the germ of this formal development may lie in Santiago, it must be conceded that the type of the royal portal appears first in Capetian territory and for many years was largely confined to that region.[110] The numerous formal debts to territories either ruled by Eleanor or associated with the pilgrimage must not, therefore, be overinterpreted. Still, it seems odd that art historians have not found it worthwhile to link these formal debts to the new dynastic and political situation which obtained in the Frankish kingdom after 1137 even though they are well aware that the movement of style in the Middle Ages often accompanied royal marriages.[111]

Current opinion holds that the Abbot Suger commissioned the western portals at Saint-Denis.[112] As is well known, the sculptors carved his portrait, a tiny kneeling figure, at the foot of the Christ-Judge in the central tympanum.[113] It has always been a puzzle, however, that Suger nowhere mentions the sculptures of the west façade, while he does refer to the fact that, at his explicit orders and "contrary to modern custom," he installed a mosaic in the tympanum of the north portal, "incongruously combined with the sculpture of an already proto-Gothic portal," as Panofsky says.[114] This looks as if a clash of wills had occurred. It certainly is a clash of styles. Would Suger, or anybody, after having commissioned a new-fangled portal adorned with full-round sculptures, thus diminish their effect by combining them with an old-fashioned mosaic? Or is it possible that the portals were the suggestion of someone else with more up-to-date tastes—someone in touch with the latest achievements of the pilgrimage roads and Santiago itself?

Whatever the source of the commission or the concept, there is little doubt that the twenty column-statues formerly lining the jambs of the portals[115] referred in some way to royalty. Because of their attributes and their crowns, they have been identified as Old Testament kings, patriarchs, and prophets—and queens, or a queen and a prophetess. For among them— an unparalleled adornment for the portal of a monastic church—are two youthful, attractive females, one wearing a sort of turban on her head, the other a crown, their faces framed by long braids, bound their full length with ribbon,[116] a contemporary hair style which aroused Saint Bernard's spleen. The elegant costumes, adorned with long modish sleeves and belted at the waist, reveal the curve of youthful bodies. The identity of these two figures is not made easier of solution by the fact that another pair of females—now headless—are to be found among the six column-statues on the contemporary portal of Notre-Dame du Fort in Etampes.[117]

Some twenty miles south of Paris, Etampes was a royal residence, where Louis VI had begun construction of a castle. An atelier of sculptors not identical with that at Saint-Denis began a single portal for the church of Notre-Dame around 1140.[118] Set up on the south flank rather than on the west end of the church, the six column-statues faced the road leading to the royal castle. Their style has been called Burgundian,[119] although the awkward articulation of the arms recalls that of the apostles from Saint-Etienne in Toulouse.[120] Links with the Porte Miègeville at Saint-Sernin in Toulouse also exist—the composition of the Ascension in the tympanum and the built-out structure of the portal.[121]

The almost simultaneous appearance of the Etampes and Saint-Denis ensembles—the earliest of all royal portals—in the environs of the capital, at sites closely associated with the royal house, and with a common link with Toulouse, certainly suggests ultimately royal inspiration for them both, but we do not know whether the royal house itself took the initiative, commissioned the sculptors, and paid the bills, or whether the initiative came from the side of the religious house. It is a possibility that the costs of erecting the portal at Etampes were borne by Henri de France, the king's brother and abbot of Notre-Dame from about 1140 to 1146.[122] There is some evidence to connect the Etampes atelier further with Saint-Denis itself. In the view of Wilhelm Voege, who based his opinion on an engraving published by Montfaucon, the Etampes Master carried out an enthroned statue of King Dagobert for the royal abbey, "the first representation of a specific French King at Saint Denis," unfortunately destroyed in the revolution.[123] With this view Sauerländer agrees, dating the statue to the time of Suger.[124] The badly damaged surface of the surviving fragment of the sculpture, which has recently been published, makes a conclusion as to date difficult, if not impossible.[125] But even if we accept the date "before 1151" for the Dagobert, we cannot be sure of the source of the commission. Nor can we be sure whether the king's brother, if he bore the costs of the portal at Etampes, did so as royal prince or as abbot, since he combined both ranks in the same person. We cannot use the example of Etampes as conclusive evidence for the view that the royal house rather than Suger commissioned and paid for the column-statues at Saint-Denis. The royal connotation of these statues, however, seems beyond question. Crosby has stated, following a suggestion by Ernst Kitzinger, that they are the "symbols, not the portraits of the Kings and Queens of France,"[126] an interpretation in accord with Capetian ideology, for Frankish kingship was sacred and had a quasi-sacerdotal character, like that of the ancient Hebrews.[127] In speaking of early Gothic figured portals as "royal," scholars are only following medieval precedent.[128] There is about these early ensembles an air of secular magnificence and an acceptance of profane and youthful feminine beauty more in accord with courtly than monastic art. While the nature of the sources and documents, then, does not permit the conclusion that Eleanor or Louis commissioned and paid for the portals at Saint-Denis, it is possible that those portals could have been the expression of the munificence and dynastic connections of the young queen whose worldly propensities so scandalized Saint Bernard.

But if Eleanor's wealth and territorial claims were in any way responsible for the presence of sculptors at Saint-Denis, why would Suger not say so? Why is he so silent on the subject? The answer must lie, in part, in the fact, disputed by no one, that the queen conducted herself badly after 1141/1142 in the affair regarding her sister and Raoul of Vermandois[129] and may have made her name a very unpopular one at the abbey. But the character of the writings which have come down to us may also bear part of the blame for the silence concerning Eleanor and Louis. Exasperatingly tantalizing—spiritual treatises rather than chronicles—they have been characterized in a recent communication by Crosby as follows: "The *De Administratione* is a curious text. . . . As an account of his [Suger's] administration, it is hopelessly incomplete. Mention of incidents is haphazard and so is their exclusion, so that objective evaluation is most difficult. Many things seem to have been taken for granted, such as royal gifts to the Abbey." [130] With these observations, applicable also to the *De Consecratione*, one must heartily agree. Unconcerned with the facts of external history, Suger's texts must be read as cautiously as certain others closely associated with the abbey, which are among the most famous literary *faux* (or spoofs) of the Middle Ages: the so-called *Descriptio*, written in the late eleventh century to authenticate the relics of the Passion claimed by the abbey and venerated at the annual feast of Lendit; [131] the *Pèlerinage de Charlemagne*, [132] written about 1150 as a spoof of the *Descriptio*; and the fraudulent charter purportedly granted by Charlemagne to the abbey in the year 813, but based upon the equally fraudulent *Pseudo-Turpin*, and possibly no earlier than 1148. [133]

It is useless, then, to expect from Suger's treatises a full accounting of the abbot's expenditures. In spite of this, they will be examined, *faute de mieux*, for the evidence they provide on this subject. From a passage in the *Ordinatio*, repeated verbatim in the *De Consecratione*, we learn the amount of annual revenue set aside by Suger and his brother monks from their income for the completion of the choir. [134] This action was taken immediately following the foundation ceremony of July 1140, when the king was present. Louis, Suger tells us, *gave his consent* to the annual expenditure of two hundred pounds, [135] an event which throws some light upon the relationship between the monarch and the abbey, although it tells us very little about the king's own contribution. We also learn that Suger was uneasy about the ability of the abbey to meet the costs of this new phase of building and that he was, in fact, in debt for the earlier structure, on which he abandoned work in order to begin the choir: "But suddenly the love and devotion of the Holy Martyrs our Patrons and Protectors roused us to enlarge and amplify the chevet of the upper church. Nor could the unfinished state of the former [structure] restrain us from beginning the latter; for we hoped to the Lord that the Omnipotence of God, either through us or through those whom He should please [to choose], would be able to provide sufficient resources for that earlier structure as well as for this later one." [136]

In launching the campaign at the east end of the church, then, Suger was living beyond his means, although it is possible that he exaggerated somewhat in order to make the completion seem all the more the work of Providence.

Similar passages from *De Administratione* support the view that funds were short. Well known is the account of the "merry but notable" miracle which occurred in connection with the decoration of the Great Cross (Ch. 32).[137] Suger needed gems, of which he had an insufficient number; and he could not provide himself with more, "for their scarcity makes them very expensive." However, by a lucky chance, monks arrived from Cîteaux with a quantity of jewels, and Suger bought the lot for four hundred pounds. Where, one would like to ask, in view of his own insufficient funds, and on seemingly short notice, did he obtain a sum equal to twice the amount of annual revenue designated by the abbey for the fabric of the church? Surely we are justified in assuming in this case the intervention of a donor of means.

But the most striking passage relating to Suger's financial situation occurs in Chapter 29 of the same treatise. Suger has told us how, after the dedication of the choir in 1144, he raised and enlarged the transept wings. He continues thus:

This done, when under the persuasion of some we had devoted our efforts to carrying on the work upon the front tower[s], the Divine Will, as we believe, diverted us to the following: we would undertake to renew the central body of the church, which is called the nave, and harmonize and equalize it with the two parts already remodeled. We would retain, however, as much as we could of the old walls. . . . The chief reason for this change was this: if in our own time or under our successors, work on the nave of the church would only be done betweenwhiles, whenever the towers would afford the opportunity, the nave would not be completed according to plan without much delay or, in case of any unlucky development, never. For no difficulty would ever embarrass those then in power but that the link between the old and the new work would suffer long postponement. However, since it has already been started with the extension of the side aisles, it will be completed either through us or through those whom the Lord shall elect. . . . For the most liberal Lord Who, among other great things, has also provided the makers of the marvelous windows, a rich supply of sapphire glass, and ready funds of about seven hundred pounds or more will not suffer that there be a lack of means for completion of the work.[138]

This strangely prescient passage raises many questions. Who, one would like to know, had the power of persuading the abbot, against his will, to resume work on the towers? To whom does he refer in speaking of "those then in power" so cynically? And who was the princely donor who provided the makers of the windows, the supply of sapphire glass, and *ready funds of more than seven hundred pounds*, a sum more than three times the abbey's annual allotment? For Suger clearly distinguishes here between what was paid for by "us," that is, the abbey or the abbot, and what was provided by "the most liberal Lord." Behind this expression must lie hidden the identity of a generous patron, who supplied the funds for the construction of the celebrated chevet with its stained-glass windows.

That Gothic incunabulum, we conclude from this passage, was paid for by some unnamed person outside the abbey. Now, writing some four years after its dedication, Suger has lost his wonted confidence and optimism. He speaks of "unlucky developments." Formerly the recipient of lavish gifts of gold and precious gems "hardly to be found among Kings," he cannot at the time of writing, about 1148, even foretell by what means the new nave will be financed or foresee a completion date. His words are not those of a man sure of his abbey's income, but of one who must establish priorities.

Considerable poignancy attaches then to this passage. It indicates that the misfortune which paralyzed construction at the abbey for the rest of the century was in 1148 already at hand. Undoubtedly the disastrous Second Crusade, which Louis had been able to mount in 1147 only by virtue of Eleanor's rich holdings,[139] was largely to blame, and time only compounded the misfortune. The death of the valiant abbot in 1151[140] deprived the abbey of the wisest and most experienced head in the kingdom. Following hard on his death came the events of 1152, when Eleanor defected to the Plantagenets, taking her rich inheritance with her.[141] Finally, in 1153, Louis turned his attention as patron and builder to the cathedral of Senlis and a short time thereafter to the reconstruction of Notre-Dame in Paris, where he had been educated.[142]

The texts of Suger's treatises, as we have seen, make clear that the western extension was carried out only with the help of an unexpected gift, consisting of a new quarry and associated with the sudden arrival of a host of skilled workmen. The luminous east end, as well, was a donation. It is tempting to believe that Eleanor, who came from a long line of generous patrons and continued that tradition as queen of the English, participated in the funding of these projects, especially the western extension. One suspects even more strongly that the king participated. The fact that documentary evidence associates the king with Senlis and Notre-Dame in Paris makes the silence of the sources relating to Saint-Denis seem anomalous indeed. Still, the historian seeks for stronger evidence than suspicions, even where there is a possibility that pertinent documents have been deliberately destroyed. Another body of written material frequently invoked in connection with the rebuilding of Saint-Denis, and one which may throw further light on the question of royal patronage, is that cleric's version of the *Song of Roland* which was referred to briefly above—the *Chronicle of Pseudo-Turpin*.[143] Composed in the form in which we have it around 1140, the *Pseudo-Turpin* purports to be the account of three—quite legendary—expeditions into Spain, carried out over a fourteen-year period by Charlemagne and undertaken at the behest of Saint James himself, who in the first chapter appears to Charles in a dream, urging him to follow the Milky Way to Galicia and there free his shrine from the infidel. During the course of these campaigns, Charles delivers the entire peninsula from Saracen dominance and, among other exploits, enlarges the abandoned shrine of Saint James at Compostela, enriching it (as well as Saint-Sernin in Toulouse and other churches) with the gold acquired in his Spanish conquest (Ch. 5). On his third expedition Charles returns to Santiago and, with nine (or according to the manuscript at Santiago, sixty) bishops, dedicates the basilica and the altar of Saint James (Ch. 19).[144] To the assembled potentates, ecclesiastical and secular, Charles announces the privileges granted the shrine: to it are allotted all Spain and Galicia, while an annual impost of four *nummi* is to be levied on every householder for its upkeep. The shrine is to be raised to the rank of apostolic see; all bishops of Spain shall receive the insignia of their office there, as well as kings their crowns. On his way back to France Charles experiences the disaster of Roncevaux. Subsequently, taking a circuitous route, he buries the bodies of the dead at Bordeaux, Blaye, Belin, and Arles. Leaving the wounded Turpin at Vienne, he returns to Paris and Saint-Denis. Chapter 30, the account of what takes place there, is a doublet of Chapter 19.[145] Convoking an assembly of bishops and princes analogous to that he had convened at Santiago, Charles accords to the abbey the same privileges: all France is to be subject to the abbey of Saint-Denis; no king shall be crowned nor any bishop ordained without the counsel of the abbot, to whom both kings and bishops owe obedience. The abbot is, in short, to be primate of France, and every householder is ordered to pay an annual impost of four *nummi* for the building of the church at Saint-Denis.

J. Bédier, Cyril Meredith-Jones, H. M. Smyser, and André de Mandach have pointed out that the structure of the *Pseudo-Turpin* is such that its second half is marked by a long series of doublets—passages which repeat almost verbatim events or situations described in the first part (Chs. 1–19). Thus the opening chapter, in which Saint James appears to Charlemagne, has its pendant in the scene described in Chapter 30 when, after the assembly at Saint-Denis, the Patron Martyr Denis appears to Charlemagne in a dream, promising the crown of martyrdom to those who leave their possessions to fight *pro divino amore* against the Saracen in Spain and healing to those who give their coins for the building of his church.[146] It has been mentioned earlier that legends circulating in Spain had, by the late eleventh century, made Santiago as much a Carolingian as a Jacobean shrine. The *Pseudo-Turpin*, returning the compliment, makes of Saint-Denis a Jacobean as well as a Dionysian one: the patron of France himself has become an advocate of the pilgrimage to Santiago and a full partner with the Apostle James in the crusade against the Moors.

One would give much to know at whose initiative the unknown author of the *Pseudo-Turpin* introduced the abbey of Saint-Denis into the orbit of the pilgrimage to Santiago and incorporated its foundation into the legendary matter of the *Song of Roland*. A recent study by Christopher Hohler, brilliantly documented, has argued that some traveling grammar master wrote it, revising the text from time to time throughout a long career of teaching, and filling it with grammatical, rhetorical, and theological "howlers" by way of teaching boys—presumably incipient clerics— to read and write Latin.[147] Here the epic heroes Roland and Charlemagne become the butt of schoolboy laughter. But of course not even Mr. Hohler's argument, however convincing, can do away with the *Song of Roland* or the legends of Charlemagne's conquests in Spain, any more than *1066 and All That* can do away with 1066. Even that literary spoof, the *Pèlerinage de Charlemagne*, and the *Descriptio* on which it was based were anchored in the historical circumstance that the abbey of Saint-Denis believed or wished to make others believe that it possessed relics brought back from Jerusalem by Charlemagne. In spite of its atrocious metaphors and deliberately comic passages, then, the *Pseudo-Turpin*, in linking Saint-Denis with Santiago and Charles's legendary conquests in Spain, seems to reflect contemporary building at the royal abbey and provides a literary analogue to what occurred there in terms of the design and the sculptures.

It was Mandach's view that the rapports between Saint-Denis and Santiago chronicled in Chapters 19 and 30 of the *Pseudo-Turpin* derived from the personality of Guy de Bourgogne,[148] later Pope Calixtus III, friend, adviser, and close relative of the Frankish and Castilian monarchs Louis VI, Alfonso VI, and Alfonso VII.[149] In 1120 Calixtus raised the see of Santiago to the rank of archbishopric, an event which seems to be reflected in Chapter 19. Calixtus was also a close friend of Suger.[150] Calixtus died, however, in 1124.[151] While it is possible that the germ of the idea to rebuild Saint-Denis on the model of the pilgrimage shrine came from Calixtus, when the *Pseudo-Turpin* was written some fifteen years after his death an entirely new set of historical circumstances prevailed at the Frankish court, the most striking of which was the Aquitanian presence there. If Calixtus, who had been trained at Cluny, helped establish a link between Saint-Denis and Santiago, such as that chronicled in the *Pseudo-Turpin*, that link can only have been reinforced by Eleanor's presence. Barton Sholod has pointed out that Aquitanian influence in Spain, on the ascendant since 1114, soon replaced even that of Cluny.[152]

Schramm[153] and von Simson,[154] who held the view that the *Pseudo-*

Turpin was in all likelihood written at Saint-Denis, regarded it, together with the false decretal of Charlemagne based upon it, as the chief literary evidence of a *renovatio imperii Karoli Magni* at the Capetian court. Hohler's article makes it necessary to re-evaluate this view. To be sure, Hohler concedes that the chronicle received its final touches in Paris, at least in the redaction which we know, "later than 1130," for use in a school in some way associated with the royal abbey.[155] The author and grammar master Hohler regards as a Poitevin,[156] and this no doubt accounts for his frequent mention of Aquitanian sites, such as Bordeaux or Belin or Blaye. Indeed, Hohler believes that this Poitevin invented the story that Charles buried Roland at Blaye and deposited his horn at Saint-Seurin at Bordeaux.[157] He composed for Saintes a second miracle of the flowering lances, a doublet of the more celebrated episode outside the walls of Pamplona, and made up out of whole cloth the "splendidly Rabelaisian" Passion of Saint Eutropius of Saintes, as a satire on the "New Testament careers recently invented, in competition, for St. Martial and St. Front, by the clergy of Limoges and Perigueux."[158] In Chapter 11 the author also treats us to what Hohler calls some "special nonsense" about the duke of Aquitaine, which is worth closer examination, for it reveals the author's Aquitanian "bias," which Hohler has also noticed.[159] The chapter consists of a roll call of Carolingian commanders, the number of their men at arms, and their titles. Devoting three and one-half lines to Turpin, two and one-half to Roland, three to Oliver, and scarcely two to the duke of Burgundy, the author gives no less than thirteen to the duke of Aquitaine, Engelerius. Not only does he praise the Aquitanian proficiency in arms ("Isti erant docti omnibus armis. . .") in distinction to his treatment of other groups; he also provides us with a brief, if apocryphal, history of the dukedom. Engelerius, he tells us, was the duke of the *city* of Aquitaine, which Augustus Caesar had founded and named and which had given its name to the entire region ("unde tota patria illa Aquitania vocatur"). After the death of Engelerius, the city of Aquitaine lapsed into ruin, because its inhabitants fell by the sword with their leader at Roncevaux.[160]

Evidence of an actual link between Aquitaine and the chronicle has already been noticed by Bédier, who calls attention to the striking parallel between its narrative core and the contents of the two false diplomas of Saint-Jean de Sorde on the French road near Dax, written between 1050 and 1120.[161] The first purports to be Charles's order to build the monastery as he was passing through on his way into Spain. The second records the dedication of the altars by Charles and Turpin and how the emperor, after having made war in Spain for seven years, returned that way to bury the body of the dead Turpin. Another charter, preserved at the abbey, even more interesting than the first two and dated 1120, carries the name of Duke William IX of Aquitaine, who confirms the privileges granted by Charlemagne in the false diplomas.[162] Obviously, these diplomas do for Saint-Jean de Sorde precisely what the *Pseudo-Turpin* does for Saint-Denis—they incorporate its foundation into the legendary campaigns of the emperor in Spain and provide imperial funding for its construction. Since these diplomas were known to William IX, frequent visitor to Santiago and patron of poets and jongleurs, it is not impossible that he or other poets in his employ told such stories of Charlemagne and Roland to Eleanor's father when he was a boy. Eleanor herself may have heard similar tales in her own childhood. Precocious scion of a lettered race, she undoubtedly had a taste for epic and *chanson* already in her teens.

The Poitevin connections of the *Pseudo-Turpin* make it necessary to ask why its author appeared in Paris in the early 1140's, at the very moment when Eleanor of Poitou and Aquitaine was queen, and why, at this point, he elaborated his story by some thirteen chapters in order to incorporate the founding of the royal abbey into Charlemagne's legendary campaigns against the Moors. And why was this elaboration achieved just as the royal abbey was in the actual process of being reconstructed on a new and grandiose scale and according to a design based upon the Jacobean shrine? Is it Eleanor's presence in Paris which explains this concatenation of events? Or are we to attribute their simultaneity to pure coincidence? Whatever answer one is inclined to give to this question, it is a fact, hitherto unnoticed, that one can document for the House of Aquitaine a direct knowledge of the narrative at three successive and critical stages in its development.

The first of these occurred in 1120, as noted above, when the duke of Aquitaine, William IX, confirmed to Saint-Jean de Sorde the privileges granted in the two false Carolingian diplomas, evidence that the Duke knew the narrative core of the *Pseudo-Turpin* even if he did not know the version of the grammar master. The second occurs in Paris in the 1140's. While this circumstance need not be causally related to Eleanor's presence, the second portion of the *Pseudo-Turpin*, as all scholars have seen, reflects official Capetian policy, evidenced by the presence at Saint-Denis in the 1140's of the false decretal of Charlemagne.[163] The third phase is directly linked to Eleanor's patronage, although it dates from her English reign. Historians have regarded the copy of the *Pseudo-Turpin* made by the abbot of Ripoll in 1173 at Santiago de Compostela as the earliest to appear outside the confines of Cluny and Santiago.[164] But a year or two before that date, Geoffrey du Breuil, prior of Vigeois near Limoges and historian of Eleanor's court at Poitiers, obtained a copy of the *Pseudo-Turpin* and revised it slightly to flatter the person of Richard, the fourteen-year-old presumptive duke of Aquitaine.[165] By means of this revision, according to Mandach, Geoffrey managed to suggest an identity between the young duke and the Emperor Charlemagne. All this makes one wonder: Did Eleanor herself give Geoffrey the commission to search out this fabulous tale, remembering it from her own youth? And was the chronicle in the Parisian version (ca. 1140) also composed for the purpose of identifying the duke of Aquitaine with Charlemagne? If so, that duke in 1140 would have been Louis VII. Such a close association between the Capetian king and the emperor was of course the ultimate aim of the Carolingian *renovatio*. At Poitiers in the 1170's, however, the *Pseudo-Turpin* served the future Lion-Heart and his Plantagenet siblings, quite rightly in view of Hohler's findings, as a piece of children's literature. Clearly the Aquitanian bias of the story was not lost upon Eleanor and her Plantagenet brood. It was at her court that, as Hohler would say, the "publication rights" were broken and the chronicle began to spread outside the confines of monastery and cathedral into courtly circles. Although this evidence of Aquitanian concern with the *Pseudo-Turpin* does not permit a firm conclusion, it is conceivable that, when it was composed in Paris in the 1140's, it represented an Aquitanian contribution to the Carolingian *renovatio* at the Capetian court.[166]

The basis of that *renovatio* had of course been laid out in the reign of Louis VI, long before Eleanor's appearance on the scene, and can be graphically demonstrated in subsequent portal and tomb programs at the abbey,[167] designed long after Eleanor's departure, to make explicit the theme implied in the architectural design, namely that the Capetian king, rather than the German emperor, represented the legitimate heir of Charlemagne. The Frankish house cultivated dynastic ties which would enhance this legitimacy, a policy which may have led to the marriage between Eleanor and Louis, for it promised once more to give the Franks a king who traced his lineage back to the great Charles.[168]

Similar considerations may have inspired the Frankish king to contract his second marriage in 1153 with Constance, daughter of Alfonso VII of Castile, emperor of Christian Spain and descended through his mother, Urraca, from the Aquitanian house. When in 1154 Louis and Constance went on pilgrimage to Santiago, Alfonso gave Louis an emerald, which the king in turn gave to Saint-Denis.[169] This well-documented gift makes the lack of such documentation for similar gifts received during Suger's abbacy even more keenly disappointing. Two other documents dating from Louis's second marriage are of interest here. In one of these (1155/1156) Louis speaks of himself as the "august emperor of the Franks [*Francorum im-*

perator augustus]."[170] In another, he states that the love of God and the
weight of vows have forced him to go on pilgrimage to the shrine of "Saint
James the Apostle and *our patron*."[171] Coming from a king whose patron
had traditionally been the Blessed Denis, this is an astonishing statement.
But it is less astonishing when one keeps in mind that Charlemagne, in his
legendary aspect at least, venerated the same saint and, indeed, according
to the *Pseudo-Turpin*, undertook his Spanish campaigns for the sole purpose of freeing the saint's bones from the infidel. Louis, as the living
embodiment of Charlemagne—as the *imperator Francorum*—would have
necessarily inherited the emperor's devotion to Saint James. In this double
patronage of the Capetian king by Saint James and Saint Denis lies the best
clue to the part-Jacobean, part-Dionysian design of the royal abbey.
Louis's assumption of the title of *emperor* and his devotion to Saint James
made Saint-Denis, like Santiago itself, an imperial foundation. In associating the construction of Saint-Denis with Charlemagne, the *Pseudo-Turpin*,
then, correctly reflects the true meaning of the new church as imperial
rather than merely monastic in character.

The question of Eleanor's participation in the rebuilding of the abbey
church can best be narrowed to that of her role in the Carolingian *renovatio*. Before the events of the Second Crusade and her inadequacy as
the bearer of Capetian kings had cleared her head, Eleanor would surely
have done her part to inspire the king with that policy of "grandeur and
illusion" which, according to Marcel Pacaut, marked the early years of
Louis' reign.[172] Indeed, it was in all likelihood the revenue from Eleanor's
territories which provided the king with the means of implementing that
policy. Pacaut has tabulated the donations to churches made by Louis
during his long reign (1137–1180) and has arrived at some interesting
figures. Acts recording such donations during the first fifteen years
(1137–1152) are twice as numerous as those made during the succeeding
twenty-eight (1152–1180). Pacaut accounts for this discrepancy as being
due to the king's increased wisdom and soberness and to his having abandoned the policy referred to above. Undoubtedly this is at least in part
correct; the king was both sadder and wiser after the Second Crusade and
after the divorce of 1152. But is it not striking that the liberality of his early
reign corresponds precisely with the years of his marriage to Eleanor and
his tenure as duke of Aquitaine? Although the documents do not permit us
to attribute this generosity to Eleanor personally, they certainly suggest
that Louis was not only more sober after 1152. Thrown back on the
narrow confines of the Capetian realm, he was comparatively hard up.

Scholars have remarked upon what seems to them a contradiction in the
history of Gothic architecture: closely associated with the rise of urban

society and typically expressed in the cathedrals which served that society, it was by a curious quirk of history created in a monastic church. But this contradiction is more apparent than real; it can be done away with if one keeps in mind that aspect of Saint-Denis which the abbey shares with the great cathedrals, such as Chartres, Rheims, and Amiens, and which this essay has been at pains to demonstrate—namely, that it was constructed with royal patronage. It is more correct to see in Saint-Denis a princely— yes, even an imperial—foundation than a monastic one. If this be granted, it would be rash indeed to deny to the Empress Eleanor a conscious role in the creation of the new visible symbol of Capetian imperial pretensions at Saint-Denis.

NOTES

1. Amy Kelly, *Eleanor of Aquitaine and the Four Kings* (Cambridge: Harvard University Press, 1950), pp. 3–15. See also Régine Pernoud, *Aliénor d'Aquitaine* (Paris: Editions Michel Albin, 1965).

2. Sumner McK. Crosby, *L'Abbaye royale de Saint-Denis* (Paris: P. Hartmann, 1953), pp. 31–56; Otto von Simson, *The Gothic Cathedral* (New York: Bollingen Foundation, 1956).

3. On the Ile-de-France as an architectural and artistic hinterland prior to the rebuilding of Saint-Denis, see von Simson, *The Gothic Cathedral*, p. 64; K. J. Conant, *Carolingian and Romanesque Architecture: 800–1200* (Baltimore: Penguin Books, 1959), pp. 276 ff.

4. For a recent expression of this view, with appropriate bibliography, see the catalogue by Stephen K. Scher, *The Renaissance of the Twelfth Century* (Providence: Museum of Art, Rhode Island School of Design, 1969), pp. 151–154.

5. On Suger's personality, see the introduction by Erwin Panofsky, ed. and trans., *Abbot Suger on the Abbey Church of St. Denis and Its Art Treasures* (Princeton, 1946). On the dates, see Panofsky, pp. 144–145; von Simson, *The Gothic Cathedral*, Ch. 3; Marcel Aubert, *Suger* (Abbaye de Saint-Wandrille 1950); Otto Cartellieri, *Abt Suger von St. Denis (1081– 1151)* (Berlin, 1855).

6. Von Simson, *The Gothic Cathedral*, pp. 96 ff.

7. Panofsky, ed. and trans., *Abbot Suger*, p. 36.

8. The term is Cartellieri's; see *Abt Suger*, p. 51. But compare this view with that of Paul Frankl, *The Gothic: Literary Sources and Interpretations through Eight Centuries* (Princeton: Princeton University Press, 1960), p. 21: "Suger. . .was no architect. He was most certainly not the designer and draftsman of the architectonic composition." In Frankl's view, Suger had two architects, one for the western extension, another for the choir.

9. Robert Fawtier, *The Capetian Kings of France* (London: Macmillan, 1960), p. 107. Suger's life of Louis VII was never completed and has been re-

worked by later hands. See Auguste
Molinier, *Vie de Louis le Gros par
Suger, suivie de l'histoire du roi Louis
VII* (Paris, 1887). For a more recent
assessment of the reign of Louis VII,
with introduction by Fawtier, see Mar-
cel Pacaut, *Louis VII et son royaume*
(Paris: S. E. V. P. E. N., 1964).

10. Albert Lecoy de la Marche, ed.,
Oeuvres complètes de Suger, Société de
l'Histoire de France, no. 139 (Paris:
Renouard, 1867) prints Suger's letters,
pp. 239–284. They begin with one
dated 1145 or 1146 to the archbishop
of Bourges regarding some property
belonging to Saint-Denis.

11. A royal abbey was one where the
king had the right of naming or ap-
proving the election of the abbot. See
R. Branner, *St. Louis and the Court
Style in Gothic Architecture* (London:
A. Zwemmer, 1965), p. 10 n.35;
Pacaut, *Louis VII*, pp. 91 ff.

12. Percy Ernst Schramm, *Der
König von Frankreich: Das Wesen der
Monarchie vom 9. zum 16. Jahrhun-
dert* (Weimar: H. Böhlaus Nachf.,
1939), pp. 131 ff.; von Simson, *The
Gothic Cathedral*, pp. 70 ff., 76 ff.

13. There is no systematic study of
royal patronage in the twelfth century
to compare with Branner's study of the
subject in the thirteenth. But see
Pacaut, *Louis VII* pp. 67 ff. To be sure,
Louis was not known for lavish gifts
out of his own purse (pp. 80 ff.). The
role of kings as patrons of church
building had, of course, been standard
since the Carolingian period (see the
catalogue *Karl der Grosse: Werk und
Wirkung*, ed. Wolfgang Braunfels
[Düsseldorf: Schwann, 1965], p. 181).
One has only to recall the role of the
Norman dukes on the Continent or the
Norman kings in Sicily and England.

Queen Emma of England supported
the construction of Saint-Hélaire at
Poitiers in the early eleventh century
and provided the architect (Conant,
*Carolingian and Romanesque Ar-
chitecture*, p. 105). Alfonso VI of Castile contributed enormous sums to
Cluny after the conquest of Toledo in
1085 (Conant, pp. 115–116). Caecilia
Davis-Weyer, *Early Medieval Art
300–1150: Sources and Documents*
(Englewood Cliffs, N.J.: Prentice-Hall,
1971), pulls together numerous
medieval references to royal and imperial *largesse*. Thomas W. Lyman has
recently explored the patronage of
Saint-Sernin in Toulouse by the Count
Guilhem IV in "The Sculpture Pro-
gramme of the Porte des Comtes Master at Saint-Sernin in Toulouse,"
*Journal of the Warburg and Courtauld
Institute* 34(1971):12–39. One has
also to recall the lavish patronage of
church building by Blanche of Castile in
the thirteenth century (Branner, *St.
Louis*, pp. 32–33, 46).

14. Pacaut, *Louis VII*, p. 34.

15. Panofsky, ed. and trans., *Abbot
Suger*, p. 113.

16. Ibid., p. 79.

17. Fawtier, *Capetian Kings* p. 106.

18. Ibid.

19. Von Simson, *The Gothic Cathedral*, p. 89; on Dionysian light
metaphysics, pp. 105 ff.; on Suger's
politics, pp. 64 ff., 82 ff.

20. Ibid., pp. 95, 80; on his travels,
see also Sumner McK. Crosby, "An International Workshop in the Twelfth
Century," *Cahiers d'Histoire Mondiale*
10(1966):19–30.

21. Schramm, *Der König*, pp. 138
ff.; von Simson, *The Gothic Cathedral*,
pp. z th bibliography p. 82 n.84.

22. On the imperial association of

the westwork in Carolingian and Romanesque architecture, see G. Bandmann, *Mittelalterliche Architektur als Bedeutungsträger* (Berlin: Gebrüder Mann, 1951), pp. 105 ff., 176, 207 ff. The original form of the westwork at Saint-Denis, however, is not precisely known; see Braunfels, ed., *Karl der Grosse: Werk und Wirkung*, p. 391.

23. On Charlemagne's participation at the consecration, February 24, 775, see Edgar Lehmann, "Die Architektur zur Zeit Karls des Grossen," in *Karl der Grosse: Lebenswerk und Nachleben*, ed. Wolfgang Braunfels, vol. 3, *Karolingische Kunst* (Düsseldorf: Schwann, 1965), pp. 301–302. Charlemagne's father, Pepin, began the church; his grandson Louis (died 867) was abbot of Saint-Denis, and another grandson, the emperor Charles the Bald (died 877) was a lay abbot there. Even in the twelfth century, the Frankish kings were lay abbots of Saint-Denis. Many of them, including Louis VI and Charles the Bald, were buried there.

24. Schramm, *Der König*, p. 137.

25. Ramón Menéndez Pidal, *La Chanson de Roland et la tradition épique des Francs*, 2d ed. (Paris: A.-J. Picard, 1960), pp. 271, 367–369.

26. Marcelin Defourneaux, *Les Français en Espagne au XIe et XIIe siècles* (Paris: Presses Universitaires de France, 1949), pp. 125–126, 129, 132, 140. On intermarriages between the ducal family of Aquitaine and the houses of Burgundy and of Spain, see Szabolcs De Vasay, "Ramire le Moine et Agnès de Poitou," in *Mélanges offerts à René Crozet*, ed. P. Gallais and Yves-Jean Riou, 2 vols. (Poitiers: Société d'Etudes Médiévales, 1966), II,

727–750. On the cooperation between Cluny and Aquitaine and their common aims in Spain, see Georges Gaillard, "La Pénétration clunisienne en Espagne dans la première moitié du XIe siècle," *Centre International d'Etudes Romanes, Bulletin Trimestriel* 4(1960):8–15.

27. Barton Sholod, *Charlemagne in Spain: The Cultural Legacy of Roncesvalles* (Geneva: Droz, 1966), p. 224.

28. Defourneaux, *Les Français*, p. 132.

29. Sholod, *Charlemagne*, p. 172.

30. Defourneaux, *Les Français*, p. 140.

31. Ibid., p. 139.

32. Ibid., pp. 32 ff.; Sholod, *Charlemagne*, pp. 73–74; Menéndez Pidal, *La Chanson de Roland*, pp. 387–388. But Pierre David has rejected the idea that the Council of León abolished Visigothic writing; see *Etudes historiques sur la Galice et le Portugal* (Coimbra, 1947), pp. 431 ff. I am grateful to Professor John Williams of the Department of Fine Arts, University of Pittsburgh, for calling this fact to my attention.

33. Defourneaux, *Les Français*, pp. 159–160.

34. Ibid., p. 166.

35. Ibid., p. 113: "Le baron français qui témoigna le plus de vénération envers l'apôtre de Galice fut, sans conteste, Guillaume X d'Aquitaine."

36. Kelly, *Eleanor of Aquitaine*, pp. 3 ff. Since William went on annual pilgrimages to Santiago, one wonders whether his motives in 1137 were so exclusively political as Kelly implies. Defourneaux regards the reports of William's death and burial, "before the great altar of Saint James" as "arranged," although possibly true. For

one account of the duke's death, see Suger, *Histoire du Roi Louis VII*, ed. A. Molinier (Paris: 1887), p. 156.

37. Kelly, *Eleanor of Aquitaine*, pp. 26 ff.

38. Defourneaux, *Les Français*, pp. 69 ff. The canons of Santiago were almost exclusively French or French-trained; see Reyna Pastor de Togneri, "Diego Gelmirez: Une Mentalité à la page; A propos du rôle de certaines élites de pouvoir," in *Mélanges offerts à René Crozet*, ed. Gallais and Riou, I, 597–608.

39. See J. Bédier, *Les Légendes épiques*, 4 vols. (Paris: H. Champion, 1912), III, 375–376.

40. Ibid., pp. 322–323.

41. Sholod, *Charlemagne*, p. 226; Cyril Meredith-Jones, ed., *Historia Karoli Magni et Rotholandi* (Paris: E. Droz, 1936), p. 48.

42. Menéndez Pidal, *La Chanson de Roland*, p. 389.

43. The well-known "Monk of Silos"; see Bédier, *Les Légendes épiques*, III, 379; Meredith-Jones, *Historia*, p. 308.

44. Defourneaux, *Les Français*, p. 98.

45. Ibid., p. 167.

46. Sholod, *Charlemagne*, p. 123.

47. Conant, *Carolingian and Romanesque Architecture*, p. 96; G. Bandmann, *Mittelalterliche Architektur*, pp. 235–236.

48. Elie Lambert, *Le Pèlerinage de Compostela* (Paris-Toulouse, 1959), pp. 1–5.

49. Conant, *Carolingian and Romanesque Architecture*, pp. 93–95; Howard Saalman, *Medieval Architecture* (New York: G. Braziller, 1965), p. 38. Such northern French churches as Saint-Remi at Rheims and the basilica of Fulbert at Chartres, both of the eleventh century, have been named as sources for elements in plan and elevation at Santiago; see Pierre Pradel, "La France et les routes de Saint-Jacques," in *L'Art roman* (Barcelona and Santiago de Compostela: Council of Europe, 1961), p. lxiv.

50. On the dates of Saint-Sernin, see Marcel Durliat, "La Construction de Saint-Sernin de Toulouse au XIᵉ siècle," *Bulletin Monumental* 121(1963): 151–170; Thomas W. Lyman, "Notes on the Porte Miègeville Capitals and the Construction of Saint-Sernin de Toulouse," *Art Bulletin* 49(1967):25–36.

51. Arthur Kingsley Porter, *Romanesque Sculpture of the Pilgrimage Roads* (Boston: Marshall Jones Co., 1923), p. 194; Conant, *Carolingian and Romanesque Architecture*, pp. 91–92; Lambert, *Le Pèlerinage*, pp. 130–133, Ch. 7.

52. Von Simson, *The Gothic Cathedral*, p. 81; see also Schramm, *Der König*, pp. 137–140.

53. Kelly, *Eleanor of Aquitaine*, p. 3.

54. Ibid., pp. 20–22.

55. See Hans Eberhard Meyer, *The Crusades* (Oxford: Oxford University Press, 1972), pp. 96–109; Kelly, *Eleanor of Aquitaine*, pp. 51, 65.

56. The inactivity of the Capetians in Spain meant, according to Menéndez Pidal, that they played no part in the elaboration of the *chansons de geste*, created on the pilgrimage routes (*La Chanson de Roland*, p. 260); see also Bédier, *Les Légendes épiques*, IV, 153, 454.

57. Porter, *Romanesque Sculpture*, p. 194.

58. The phrase is taken from the *Pilgrim's Guide* (Jeanne Vielliard, *Le*

Guide du pèlerin de Saint-Jacques de Compostela, 3d ed. [Mâcon: Protat Frères, 1963], p. 60), where it is said of Saint-Martin in Tours.

59. Lambert, *Le Pèlerinage*, p. 142; Conant, *Carolingian and Romanesque Architecture*, p. 93.

60. Consult Crosby's plan, *L'Abbaye royale*, p. 68.

61. Carl K. Hersey, "The Church of St. Martin at Tours (903–1150)," *Art Bulletin* 25(1943):1–39; F. Lesueur, "Saint Martin de Tours et les origines de l'art roman," *Bulletin Monumental* 107(1949):7–84. See also Sumner McK. Crosby, "Crypt and Choir Plans at Saint-Denis," *Gesta* 5(1966):4–6.

62. As dukes of Francia, the Capetians were lay abbots of Saint-Martin; see Lesueur, "Saint Martin." It is of interest that the one journey made by Suger outside Paris during the construction of the chevet at Saint-Denis was to Tours; see Cartellieri, *Abt Suger*, p. 101.

63. Charles LeLong, "La Date du déambulatoire de Saint-Martin de Tours," *Bulletin Monumental* 131(1973):297–309.

64. Lambert, *Le Pèlerinage*, p. 157.

65. Conant calls attention to this placement (*Carolingian and Romanesque Architecture*, p. 100). For Charlieu, see Conant, p. 304 n. 16; Marcel Aubert, *La Bourgogne, La Sculpture*, 3 vols., Les Richesses d'Art de la France (Paris: G. van Oest, 1930), pl. 193; E. R. Sunderland, "The History and Architecture of the Church of St. Fortunatus at Charlieu in Burgundy," *Art Bulletin* 21(1939):61–88. On Cluny, see J. Talobre, "La Reconstitution du portail de l'église abbatiale de Cluny," *Bulletin Monumental* 102(1944): 225–240.

66. Porter, *Romanesque Sculpture*, pls. 696–701.

67. Ibid., I, 63; pls. 677–691; George Zarnecki, "Plastik im 12. Jahrhundert," in *Das Mittelalter I*, ed. Hermann Fillitz, vol. 5 of *Propylaenkunstgeschichte* (Berlin: Propylaen Verlag, 1969), pl. 294.

68. See Durliat, "La Construction"; Lyman, "Notes."

69. Panofsky, ed. and trans., *Abbot Suger*, pp. 86–89 (*De Consecratione*, Ch. 2); Crosby, *L'Abbaye royale*, p. 31.

70. Crosby, *L'Abbaye royale*, p. 32.

71. Panofsky, ed. and trans., *Abbot Suger*, p. 42; see also Crosby, *L'Abbaye royale*, p. 32.

72. Saalman, *Medieval Architecture*, p. 39.

73. Panofsky, ed. and trans., *Abbot Suger*, pp. 43–45 (*De Administratione*, Ch. 25).

74. Crosby, *L'Abbaye royale*, p. 32. For the testament, see Lecoy de la Marche, ed., *Oeuvres*, pp. 333–341; Aubert, *Suger*, pp. 19–21.

75. Crosby, *L'Abbaye royale*, Fig. 25, pp. 68–69.

76. Panofsky, ed. and trans., *Abbot Suger*, p. 91 (*De Consecratione*, Ch. 2).

77. Kelly, *Eleanor of Aquitaine*, pp. 6–13.

78. Lecoy de la Marche, ed., *Oeuvres*, p. 336: ". . .videlicet in novi et magni aedificii ecclesiae augmentatione, in aedificatione magnae et caritative domus hospitum, in reparatione et renovatione dormitorii et refectorii, et in augmentatione obedientiae thesauri, et in multis aliis tam ecclesiae quam officinarum sumptuosis operibus [(I have endowed the abbey) through augmenting the church with a great new building, through the construction of a

great and charitable hospice, by repairing and renovating the dormitory and refectory, and by enlarging the treasury, and by many other sumptuous works]." The "great new building" mentioned by Suger was, in June of 1137, largely still in the planning stages; the old western entrance was probably already dismantled, and the walls of the extension of the nave may have been, in part at least, standing.

79. Panofsky, ed. and trans., *Abbot Suger*, p. 91.

80. Ibid. This is the single mention of sculptors in all of Suger's treatises.

81. Crosby, *L'Abbaye royale*, p. 32; Aubert, *Suger*, p. 131.

82. Panofsky, ed. and trans., *Abbot Suger*, p. 49 (*De Administratione*, Ch. 28).

83. Panofsky, ed. and trans., *Abbot Suger*, p. 51 (*De Administratione*, Ch. 29).

84. Crosby, *L'Abbaye royale*, p. 33.

85. Paul Frankl, *Gothic Architecture* (Harmondsworth: Penguin, 1962), pp. 34 ff., 79 ff.

86. Crosby, *L'Abbaye royale*, p. 59.

87. Panofsky, ed. and trans., *Abbot Suger*, pp. 82–111.

88. Ibid., p. 90.

89. Sumner McK. Crosby, "The West Portals of St. Denis and the St. Denis Style," *Gesta* 9(1970):10. The presence of Normans among the workmen need not be taken as an argument for the view that they came directly from Normandy or England. The influence of the Normans in Castile and Galicia was sufficient to seduce the bishop of Santiago, Diego Pelaez, into treason in 1088, and Norman knights had fought throughout the eleventh century in the reconquest, where Norman masons

may have followed them. On the probable French or Norman origin of the master builders of Santiago, see Porter, *Romanesque Sculpture*, p. 193; Manuel Chamoso Lamas, "Eléments romans de la cathédrale de Saint-Jacques de Compostela," in *L'Art roman* (Barcelona and Santiago de Compostela: Council of Europe, 1961), p. lxxv.

90. Porter, in his monumental study of romanesque sculpture, completely omits Normandy.

91. Willibald Sauerländer, *Gothic Sculpture in France, 1140–1270* (London: Thames and Hudson, 1972), p. 379. Some very primitive statues associated with columns are in the museum at Beauvais (Porter, *Romanesque Sculpture*, pls. 1431–1433), but the date is uncertain.

92. Wilhelm Voege, *Die Anfänge des Monumentalenstiles im Mittelalter* (Strasburg, 1894).

93. Willibald Sauerländer, "Sculpture on Early Gothic Churches: The State of Research and Open Questions," *Gesta* 9(1970):36.

94. Ibid.; Porter, *Romanesque Sculpture*, pp. 197–198; Paul Deschamps, *French Sculptors of the Romanesque Period: Eleventh and Twelfth Centuries* (1930; reprint, New York: Hacker, 1972). In a recent note, "The Pilgrimage Roads Revisited?" *Bulletin Monumental* 129(1971):113–120, Marcel Durliat rejects the notion of a pilgrimage "school," insisting on the originality and creativeness of each center.

95. Sumner McK. Crosby, "An International Workshop," pp. 23–24.

96. Zarnecki, "Plastik," pp. 99, 241.

97. Kelly, *Eleanor of Aquitaine*, pp. 20–21, 140; Aubert, *Suger*, p. 94.

98. Fawtier, *The Capetian Kings*, p. 138. But see Pacaut, *Louis VII*, p. 42.

99. Emile Mâle, *L'Art religieux du xii⁴ siècle en France*, pp. 148–149, 180; Porter, *Romanesque Sculpture*, p. 194.

100. Zarnecki, "Plastik," p. 87, Fig. 287; an observation first made by Wolfgang Graf Rothkirk, *Architektur und monumentale Darstellung im Mittelalter* (Leipzig, 1938).

101. Adolf Katzenellenbogen, *The Sculptural Programs of Chartres Cathedral: Christ-Mary-Ecclesia* (Baltimore: Johns Hopkins Press, 1959), p. 4.

102. Sauerländer, *Gothic Sculpture*, p. 381.

103. See note 65 above.

104. George Zarnecki, *Romanik* (Stuttgart: Belser, 1970), p. 61. See also Georges Gaillard, "Les Statues-colonnes d'Antealtares à Saint-Jacques de Compostelle," *Bulletin de la Société Nationale des Antiquaires de France* 1957:171–179. Gaillard also compares some spiral columns preserved in the museum of the cathedral and ornamented with vine scrolls inhabited by *putti* with similar ones from Saint-Denis now in the Musée de Cluny, Paris.

105. Porter, *Romanesque Sculptures*, pls. 686, 687, 688, 690, 691. Porter dated these columns around 1140, but they appeared to him to be archaic in style.

106. Bernhard Kerber, *Burgund und die Entwicklung der französischen Kathedralskulptur im 12. Jahrhundert* (Recklinghausen: Bongers, 1966), p. 31.

107. Linda Seidel, "A Romantic Forgery: The Romanesque 'Portal' of Saint-Etienne in Toulouse," *Art Bulletin* 50(1968):33–41. Seidel's conclusions are accepted by Leon Pressouyre,

"Chronique," *Bulletin Monumental* 127(1969):241–242.

108. D. M. Robb, "Niccolò: A North Italian Sculptor," *Art Bulletin* 12(1930):374–420.

109. The description in the *Pilgrim's Guide* expressly mentions marble columns and closely associates them with images of men and women, as well as animals, birds, and "saints" (Vielliard, *Le Guide du pèlerin*, pp. 102 ff.). Kerber claims for the figure of Saint John the Baptist on the trumeau at Vézelay the distinction of being "die älteste uns bekannte Säulenfigur [the oldest known column-statue]" (*Burgund*, p. 20). Kerber, following Francis Salet, dates this figure ca. 1125. Undoubtedly the ensemble at Vézelay marks an important stage in the development of the column-statue, but no influence of that ensemble on Saint-Denis has been detected. See Sauerländer, "Sculpture," p. 34.

110. Early Burgundian examples stand under the influence of the Ile de France and immediately adjoining territory: Dijon, Bourges, Avallon, and elsewhere. See Bernhard Kerber and André Lapeyre, *Des façades occidentales de Saint-Denis et de Chartres aux portails de Laon* (Mâcon, 1960).

111. One may cite, among many possible examples of this phenomenon, two, one from the early, one from the late Middle Ages—Hans Wentzel, "Das byzantinische Erbe der ottonischen Kaiser: Hypothesen über den Brautschatz der Theophano," *Aachener Kunstblätter* 43(1972):11–96, on the coming of Byzantine style and artifacts to the West; Margaret Rickert, *Painting in Britain in the Middle Ages* (Harmondsworth: Penguin, 1954), pp.

173–174: "Anne of Bohemia took a large train. . .when she came to England in 1382 to marry Richard II." In that train, as is well known, Anne brought an artist who was of importance for subsequent developments in English painting.

112. Sauerländer, *Gothic Sculpture*, pp. 49, 379; Scher, *The Renaissance*, p. 157.

113. Sumner McK. Crosby and Pamela Z. Blum, "Le Portail central de la façade occidentale de Saint Denis," *Bulletin Monumental* 131(1973):220, Fig. 4.

114. Panofsky, ed. and trans., *Abbot Suger*, pp. 26, 47.

115. Destroyed in the French Revolution, the column-statues are known only through eighteenth-century drawings and engravings, the latter published by Bernard de Montfaucon, *Les Monumens de la monarchie françois* (Paris, 1729), I, pls. 16–18.

116. Sauerländer, *Gothic Sculpture*, p. 379; Porter, *Romanesque Sculpture*, pls. 1445–1457.

117. Sauerländer, *Gothic Sculpture*, pl. 31, p. 398; Porter, *Romanesque Sculpture*, pls. 1460, 1463, 1464.

118. Kerber, *Burgund*, pp. 34–35. See this work for the older bibliography.

119. Ibid.; Sauerländer, *Gothic Sculpture*, p. 398.

120. Such a fusion of Burgundian and Western elements could have occurred at Châteaudun, where in the 1130's a Burgundian atelier seems to have been at work which came from there to Etampes. The statues on the north facade of the church of the Madeleine at Châteaudun no longer survive, but they were scattered over the facade after the manner of the West; see Kerber, *Burgund*, p. 34, and the literature cited there.

121. Sauerländer, *Gothic Sculpture*, p. 398.

122. Kerber, *Burgund*, p. 38, citing Eugène-Louis Lefevre-Pontalis, *Le Portail royal d'Etampes* (Paris, 1908). Notre-Dame du Fort is today a collegiate church.

123. Voege, *Die Anfänge*, pp. 233–234. Cf. the article cited in note 126 below.

124. Sauerländer, *Gothic Sculpture*, p. 382.

125. Georgia Sommers Wright, "A Royal Tomb Program in the Reign of St. Louis," *Art Bulletin* 56(1974):229–230.

126. Crosby, *L'Abbaye royale*, p. 37; Ernst Kitzinger, "The Mosaics of the Capella Palatina at Palermo: An Essay on the Choice and Arrangement of Subjects," *Art Bulletin* 31(1949):269–292. The recent Columbia dissertation on the iconography of the west facade at Saint-Denis by Paula Gerson was not available to me.

127. In addition to the studies cited in the preceding note, see Joel T. Rosenthal, "The Education of the Early Capetians," *Traditio* 25(1969):366–376, and Pacaut, *Louis VII*, p. 35.

128. Crosby and Blum, "Le Portail," p. 209.

129. See Pacaut, *Louis VII*, p. 43.

130. Letter dated May 23, 1973.

131. *Descriptio qualiter Karolus magnus, clarum et coronam a Constantinopli aquis grani detulerit qualiterque Karolus Calvus hec ad Sanctum Dyonisium retulerit*, Publikationen der Gesellschaft für Rheinische Geschichtskunde, vol. 7 (Leipzig, 1890).

132. A. J. Cooper, ed., *Le Pèlerinage de Charlemagne* (Paris, 1925).

133. On the *Pseudo-Turpin*, see note 143 below. On the false charter based upon it, see Meredith-Jones, *Historia*, pp. 324–327, 348–349; Schramm, *Der König*, pp. 134–136; and note 163 below.

134. On the repetition of this passage of some forty lines, see Panofsky, ed. and trans., *Abbot Suger*, p. 134 n.22.

135. Ibid., p. 103. Suger specifies those possessions whose income he is transferring to the cost of building. He adds: "And we decreed that these two hundred pounds, in addition to anything which will be brought to the collection box through the devotion of the faithful or might be offered *specifically for the two structures*, be applied to the continuation of these works."

136. Ibid., p. 134.

137. Ibid., p. 59. On this celebrated object of the goldsmith's art, dedicated by Pope Eugenius III on Easter day 1147, see Philippe Verdier, "La Grande Croix de l'abbé Suger à Saint-Denis," *Cahiers de Civilisation Médiévale* 13(1970):1–31.

138. Panofsky, ed. and trans., *Abbot Suger*, pp. 51–52.

139. Kelly, *Eleanor of Aquitaine*, pp. 103–106.

140. Panofsky, ed. and trans., *Abbot Suger*, p. 37.

141. Kelly, *Eleanor of Aquitaine*.

142. The date usually given for the beginning of construction in Paris is 1163 (Frankl, *Gothic Architecture*, p. 45; see also Pacaut, *Louis VII*, 77). Louis, it seems, wrote letters in 1153 to the archbishops, bishops, abbots, and clerics of the realm, urging their assistance in the rebuilding of Senlis, an expense too great for the local clergy. One

wonders, can Louis have done less for Saint-Denis? If he did do as much, the letters do not survive.

143. Meredith-Jones, *Historia*, published the oldest existing manuscript, that in the Codex Calixtinus at Santiago de Compostela, as well as Bibliothèque Nationale *latin* 13774. For a bibliography of editions of the *Pseudo-Turpin*, see Christopher Hohler, "A Note on Jacobus," *Journal of the Warburg and Courtauld Institute* 35(1972):31–80.

144. Meredith-Jones, *Historia*, p. 168.

145. See Bédier, *Les Légendes épiques*, III, 50; IV, 173; André Bernard de Mandach, *Naissance et développement de la chanson de geste en Europe*, 2 vols. (Geneva: Droz, 1961), II, 15.

146. Meredith-Jones, *Historia*, pp. 216 ff.

147. Hohler, "A Note on Jacobus," p. 33.

148. Mandach, *Naissance*, I, 84; cf. Bédier, *Les Légendes épiques*, III, 82 ff.

149. Von Simson, *The Gothic Cathedral*, p. 85.

150. Aubert, *Suger*, p. 81.

151. Geoffrey Barraclough, *The Medieval Papacy* (Norwich: Harcourt Brace, 1968), p. 97.

152. Sholod, *Charlemagne*, p. 89 n.139; Defourneaux, *Les Français*, pp. 129, 132, 159.

153. Schramm, *Der König*, pp. 134–139.

154. Von Simson, *The Gothic Cathedral*, p. 84.

155. Hohler, "A Note on Jacobus," p. 37.

156. Ibid., p. 40.

157. Ibid., p. 50.

158. Ibid.

159. Ibid.

160. Meredith-Jones, *Historia*, p. 109.

161. Bédier, *Les Légendes épiques*, III, 33–36, 340.

162. Ibid., p. 339 n.2.

163. See note 133 above and Robert Barroux, "L'Abbé Suger et la vassalité du Vexin en 1124," *Le Moyen Age* 64(1958):1–26; Max Buchner, "Die gefälschte Karlsprivileg für St.-Denis," *Historisches Jahrbuch* 52(1922):12–28, 250–265; C. van de Kieft, "Deux diplômes faux de Charlemagne pour Saint-Denis du XIIe siècle," *Le Moyen Age* 64(1958):401–436; and now Hohler, who relates the charter to the east end of the church and dates it therefore to 1140–1143 ("A Note on Jacobus"). Indeed, in Hohler's opinion, the manuscript of the *Pseudo-Turpin* now in Santiago may have actually been in the *early* 1150's at Saint-Denis ("A Note on Jacobus," p. 63).

164. Hohler, contrary to previous scholarship, does not believe that the abbot of Ripoll found the *Pseudo-Turpin* at Santiago ("A Note on Jacobus," pp. 62, 69).

165. Mandach, *Naissance*, I, 130; see also I, 385–392.

166. Rita Lejeune, "Rôle littéraire d'Aliénor d'Aquitaine et de sa famille," *Cultura Neolatina* 14(1954):7–12, suggests that there was some connection between the composition of the *Liber Sancti Jacobi* (or *Pilgrim's Guide*) and the *Pseudo-Turpin* and the death of William X at Compostela in 1137. Both works make special mention of Belin, Eleanor's probable birthplace.

167. Wright, "A Royal Tomb Program," pp. 224–243.

168. Founder of the Aquitanian house was Theodaric, a Carolingian commander and apparently a blood relation of Charlemagne; see Melriah V. Rosenberg, *Eleanor of Aquitaine, Queen of the Troubadours and Courts of Love* (Boston: Houghton Mifflin, 1937), p. 5.

169. Jules Horrent, "Chroniques espagnoles et chansons de geste," *Le Moyen Age* 53(1947):287–302. For this reference I am indebted to Professor John Williams, Department of Fine Arts, University of Pittsburgh.

170. Pacaut, *Louis VII*, pp. 35–36.

171. Defourneaux, *Les Français*, p. 114.

172. Pacaut, *Louis VII*, p. 83.

5. English Painting and the Continent during the Reign of Henry II and Eleanor

LARRY M. AYRES

The life span of Eleanor of Aquitaine (1122–1204) bridges for art historians a most significant period, the transition from the late spring to the early summer of medieval art. She lived to see the maturation of the first international style of medieval art, Romanesque. She stood at the threshold of "first Gothic" at Saint-Denis and died after the first High Gothic edifice, Chartres Cathedral, was planned and under construction. This article is an attempt to evaluate the relationship of artists working in England to Continental developments during the reign of Henry II and Eleanor, thereby setting the chronological bounds of my study at the years 1154 and 1189, the year of Henry's death. From the start we should realize that, as far as English painting of the period is concerned, Henry and Eleanor in no way created a "court school" in the sense that we understand the meaning of the term as regards Charlemagne's Palace School.[1] I also wish to make clear that I plan to deal with art in terms of art but that, when factors external to stylistic developments seem relevant, they will be brought into play. I will essentially limit my investigation to aspects of the decorative programs of illuminated manuscripts which were executed in English monastic communities at Winchester, Bury St. Edmunds, Canterbury, and Saint Albans. Miniatures will be the primary evidence, and I will argue that there are three major tracks along which we should gauge or evaluate English painting in light of contemporary Continental developments.

Carl Nordenfalk once mentioned that the history of twelfth-century book illustration might well be written by studying the giant copies of the Vulgate which were owned by monastic foundations throughout Europe, and I would like to begin this discussion by examining the work of one of the illuminators of the book which Nordenfalk has called the finest of all

Romanesque Bibles, the Winchester Bible, now housed in Winchester Cathedral Library and without a doubt a product of the Benedictine cathedral priory scriptorium at Winchester.[2] The artist in question has sometimes been called the Master of the Apocrypha Drawings, because he designed two great frontispieces before the books of Judith and I Book of Maccabees in the Winchester Bible; for the sake of brevity, I will call him the Apocrypha Master. He is a painter who has been much neglected by art historians. This may be partly due to the enchanting quality of his frontispiece drawings, which were never painted and which still call out for more detailed study, but I would like to concentrate on the Apocrypha Master's painted, historiated initials in the manuscript. Two miniatures, in particular, those which preface the books of Hosea and Joel (Figs. 1 and 2) present important clues to his artistic antecedents and have a special relevance for understanding the relationship between English painting and the Continental centers of the Angevin empire.

In his discussion of stylistic trends in English painting of the second half of the twelfth century, T. S. R. Boase observed links which existed between insular and Continental ateliers during the period. His investigations greatly enhanced our knowledge of the "marked affinities of English work. . .with books produced in the Capetian areas of Ponthieu, Vermandois, Flanders, and Paris."[3] Our first line of inquiry, however, will turn toward Henry II and Eleanor's Angevin empire, and I will suggest that the work of the Apocrypha Master represents the invasion into insular soil of a style which developed in Poitou, Anjou, Aquitaine, and Touraine in the late eleventh and early twelfth centuries. Second, I think this style asserted itself in English developments more clearly and dramatically after Henry II and Eleanor became king and queen of England—in other words, that its reception was related to an altered political situation.

The first miniature by the Apocrypha Master which I would like to consider prefaces the Book of Hosea in the Winchester Bible and depicts the prophet standing at the far left (Fig. 1). This is the best preserved example of the Apocrypha Master's painted work. There are a number of features which are conservative or even archaic in his style, such as the manner in which highlights are applied to the right arm of the prophet. This is not true modeling; the highlights appear glued on. The patterns of highlights seem to originate from a whirlpool of light at the top of Hosea's right arm and then descend, forming crescents along the edge of the arm. The same technique is used in the application of light patterns on the prophet's right leg. Here we see a bright knob at the knee exploding into a series of glistening cascades which sit on the surface rather than give an impression of plasticity or rotundity to the figure. Note also the prevalence of linear devices in the way the lower edges of Hosea's tunic and mantle are caught as though by a breeze to form a series of cusplike folds which appear in suspended animation, immune from the laws of gravity. The Apocrypha Master is not composing in terms of the twelfth-century stylistic idiom that Wilhelm Koehler labeled "damp fold," a formal outlook which is found in English painting from the second quarter of the twelfth century onward, the great exemplars being the miniatures of the Bury and Lambeth Bibles and the wall painting of Saint Paul and the Viper at Canterbury Cathedral.[4] A colleague of the Apocrypha Master at Winchester, one of his teammates in the decoration of the Winchester Bible, who has been called by Walter Oakeshott the Master of the Leaping Figures, was one of the most gifted interpreters of the "damp-fold style" on English soil (Fig. 3).[5] The Master of the Leaping Figures is more sensitive to tactile values and modeling than the Apocrypha Master, and, to borrow K. H. Usener's apt phrase, his "damp folds" endow the figures with a plasticity which begins and ends at the edges of their contours.[6] A stylistic gulf separates these collaborators at Winchester.

The Apocrypha Master's formal orientation may be regarded as the "swan song" of an artistic movement which originated and blossomed in the West and Southwest of France in the late eleventh and early twelfth centuries.[7] It was confined neither by feudal nor by ecclesiastical boundaries and reached one of its summits around 1100 in the mural paintings of Saint-Savin-sur-Gartempe and Notre-Dame-la-Grande in Poitiers and in illustrated manuscripts from Tours and the province of Anjou.[8] Scholars have accepted the presence of a "regional school" which we will call the "Angevin style" in the vicinity of Poitiers by the end of the eleventh century. As André Grabar has pointed out, within a radius of fifty kilometers from Poitiers we are presented with both mural paintings and manuscript illuminations which stylistically share a striking family resemblance. If we compare the Apocrypha Master's image of Hosea with paintings from the crypt and porch of Saint-Savin (Figs. 4 and 5), stylistic resemblances abound.[9] Highlights traverse the surfaces of the figures like metallic lusters. The square-jawed visages of the Apocrypha Master's figures and his method of rendering highlights as hard-edged patterns can also be found in miniature decorations, such as the Logos portrait in a Gospel Book from Angers (Fig. 6)[10] and the initial depicting David's struggle with the lion in a Limoges manuscript (Fig. 7).[11]

Assuming that the Apocrypha Master's style is indeed grounded in the principles of the "Angevin style," there is a problem of chronology, since

I have been comparing his work, which I place in the late 1170's or early 1180's, with monuments which are usually dated to the late eleventh or the first half of the twelfth century. Nevertheless, Otto Demus in his study of Romanesque mural painting has noted that the "Angevin style" did not die out quickly but continued to develop and by the third quarter of the twelfth century entered a mannered phase which can be observed in the frescoes at Saint-Aignan-sur-Cher.[12] In the realm of manuscript illustration, we can also verify the longevity of the "Angevin style" by looking at a West of France manuscript containing a collection of Lives of Saints and now in Paris.[13] The earliest date which this manuscript has been given is "mid-twelfth" century and it has been placed even later by some scholars. I would like to compare the figure which holds a large fish, thus forming an initial *T* (Fig. 8), from the Lives of Saints manuscript with that of Matthias decapitating a soldier from the Maccabean frontispiece by the Apocrypha Master in the Winchester Bible (Fig. 9). Here there is no need to belabor the obvious congruities in formal outlook, because both these artists ultimately emerge from the orbit of the "Angevin style." The Paris manuscript is assumed to have originated in West or West-Central France, and some of its initials have affiliations with Limoges traditions.

We may now ask whether we know anything about the Apocrypha Master's activity before he worked on the Winchester Bible. L. W. Jones and C. R. Morey proposed in their study of illustrated Terence manuscripts that the Apocrypha Master was probably the "headmaster" of a team of artists who illustrated a Terence manuscript which bears a Saint Albans *anathema*.[14] They thought that the Apocrypha Master was probably recruited from Winchester to work on the Saint Albans Terence; but there is reason to believe that the Apocrypha Master is more likely to have migrated to Winchester after he had been resident at Saint Albans. The pedigree of the Terence manuscript which the Apocrypha Master used as a model at Saint Albans is most relevant to our investigation. He copied from an illustrated Carolingian manuscript of Terence's plays which is thought to have been produced at Reims in the ninth century (Paris, Bibliothèque Nationale, MS. lat. 7899). However, the Carolingian exemplar which the Apocrypha Master copied was not brought directly to Saint Albans from Rheims. In the ninth century it was taken and in part copied at Fleury; and, around 1100, portions of the Carolingian model, later used by the Apocrypha Master, were again copied in France by an artist believed to be an exponent of the "Angevin style" (Vatican Library, MS. lat. 3305).[15] The miniatures of the Vatican Terence display a close correspondence in style to a series of drawings on a leaf in Auxerre

Cathedral, which Meyer Schapiro localized to Tours and dated to the years around 1100.[16] Consequently, it appears that the Carolingian Terence, which was later copied by the Apocrypha Master at Saint Albans, was employed around 1100 in a center, perhaps Tours, where the "Angevin style" was current usage.

There is no historical evidence to indicate by what route the Carolingian exemplar of Terence's plays which was employed in the West of France around 1100 reached Saint Albans, probably in the 1170's. However, in light of the Apocrypha Master's stylistic affiliations with prior artistic developments in the Angevin realm, he could well be a prime suspect in a move to fill this historical lacuna. His stylistic antecedents certainly do not stand in the way of identifying him as the vehicle of transmission not only of the Carolingian exemplar but also of a distinct stylistic profile across the Channel. He could well have been a "British subject," because the West of France and Aquitaine were Angevin dominions which Henry II valued highly. The Apocrypha Master's work at Saint Albans and Winchester establishes a link between insular and Continental art which is entirely consonant with the political dynamics of the Angevin empire. The "Angevin style" did not pervade English painting in the first half of the twelfth century; only after the ascendance of Henry and Eleanor in 1154 did it boldly assert itself in various centers. Could it be, in this instance, that new arrangements in the political sphere favored the adoption of the "Angevin style" which, as it were, invaded two major English centers, Winchester and Saint Albans? There are further examples which might verify such an assumption, but I would now like to call attention to another group of illuminated manuscripts in which it is more difficult to establish whether Continental art was influencing English production or vice versa, a problem which introduces the notion of the "Channel style."

The Saint Albans Terence manuscript probably belongs to the period of the reforming activities of Abbot Simon between 1167 and 1183.[17] Other manuscripts which were illuminated at Saint Albans during this period clearly bring into play Boase's notion of the "Channel style."[18] Art historians have begun to reconstruct the work of an artist who illuminated some of Abbot Simon's books, and this illuminator has been dubbed the Simon Master by Walter Cahn.[19] The chronicle of the abbey speaks of Abbot Simon employing professional scribes, and the Simon Master decorated at least one of Simon's books written by a professional scribe.[20] Can this evidence lead us to speculate as to whether or not the Simon Master too was a lay employee rather than a monastic artist? In the life of Saint Hugh of Lincoln, for example, it is recorded that Henry

II once advised Saint Hugh when he was prior of the Carthusian house at Witham between 1179/1180 and 1186 to use professional scribes.[21]

The Simon Master also worked on the Continent and was responsible for many historiated initials in a twelfth-century Bible now in Paris (Bibliothèque Nationale, MSS. lat. 16743–16746). The Simon Master's work therefore epitomizes what Boase has called the "Channel style," as this artist worked on both sides of the Channel and it is no easy matter to establish conclusively his national origins and direct stylistic antecedents. C. R. Dodwell and Arthur Watson have noted iconographical correspondences between the illustrations of the Tree of Jesse in the Capucins Bible and that of the Lambeth Bible (London, Lambeth Palace, MS. 3) from Canterbury, which is considered earlier than the Capucins Bible by at least a decade.[22] The Simon Master's historiated initial which opens the Book of Ezekiel in the Capucins Bible contains an episode from the prophet's life (Ezekiel following the Lord's instructions and obediently devouring the unfurled book, Ezek. 2:9–3:3), which is also depicted in the miniature before the Book of Ezekiel in the Lambeth Bible (Figs. 10 and 11).[23] The similarity in imagery, however, is not paralleled by a close stylistic correspondence between the art of the Simon and Lambeth Masters. Dodwell suggests the possibility that the Tree of Jesse imagery of the Lambeth Bible, which he believes was illuminated at Canterbury, may have been transmitted across the Channel to Saint Bertin when some Canterbury monks went to Saint Bertin in 1164 during the Becket controversy.[24] It is not without interest that some of the Simon Master's earliest miniatures are found in a book which has been associated with Saint Bertin. The Simon Master, whatever his nationality, remains an essential line of communication between England and the Continent during the period 1154–1189 and may indeed serve as an index for "Channel-style" developments.

Mention of the Lambeth Bible introduces another problem regarding the relationship of English and Continental painting. The question of where the Lambeth Master received his training cannot be solved, if ever, until an intensive study of North French and Parisian manuscripts of the twelfth century has been conducted, but I will here draw the general outlines of the issue. It seems that the Lambeth Master worked on the Continent before he illustrated the Lambeth Bible, and the problem of the chronology of his work will ultimately have to be gauged within the context of a "Channel school." The "Englishness" of his art in the meantime needs to be defined more precisely.

Two leaves from a now lost Gospel Book which belonged to the abbey of Liessies in Hainaut show that the Lambeth Master was active on the

1. Initial to Hosea, Winchester Bible, fol. 198, Winchester Cathedral Library. Courtesy Dean and Chapter, Winchester Cathedral.

2

di muulnuf mcum: & uucnc īnūuoie
Et eiaiaf. Audue ceu & aurtbuf pape
INCIPIT IObEL PROPh

ER

DOM

QVE

FACTUM EST AD IObEL filium Bathuel

3

dei touidie.
nfidianf cogitat lingua fua· quafi nouacula·

2. Initial to Joel, Winchester Bible, fol. 200v, Winchester Cathedral Library. Courtesy Dean and Chapter, Winchester Cathedral.

3. Initial to Psalm 51, Winchester Bible, fol. 232, Winchester Cathedral Library. Courtesy Dean and Chapter, Winchester Cathedral.

4. Martyrdom of Saint Savin, fresco from crypt, Saint-Savin-sur-Gartempe. Photo: Archives Photographiques, Paris.

5. Trumpeting Angel, porch fresco, Saint-Savin-sur-Gartempe. Photo: Archives Photographiques, Paris.

6. Christ "Logos," initial to Gospel of Saint John, Angers, Bibliothèque Municipale, MS. 25, fol. 85v. Courtesy Bibliothèque Municipale, Angers.

7. David and the Lion, Paris, Bibliothèque Nationale, MS. lat. 1987, fol. 56v. Courtesy Bibliothèque Nationale.

8. "T" initial, Lives of Saints, Paris, Bibliothèque Nationale, MS. lat. 5323, fol. 48v. Courtesy Bibliothèque Nationale.

anno·inqrco mense·inquinca m̄
cum eē m inmedio caprinorₛ iur

9. Matthias scene, Maccabean frontispiece, Winchester Bible, fol. 350v, Winchester Cathedral Library. Courtesy Dean and Chapter, Winchester Cathedral.

10. Initial to Ezekiel, Lambeth Bible, Lambeth Palace Library, MS. 3, fol. 258v. Courtesy Archbishop of Canterbury and Trustees of Lambeth Palace Library.

11

12

11. Initial to Ezekiel, Capucins Bible, Paris, Bibliothèque Nationale, MS. lat. 16744, fol. 81. Courtesy Bibliothèque Nationale.

12. Labor for July, Saint Albans calendar, Oxford, Bodleian Library, MS. Auct. D.2.6, fol. 4v. Courtesy Bodleian Library.

13. *Beatus* initial, Douai, Bibliothèque Municipale, MS. 250, fol. 2v. Courtesy Bibliothèque Municipale de Douai. Photo: Archives Photographiques, Paris.

14. Initial to Isaiah, Lambeth Bible, Lambeth Palace Library, MS. 3, fol. 198v. Courtesy Archbishop of Canterbury and Trustees of Lambeth Palace Library.

filii amos qm uidit sup iudam &
ierlin·in diebz ozie·ioatham·achai

15. Initial to Leviticus, glossed Leviticus, Paris, Bibliothèque Nationale, MS. lat. 14771, fol. 1. Courtesy Bibliothèque Nationale.

16. Frontispiece to Deuteronomy, Bury Bible, Cambridge, Corpus Christi College, MS. 2, fol. 94. Courtesy Master and Fellows, Corpus Christi College, Cambridge.

17. Initials to Psalm 109, Winchester Bible, fol. 250, Winchester Cathedral Library. Courtesy Dean and Chapter, Winchester Cathedral.

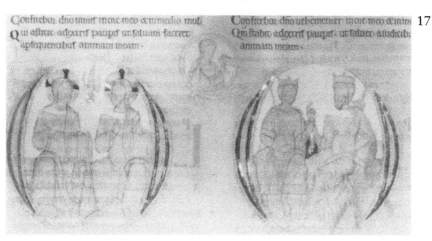

Confitebor dño nimis in ore meo & in medio multi
Qui astitit adextris paupis ut saluam facteet
apsequentibus animam meam·

Confitebor dño uehementer in ore meo & in m
Qm stabit adextris paupis· ut saluet a iudicib:
animam meam·

18. Jeremiah's Lamentation, Winchester Bible, fol. 169, Winchester Cathedral Library. Courtesy Dean and Chapter, Winchester Cathedral.

Continent.[25] The Gospel Book itself was destroyed during World War II, but two leaves from the manuscript, depicting Evangelist portraits, are preserved in the Société Archéologique at Avesnes. The more famous leaf represents Saint John the Evangelist dipping his quill in an inkhorn held out to him by Wedric, abbot of Liessies between 1124 and 1147. Fortunately, a colophon existed in the manuscript, according to which the book was written by a scribe named John in 1146 and, consequently, the Wedricus page must date to 1146/1147. The Lambeth Master's style as exemplified by the Avesnes leaves is a rather mannered variant of the "damp-fold style," which curiously denies many of the tactile qualities found in other examples of the "damp-fold" idiom in favor of an almost metallic stiffness that seems quite planar. Dodwell assumes that the Lambeth Master's miniatures in the Lambeth Bible postdate his work on the Continent on Abbot Wedric's Gospel Book, and he dates the Lambeth Master's activity at Canterbury to the years around 1150.[26]

Other factors may nevertheless indicate that the Lambeth Bible was illuminated somewhat later and therefore that its miniatures would have been created during the reign of Henry and Eleanor. For example, Dodwell has used mosaic decorations of Norman court art in Sicily, notably those of the Cappella Palatina in Palermo, to account for Byzantine influences on the Canterbury School of illumination.[27] This is particularly evident when he compares mosaic scenes from the lives of Abraham and Jacob on the nave walls of the Cappella Palatina with miniatures in the Lambeth Bible. Ernst Kitzinger, on the other hand, noted that the execution of the cycle of nave mosaics in the Cappella Palatina may not have been under way until the 1150's. He suggests that if Dodwell wishes to hold to the Cappella Palatina mosaics as sources of influence on the Lambeth Master, the Lambeth Bible would have to be placed perhaps a decade or so later.[28]

Otto Pächt and J. J. G. Alexander have recently attributed a series of illustrations depicting Labors of the Months in a Saint Albans calendar (Fig. 12) to the hand of the Lambeth Master, calling it "an early work of the Master of the Lambeth Bible."[29] The Saint Albans calendar (Oxford, Bodleian Library, MS. Auct. D.2.6) would appear to have been written between 1140 and 1158, and Pächt has already proposed that a bridge existed between Saint Albans and Canterbury ateliers toward the middle of the twelfth century.[30] However, in order for an artist of the Saint Albans calendar to mature into the Lambeth Master, he would have to have experienced a strong dose of the "damp-fold" idiom either by direct adaptation from Byzantine originals or via Western intermediary sources. Dodwell apparently recognized this when he argued that "stylistically, the illumination of the Lambeth Bible derives largely from the Bury Bible."[31]

Another work that should be taken into consideration is a historiated *Beatus* initial which was published by Albert Boeckler over forty years ago and associated with the Lambeth Bible's decorative program by him (Fig. 13).[32] The miniature decorates a copy of Saint Augustine's Commentary on the Psalms which belonged to the North French house of Marchiennes.[33] The manuscript now forms part of the collection of the Bibliothèque Municipale at Douai (MS. 250) and is dated towards the middle of the twelfth century by Boeckler, Jean Porcher, and others. In the upper register of the initial, we see the Apocalyptic Christ, and below sits King David accompanied by two musicians. It is instructive to compare the figure of Christ from the Marchiennes initial with that of King Manasseh which inhabits the initial before the Book of Isaiah in the Lambeth Bible (Fig. 14).[34] To be sure, the Marchiennes initial lacks the more lofty, accomplished look of the Lambeth Master's illumination. Nevertheless, the harsh, metallic interpretations of the "damp-fold" idiom in the rendition of the Marchiennes Christ and the Lambeth Manasseh are undeniably similar, and perhaps North French works figure in the artistic antecedents of the Lambeth Master. Victor Leroquais and André Boutemy have already provided much of the groundwork for art historians to investigate these North French scriptoria and the impact which they may have had on the formation of the style of the Lambeth Master.[35] The work of the Simon Master and the Lambeth Master demonstrates how difficult it is in these cases to establish stylistic priorities in terms of national identities, because we have individual artists working on both sides of the Channel. We may have ultimately to view their position in terms of "cross-fertilization," to borrow a phrase from Erwin Panofsky.

The complexity of the situation is further demonstrated by an artistic personality whose work represents one of the peaks of English Romanesque illumination: Master Hugo, whose miniatures in the Bury Bible have always been considered one of the touchstones of the "damp-fold style."[36] Master Hugo's work at Bury St. Edmunds is usually dated between 1135 and 1145,[37] but his style, perhaps even his own hand, appears in a miniature of a glossed Bible text which now belongs to the Bibliothèque Nationale (Fig. 15; MS. lat. 14771). This glossed copy of Leviticus probably formed part of a series of glossed books of the Bible which once belonged to Magister Gervase of the house of Saint Augustine, Canterbury.[38] Gervase had presumably studied in the schools of Paris and gave glossed copies of Old and New Testament books, among others, to the abbey of Saint-Victor in Paris. The glossed Leviticus probably belonged to Gervase's benefaction and fortunately contains a historiated initial which shows Moses counseling the Israelites. The style of the illuminator who executed the scene is certainly close to that of Master Hugo in the Bury Bible, and it may indeed be by his hand (cf. Fig. 16). The glossed Leviticus does not strike me as an English book of the first half of the twelfth century, and the question arises as to whether Gervase's glossed texts were illuminated in Paris, where he presumably studied, or at Canterbury. If the glossed Leviticus was written and illustrated in Paris, then Master Hugo's work must also be assessed in the context of Channel developments of the second half of the twelfth century. The miniature of Moses and the Israelites testifies to the longevity of Master Hugo's style either in England or on the Continent. We know that Master Hugo was a lay artist,[39] and he may have migrated to Canterbury or Paris after finishing his artistic campaign at Bury St. Edmunds. If he executed the Leviticus initial in Paris, do we assume he was working in home territory? On the other hand, if he illuminated Gervase's Leviticus at Canterbury after concluding his work at Bury, would he have come into contact with the illuminator of the Saint Albans calendar in the Bodleian (MS. Auct. D.2.6) whom Pächt and Alexander have identified as the young Lambeth Master? Is the blending of Saint Albans trends with Master Hugo's "damp-fold" idiom sufficient to explain the emergence of the Lambeth Master's style? If Gervase's glossed book was illuminated at Canterbury, it would certainly enhance Dodwell's observation that the Lambeth Master's style was to a considerable extent based on the solutions of Master Hugo's work in the Bury Bible[40] and Demus's suggestion that the fresco of Saint Paul and the viper in the Chapel of Saint Anselm at Canterbury Cathedral "must be attributed to a pupil of Master Hugo."[41] Can Canterbury therefore be regarded as an artistic crossroads where various traditions stemming from Saint Albans, Bury St. Edmunds, Byzantinizing court art in Sicily, and perhaps even Paris met in the first decade of the second half of the twelfth century?

To recapitulate, in discussing the Simon Master, Lambeth Master, and Master Hugo (or his atelier), we face the question of deciding which side of the Channel can claim priority for the origin of their styles. Perhaps surviving evidence will never allow us to cut so fine a distinction and Boase's "Channel style" must remain the caption under which this period of English illumination falls. One thing seems certain: the foregoing discussion forces us to take pause at François Masai's observation that in the twelfth century we must at least recognize the possibility that lay artists were called upon frequently to decorate luxury manuscripts.[42] As far as stylistic developments in the last decade of Henry II's reign are concerned, the Simon and Lambeth Masters and Master Hugo were not the wave of the future. Their solutions, enchanting as they may be, do not lead or even contribute to the birth of Gothic painting in England at Winchester in the early 1180's. Certainly, the "damp-fold" current could no longer be considered a progressive trend by the second half of the twelfth century, since it had already surfaced at Cluny and other Continental centers in the first quarter of the twelfth century.[43]

In the early 1180's English artists began to break with traditional formulas and participate in a classicizing trend as far as style was concerned.[44] It will be recalled that, first, the Apocrypha Master's work in the Winchester Bible has been discussed as an Angevin invasion in which a Continental style was transplanted to England, a situation of direct influence from the Continent which may have been encouraged by the ascendancy of Henry and Eleanor in England after 1154. Second, in the case of the decoration of Abbot Simon's books at Saint Albans and the Lambeth Bible at Canterbury, the direction in which artistic currents flowed across the Channel is not as easily perceived in a lineal sense as in the Apocrypha Master's works. In the second group we must speak in terms of "cross-fertilization" until further research on Parisian and North French scriptoria can be done. In this second group, the derivative character of English painting is not as clear as in the first group, and the problem of "national origins" and "stylistic sources" remains to be further investigated.

In the third phase, classicizing stylistic outlooks emerged on both sides of the Channel. This marked stylistic shift can be observed in England in miniatures by the Morgan Master in the Winchester Bible and on the Continent in the enamels of Nicholas of Verdun's Klosterneuburg ambo of 1181.[45] In these cases neither "direct influence" nor "cross-fertilization" seems to be of primary importance in the relationship of English painting to that of the Continent.[46] Rather, it is appropriate to think in terms of parallelism of developments on both sides of the Channel. Around 1180 there appears to have been a "style-break" or "mutational change" in the figurative styles of painting, sculpture, and metalwork in Northwest Europe.[47] It was in this period that English Gothic painting took its first step forward without debts to French prototypes. The earliest exponent in English painting of this new classicizing idiom was the Morgan Master, who participated in the decoration of the Winchester Bible in the early 1180's.[48]

Figures 17 and 18 show three miniatures by the Morgan Master in the Winchester Bible: two are drawings before Psalm 109 and the other a painted initial before Jeremiah's Lamentations (5:1). The painted miniature shows that the Morgan Master was indebted to Byzantine models in the manner in which his faces are drawn and treated, and such scholars as Kitzinger, Demus, and Oakeshott have argued that he received essential impulses for the resolution of his style in the court art of Norman Sicily, where Byzantine mosaic artists were employed.[49] What appears to have taken place in the Morgan Master's career is that, after his return to England, he gradually weaned himself from Byzantine canons and ultimately extracted the classical core from his Byzantine models or rediscovered for himself the language of classical values. By this I mean the serene demeanor, proportions which express a harmony of parts, the plastic validity of the enthroned figures of the drawings, and their statuesque character. The figures appear self-contained and exist within themselves independent of effects of patternization. A "restraint of emotional factors" invades the Morgan Master's vision at Psalm 109, and the same sense of classical equilibrium underlies the sculptured Coronation of the Virgin group at Chartres Cathedral, which was executed probably after 1204.[50] This is what I mean by the new parallelism of developments in English and French centers.

To be sure, the Morgan Master was much indebted to the Byzantinizing milieu of Norman Sicily; but what is equally important is how he liberated his style from Byzantine prototypes and struck out in a new direction. In the miniature before Lamentations (5:1), the figure of the Pantocrator above the lamenting prophet presupposes a monumental prototype which could be found in the Sicilian cycles.[51] However, the Morgan Master abandoned any references to Byzantine cloisonné folds and treated his drapery more naturalistically, in smoother, softer, more flowing lines. This is only one of the initial steps by which this master began to depart from his models in his quest to arrive at a formal parity with antique values. The impulse from the Byzantine mosaic workshops of Norman Sicily was all-important for the Morgan Master's stylistic posture, and one wonders whether his presence there was in some manner related to the marriage of Joanna of England, daughter of Henry II and Eleanor, to William II of Sicily in 1177. The Sicilian ambassadors glimpsed their future queen for the first time at Winchester in 1176.[52] Richard of Ilchester, Bishop of Winchester, was responsible for many arrangements surrounding the marriage.[53] Monreale, in Sicily, was a royal foundation of William II and would have been under construction probably shortly before and certainly after his marriage to Princess Joanna of England.[54] Contacts between England and the Norman island kingdom reached a high-water mark during the late 1170's as a result. It is difficult, though, to evaluate whether the dynastic connections of Eleanor's daughter were a factor in the Morgan Master's sojourn in Sicily. However, the classicizing style which he and his immediate English successors evolved was part of a much broader artistic movement which infected Northwest

Europe in the late twelfth century, and court art of Norman Sicily cannot be seen as the *fons vitae* of the entire movement,[55] even though its monuments may have inspired the first English painter to enter the Gothic world.

In conclusion, we have examined three aspects of the relationship between English painting and the Continent during the reign of Henry II and Eleanor. As for the "Angevin style" practiced by the Apocrypha Master in the Winchester Bible, I note a greater receptivity of this current in English centers after the advent of Henry and Eleanor on insular soil in 1154. Here a new set of political arrangements may have prepared the way for or encouraged the cultivation of an artistic style which had its birth and first flowering on the Continent rather than in England.

Second, we have examined aspects of the "Channel style" with reference to such works as the Lambeth and Bury Bibles and the work of the Simon Master. Here the priorities for training and innovation are not as clear, but I would not be surprised if French ateliers were eventually given more credit than is at present awarded them when all the evidence has been assembled and sifted through. Whatever the case may be, the Bury and Lambeth Bibles remain among the crown jewels of English Romanesque books.

Finally, we arrive at the new dynastic connections with Sicily and the Byzantinizing masters of the Winchester Bible. In this period, English artists were among the most avant-garde in Europe and developed stylistic outlooks along classicizing lines parallel to similar artistic developments on the Continent. In this instance, late in the reign of Henry II, there was a new assertion of stylistic independence in English centers, and for some decades afterward English artists were less inclined to borrow or be dependent on lessons from either the Continental or the Mediterranean sphere.

NOTES

1. See, in general, T. S. R. Boase, *English Art, 1100–1216* (Oxford: Clarendon Press, 1953), pp. 196–197, 205; M.-M. Gauthier, "Le Goût Plantagenet," in *Stil und Überlieferung in der Kunst des Abendlandes*, Akten des 21. Internationalen Kongresses für Kunstgeschichte in Bonn 1964 (Berlin: Verlag Gebr. Mann, 1967), I, 139–155.

2. Carl Nordenfalk, in *Romanesque Painting*, by idem and André Grabar

(Lausanne: Skira, 1958), p. 163.

3. Boase, *English Art*, p. 183.

4. Wilhelm Koehler, "Byzantine Art in the West," *Dumbarton Oaks Papers* 1(1941):63–87; Otto Demus, *Romanesque Mural Painting*, trans. Mary Whittall (London: Thames and Hudson, 1970), p. 124.

5. Walter Oakeshott, *The Artists of the Winchester Bible* (London: Faber and Faber, 1945), pl. 1.

6. K. H. Usener, "Les Débuts du

style roman dans l'art mosan," in *L'Art mosan*, ed. P. Francastel (Paris: Armand Colin, 1953), pp. 107–108.

7. For a more detailed analysis of the Apocrypha Master's work, see L. M. Ayres, "The Role of an Angevin Style in English Romanesque Painting," *Zeitschrift für Kunstgeschichte* 37 (1974):193–223.

8. André Grabar, "L'Etude des fresques romanes," *Cahiers Archéologiques* 2(1947):174–175; Demus, *Romanesque Mural Painting*, pp. 101–104.

9. For Saint-Savin, with references to earlier bibliography, see Demus, *Romanesque Mural Painting*, pp.420–423.

10. Jean Porcher, *Les Manuscrits à peintures en France du VIIe au XIIe siècle* (Paris: Bibliothèque Nationale, 1954), no. 226, p. 82; J. J. G. Alexander, *Norman Illumination at Mont St. Michel* (Oxford: Clarendon Press, 1970), p. 203 n.3.

11. D. Gaborit-Chopin, *La Décoration des manuscrits à Saint-Martial de Limoges et en Limousin du IXe au XIIe siècle* (Paris and Geneva: Droz, 1969), p. 119.

12. Demus, *Romanesque Mural Painting*, pp. 104–106.

13. Bibliothèque Nationale, MS. lat. 5323; Gaborit-Chopin, *La Décoration*, pp. 148–149 n.37.

14. L. W. Jones and C. R. Morey, *The Miniatures of the Manuscripts of Terence prior to the Thirteenth Century* (Princeton: Princeton University Press, 1931), pp. 68–93, esp. pp. 91–93. The manuscript is MS. Auct. F.2.13 in the Bodleian Library, Oxford.

15. Jones and Morey, *The Miniatures*, pp. 17–74, 213–214.

16. Meyer Schapiro, "Two Romanesque Drawings in Auxerre and Some Iconographical Problems," in *Studies in Art and Literature for Belle da Costa Greene*, ed. D. Miner (Princeton: Princeton University Press, 1954), pp. 348–349, Figs. 254–255, 264. For the leaf, see (more recently) M. W. Evans, *Medieval Drawings* (London: Hamlyn, 1969), p. 27, pl. 41.

17. For Abbot Simon, see D. Knowles, *The Monastic Order in England, 940–1216*, 2d ed. (Cambridge: Cambridge University Press, 1963), pp. 310, 502; T. G. Frisch, *Gothic Art, 1140–c. 1450: Sources and Documents*, ed. H. W. Janson (Englewood Cliffs, N. J.: Prentice-Hall, 1971), p. 39.

18. Boase, *English Art*, p. 183.

19. Walter Cahn, "An Illustrated Josephus from the Meuse Region in Merton College, Oxford," *Zeitschrift für Kunstgeschichte* 29(1966): 308 n.28; L. M. Ayres, "A Miniature from Jumièges and Trends in Manuscript Illumination around 1200," in *Intuition und Kunstwissenschaft: Festschrift für Hanns Swarzenski*, ed. P. Bloch, Tilmann Buddensieg, Alfred Hentzen, and Theodor Müller (Berlin: Verlag Gebr. Mann, 1973), pp. 120–122.

20. L. M. Ayres, "A Tanner Manuscript in the Bodleian Library and Some Notes on English Painting of the Late Twelfth Century," *Journal of the Warburg and Courtauld Institute* 32 (1969):51 n.43.

21. *Magna Vita Sancti Hugonis*, ed. and trans. D. L. Douie and H. Farmer, 2 vols. (London and New York: Nelson, 1961), I, 84–85.

22. A. Watson, *The Early Iconography of the Tree of Jesse* (London: Oxford University Press, 1934), pp.

110–112, pl. 23; C. R. Dodwell, *The Canterbury School of Illumination, 1066–1200* (Cambridge: Cambridge University Press, 1954), pp. 50, 110–111.

23. Dodwell, *The Canterbury School*, pp. 54–55, pl. 31a.

24. Ibid., pp. 110–111.

25. Hanns Swarzenski, *Monuments of Romanesque Art*, 2d ed. (London: Faber and Faber, 1967), p. 62, pl. 132; J. J. G. Alexander and C. M. Kauffmann, *English Illuminated Manuscripts, 700–1500* (exhibition catalogue, Brussels, 1973), no. 31.

26. C. R. Dodwell, *The Great Lambeth Bible* (London: Faber and Faber, 1959), pp. 16–19, pls. 7–8; see also J. Leclercq, "Les Manuscrits de l'abbaye de Liessies," *Scriptorium 6* (1952):pls. 4–7.

27. Dodwell, *The Canterbury School*, pp. 81–83.

28. Ernst Kitzinger, "Norman Sicily as a Source of Byzantine Influence on Western Art in the Twelfth Century," in *Byzantine Art—An European Art: Lectures Given on the Occasion of the Ninth Exhibition of the Council of Europe* (Athens, 1966), pp. 136–137. Dorothy Eastman has explored the question of relative chronology in her unpublished M.A. thesis on Channel School problems (University of California at Santa Barbara, 1972).

29. Otto Pächt and J. J. G. Alexander, *Illuminated Manuscripts in the Bodleian Library*, vol. 3, *British, Irish, Icelandic Schools with Addenda to Volumes I and II* (Oxford: Clarendon Press, 1973), no. 117, p. 14, pl. 11.

30. Otto Pächt, C. R. Dodwell, and F. Wormald, *The St. Albans Psalter* (London: The Warburg Institute, University of London, 1960), p. 158 n.3.

31. Dodwell, *Lambeth Bible*, p. 8.

32. Albert Boeckler, *Abendländische Miniaturen bis zum Ausgang der romanischen Zeit* (Berlin: Verlag von Walter de Gruyter Co., 1930), p. 95, pl. 96.

33. Porcher, *Les Manuscrits*, no. 148, p. 63; Florentine Mütherich, "Malerei im 12. Jahrhundert," in *Das Mittelalter I*, ed. Hermann Fillitz, Propyläen Kunstgeschichte, vol. 5 (Berlin: Propyläen Verlag, 1969), p. 275, pl. 53; Alexander and Kauffmann, *English Illuminated Manuscripts*, no. 31, pp. 58–59.

34. Dodwell, *The Canterbury School*, p. 84, pl. 52a.

35. Studies by Victor Leroquais, listed in Porcher, *Les Manuscrits*, p. 132; André Boutemy, "Un Trésor injustement oublié: Les Manuscrits enluminés du Nord de la France," *Scriptorium* 3(1949):110–122.

36. C. M. Kauffmann, "The Bury Bible," *Journal of the Warburg and Courtauld Institute* 29(1966): 74–81.

37. The date 1137 has been proposed for the execution of the Bury Bible by R. M. Thompson, "Early Romanesque Book-Illustration in England: The Dates of the Pierpont Morgan 'Vitae Sancti Edmundi,' and the Bury Bible," *Viator* 2(1971):220–224.

38. L. Delisle, *Le Cabinet des manuscrits de la Bibliothèque Nationale*, 4 vols. (Paris, 1874), II, 213. I am indebted to François Avril for the knowledge of this manuscript and its relatives.

39. Kauffmann, "The Bury Bible," pp. 62–64.

40. Thompson, "Early Romanesque Book-Illustration," p. 223, argues in favor of Master Hugo's "continuous

residence at Bury circa 1130–1155."
41. Demus, *Romanesque Mural Painting*, pp. 124, 509, colorplate on p. 121; Demus places the fresco in the third quarter of the twelfth century. Documentary references verifying the presence of goldsmiths and painters at Canterbury in the twelfth century have been published by W. Urry, *Canterbury under the Angevin Kings* (London: Athlone Press, University of London, 1967), pp. 112–113, 121.
42. François Masai, "Les Manuscrits à peintures de Sambre et Meuse aux XIᵉ et XIIᵉ siècles," *Cahiers de Civilisation Médiévale* 3(1960):188–189.
43. Koehler, "Byzantine Art," pp. 68–70; K. Weitzmann, "Various Aspects of Byzantine Influence on the Latin Countries from the Sixth to the Twelfth Century," *Dumbarton Oaks Papers* 20(1966):20–22.
44. See, with references to earlier bibliography, Ayres, "A Miniature from Jumièges," pp. 132–134.
45. For a review of Nicholas of Verdun's career, see Otto Demus, "Nicholas of Verdun," in *Encyclopedia of World Art*, X, cols. 634–640. For the Klosterneuburg ambo, see F. Röhrig, *Der Verduner Altar* (Vienna and Munich: Verlag Herold, 1955).
46. Ayres, "A Tanner Manuscript," pp. 50–54.
47. Ernst Kitzinger, "The Byzantine Contribution to Western Art of the Twelfth and Thirteenth Centuries," *Dumbarton Oaks Papers* 20 (1966):37–43; K. Hoffmann, "Introduction," in *The Year 1200*, 3 vols. (exhibition catalogue, New York, 1970), I, xxxiii–xliii.
48. L. M. Ayres, "The Work of the Morgan Master at Winchester and English Painting of the Early Gothic Period," *The Art Bulletin* 56(1974):201–223.
49. Kitzinger, "Norman Sicily," pp. 137–138; Otto Demus, *The Mosaics of Norman Sicily* (London: Routledge and Kegan Paul, 1949), pp. 450–451; idem, *Byzantine Art and the West* (New York: New York University Press, 1970), pp. 154–158; Walter Oakeshott, *Sigena Romanesque Paintings in Spain and the Winchester Bible Artists* (London: Harvey Miller and Medcalf, 1972), pp. 107–116. Strong Byzantinizing influences have long been acknowledged in the miniatures of a Winchester psalter (British Museum, Cotton MS. Nero C. IV) which antedates the Morgan Master's work in the Winchester Bible. See, more recently, F. Wormald, "Continental Influences on English Medieval Illumination," *Transactions of the Fourth International Congress of Bibliophiles*, ed. A. R. A. Hobson (London, 1967), pp. 11–12; F. Wormald, *The Winchester Psalter* (London: Harvey Miller and Medcalf, 1973), pp. 77–91; Demus, *Byzantine Art and the West*, pp. 159–161.
50. The analogy was made by Otto Pächt, "A Cycle of English Frescoes in Spain," *Burlington Magazine* 103(1961):172 n.42, and Ayres, "A Tanner Manuscript," pls. 8a, 8c. For sculpture at Chartres, see Adolf Katzenellenbogen, *The Sculptural Programs of Chartres Cathedral* (New York: Norton, 1964), and Willibald Sauerländer, *Gothic Sculpture in France, 1140–1270*, trans. Janet Sondheimer (London: Thames and Hudson, 1972), pp. 430–440.
51. Demus, *Mosaics of Norman Sicily*, p. 114, pl. 61; see also the comparison in Ayres, "The Work of the Morgan Master," Figs. 7, 21.

52. Boase, *English Art*, p. 190.

53. Régine Pernoud, *Eleanor of Aquitaine*, trans. Peter Wiles (New York: Coward-McCann, 1968), pp. 172–173.

54. W. Krönig, *Il duomo di Monreale e l'architettura normanna in Sicilia* (Palermo: Flaccovio, 1965), pp. 15–16.

55. Kitzinger, "Norman Sicily," pp. 141–143.

6. The Vintner's Son:

French Wine in English Bottles

ROSSELL HOPE ROBBINS

Tous les romanistes la connaissent pour avoir souvent vu se profiler son nom dans des travaux fort divers, sur les troubadours ou sur les chroniqueurs, sur les romanciers ou sur les cours d'amour.[1]

It is true that Queen Eleanor's name is better known to *les romanistes* than it is to *les anglicistes*. Yet she was a famous *English* queen, and her ghost remained lively in the island kingdom long after her body's interment at Fontevrault in 1204. I would like to consider, therefore, the impact of Queen Eleanor on the writings produced in England after her death and, bearing in mind this influence, to offer a tentative reappraisal of Middle English literature between 1200 and 1530.

While some parts of this reappraisal may seem a little unorthodox, the facts on which it is based are not in dispute; only the implications are innovative and hypothetical. This essay is frankly exploratory: it is written to raise questions—about Geoffrey Chaucer even more than about Queen Eleanor. What I am concerned about is the whole problem of the continuity of English poetry, especially court poetry, and how English poetry entered the main stream of European literature in its own creative right, not in its secondary role of translation from the French.

To link Chaucer to Queen Eleanor is not easy: in no book about Chaucer have I found her name mentioned. And the converse holds. Yet, curiously, Eleanor and Chaucer were both distant relatives of King Henry VII and Elizabeth of York. Had they been present at that wedding in 1486, each would have had a choice on which side of the church to sit, with the relatives of the bride or with the relatives of the groom. Eleanor was an ancestor, ten generations back, of both Henry and Elizabeth. For his part, Chaucer was the brother-in-law of the duchess of Lancaster, great-great-grandmother of King Henry VII, and the great-grandfather of John, second duke of Suffolk, uncle of Elizabeth of York. As Eleanor might have quipped, she and Chaucer were almost kissing cousins.

Charles Muscatine devotes much of the second chapter of his *Chaucer and the French Tradition* to the romances of Chrétien de Troyes, but finds no evidence of literary affinity between the two squires of the royal households: "There was not enough of this manipulation of style [as in *Yvain*] in later courtly literature to create what we could call an actual tradition leading from the *Yvain* to—as the reader may have guessed—Chaucer's *Troilus and Criseyde*."[2] In a more recent study, Patricia M. Kean wonders why Chaucer "shows so little interest in the greatest achievements of the French romance writers." Parenthetically, the answer of course is obvious: by the second half of the fourteenth century, these romances were no longer fashionable. Kean continues, "It is possible that [Chaucer] knew the romances of Chrétien de Troyes and learnt, directly, from their technique, but he shows no obvious sign of having done so and never attempts to write anything of the same kind."[3]

Yet it is possible to find a few links from Chaucer directly to the queen's circle, even to Chrétien de Troyes, who had no doubt spent some time visiting England.[4] D. S. Brewer, for example, takes two long shots: he sees the joking remarks in the *Nun's Priest's Tale* (VII. 3212–3213) to "the book of Launcelot de Lake / That wommen holde in ful greet reverence" as Chaucer's spontaneous reaction to Chrétien's *Lancelot* and interprets in similar fashion another light-hearted allusion to Lancelot in the *Squire's Tale*.[5] P. J. Frankis has pointed out that, in describing the Franklin, Chaucer uses *vavasour*, an uncommon word, generally restricted to the north of England. It is equally uncommon in French. Only in two of his poems (*Yvain*, *Erec*) does Chrétien use it, and in both in the same sense as Chaucer, for a model of hospitality: each character is open-handed and has white hair and is a skilled cook.[6] The Middle English romance translated from Chrétien's *Yvain* does not retain the French *vavasour* but translates it *knight*. Henry Barrett Hinckley, however, nearly seventy years ago, discussing the Middle English *Ywain and Gawain*, thought "nothing could have been more natural than for the young Chaucer to study it carefully if he ever saw it."[7] And then Hinckley adduces what is to me a convincing parallel in the translation and in Chaucer's *Knight's Tale*, both passages occurring in similar contexts. In the translation:

And then he bar me sone bi strenkith
Out of my sadel my speres lenkith. (lines 421–422)

and in Chaucer:

And kyng Emetreus, for al his strengthe,
Is born out of his sadel a swerdes lengthe. (I. 2645–2646)

All these resemblances may be speculative, but surely most critics would agree with Eleanor Prescott Hammond: " . . . no student of literature can read the dialogues between Troilus and Pandarus without turning again to Chrétien's *Yvain* and pondering the conversations between the hesitating widow and her sprightly maid. Nor can a student refrain from drawing the spiritual comparison, whether contact between the two writers be proved or not." [8]

Another and firmly established connection between Eleanor and Chaucer is through Benoît de Sainte-Maure, whose *Roman de Troye* (ca. 1160–1165) Chaucer used as his main secondary source for *Troilus and Criseyde* whenever he departed from Boccaccio's *Filostrato*. He obviously drew on both authors, selecting materials from either as best suited his purpose. Thus, in Chaucer's description of Criseyde's gifts to Diomede, the bay steed and the "pencel of here sleve" (lines 1038, 1043) are taken from Benoît, while the brooch (line 1040) comes from Boccaccio. [9] And other examples of Chaucer's "considerable use" of Benoît may be discovered. [10] Of course, Boccaccio's *Filostrato* itself largely followed Benoît de Sainte-Maure, [11] so that even by that indirect route the link between Chaucer and the court writers of Eleanor still holds.

Literature produced in England during the period roughly from 1100 to 1530 falls into seven broad areas. I would like briefly to categorize these seven areas in order to emphasize whatever indebtedness each may owe to Eleanor of Aquitaine as the driving force of secular poetry of the twelfth century and so trace the continuity of secular court verse in English.

1. 1100–1350: French Court Literature

From 1100 to 1350, literature in England was predominantly in French (Anglo-Norman, Anglo-French, or Old French, in which Chrétien de Troyes wrote), simply because the ruling classes in England (the nobility and gentry, the clergy, the wealthy burghers) spoke and read French. Literature followed literary decorum. It is curious that the adventures of Horn and Havelok, now regarded as essentially English in their point of view, were nevertheless first composed for a French-speaking Norman audience. As had happened at other times and other places, the *nouveaux-arrivés* assumed the traditions of the invaded. It might be noted, however, that even before the conquest, in 1042 Edward the Confessor (whose mother was Emma of Normandy) supplanted the Anglo-Saxons and Danes at his court with French-speaking favorites.

Under Henry II and Eleanor, England and most of France were, with the exception of the "unfree" (more than half the population),[12] theoretically one political unit and actually one symbiotic literary unit. "The continued union of England and Normandy," according to R. M. Wilson, "and—equally important—the later French empire of the Angevin kings, had opened the way for the unrestricted entrance of French literary influence into England."[13] The famous French *Song of Roland* appeared in an English manuscript about 1130–1150, and part of it was even translated into English about 1400.[14]

Partly fortuitously and partly by design, a circle of writers had formed, or been encouraged to form, around the queen. Some of them accompanied her to England. At the English palace, V. H. Galbraith has noted, Henry II assembled "the most dazzling group of literary men the Middle Ages had ever known."[15] And Charles H. Haskins has listed no less than twenty distinguished men of letters who at one time or another were on the king's payroll.[16]

The queen's entourage, later reinforced by Andreas Capellanus at the court of her daughter Marie de Champagne, developed, whether in game or in earnest, the conception of *fin'amors* (or "aristocratic love"). Constance West sums up the situation: "The marriages of Eleanor of Aquitaine herself . . . and of her daughters . . . probably contributed as much as any single cause to the development of courtly poetry in Northern France."[17] She might well have added, "and in England too." Subsequent court literature for diversion, in contrast to literature for edification (like St. Edmund's *Merure de Seinte Eglise* or *Sawles Warde* or the *Ancren Riwle*), was thenceforward to be identified with the dominant and continuing vogue of "the relations of the sexes and the problems, especially the emotional problems, of individuals."[18]

Eleanor's protégés established the high-society genres that later appeared in English: Chrétien de Troyes, the romance; Benoît de Sainte-Maure, the chronicle (*Le Roman de Troye* developing the first stage of the Troilus and Criseyde love theme); Bernart de Ventadorn, the lyric; and Marie de France, the lai.[19]

This precious attitude toward love was further developed by other French romances, such as *Ille et Galeron* by Gautier d'Arras (1182–1184, including *demandes d'amour*); *Amadas et Ydoine* (late twelfth century, written in England); *Durmart li gallois*; *Guillaume de Dole* by Jehan Renart (ca. 1230, with inserted lyrics); *Jehan et Blonde* by Philippe de Rémi, sire de Beaumanoir (ca. 1260–1280); *Chastelain de Couci* by Jakemon Sakesep (late thirteenth century, with inserted lyrics); and *Roman de la violette* (ca. 1284, with many inserted lyrics).

Only a few of the extant Anglo-Norman texts deal with romantic love (the majority are religious, historical, didactic). One late twelfth-century Anglo-Norman poem, *Le Donnei des amants*, Provençal inspired, in some respects heralds Chaucer's love poems. A clerk, "wandering in a meadow in the springtime,"[20] overhears a dialogue between a gentlewoman and a clerk, in which they dispute the roles and obligations of lovers. It includes elements (not always found in romances) which were to become part of the standard equipment of any fifteenth-century English love *aunter*, or adventure—the spring opening, the catalogue of birds, a list of forsaken lovers, a series of exempla, and, here, a pseudo-etymological explanation of *jalous* ("Gelus es nomé de gelee [*Jealous* is derived from *frost*]") recalling the etymology of *cukcold* in *The Remedy of Love* (st. 43–44): A cold old *k*nave and a *c*alot of *l*ewd *d*emeanor. The lady parries the clerk's advances, but her reasons are very practical:

Ben le sachez de verité
Ke tote vostre volunté
Feïsse jo sanz [nul] retur,
Ne dotasse perdre m'onur.
Je ferai quant jo pora[i] fere,
E ren ne me vodra retrere;
Mès liu a tens dei[t ben] gaiter
Ki grant chose volt comencer.[21]

This Anglo-Norman debate anticipates that of the two lovers "in the moneth of may erly in a mornyng" in the late-fifteenth-century Middle English *Craft of Lovers*, where a very practical young lady tells her courtly suitor that she is sick and tired of the circumlocutions of courtly love, knows that he really wants to "break the virginite of the virgynal Innocent," and surprisingly welcomes his frank speech and considers his request. But, as in *Le Donnei des amants*, the lady is wary for her reputation:

Vnto youre plesure I wold be at youre call,
But euer I feere me of chauncis casuall,
Of froward disceyt, and langage insolent;
Than were I sure my virgynite were shent.[22]

The significance of *Le Donnei des amants* is well expressed, I believe, by M. Dominica Legge, who says that, whether satiric or not, the poem "was written for an audience well broken in to the pastime of discussing love."[23] This tradition formed the French wine for which English-writing poets had to fashion the bottles.

Another Anglo-Norman poem, toward the end of the thirteenth century, entitled by its editor *Un Art d'aimer*,[24] likewise presupposes an audience familiar with love pastimes and the features of Guillaume de Lorris's *Roman de la rose*, such as dream vision, springtime opening, forest, symbolic roses, a roster of allegorical figures and symbolic objects (towers and hills), and definitions of love. The bulk of the poem consists of an involved description of a crowned blind child holding a dart and a brand; this of course is the god of love. The poet enumerates the expected qualities of love—its suddenness, inexplicability, irresistibility, ennobling effects, and physical passion. The poem concludes with listing the five characteristics of a *fine amaunt*: fidelity, courtesy, discretion, chastity, and obedience. By observing these requisites, the lover will better serve our Savior, "Que morust pur nostre amour [Who died for our love]. Amen."

In my opinion, the *Art d'aimer* is not ironic, but a straightforward manual for the beginning lover; its tone is similar to that of Chaucer's early court poems, the *Troilus and Criseyde*, and the love *aunters* of the fifteenth century.

One might add that the manuscript containing this *Art d'aimer*, College of Arms Arundel XIV, also contains *Le Lai d'Haveloc* and *Le Roman de Brut de Wace*. Their appearance together in a late-fourteenth-century manuscript testifies to the continuing interest in these works written almost two centuries earlier. The literature composed and read in England by the ruling classes up to 1350, therefore, was in French, and approximated closely that of the comparable classes on the mainland.

2. 1200–1350: Latin Literature

Although they had little immediate impact on the courtly-love traditions, writers in Latin must be included in any survey of English medieval literature, because their works were by scholars who set its philosophical and religious background. For example, their neoplatonic philosophy probably encouraged the formal description, not of a real mistress, but of an abstraction of perfect womanhood, with all the rhetorical devices of *notatio* and *effictio*. Furthermore, these Latin writers often carried forward a style or genre from earlier centuries, such as the use of allegorical figures, going back to Prudentius in the fourth century, or the use of the complaint genre in John de Hanville's *Architrenius* (possibly influencing Chaucer's *Parlement of Foules*). Even the recital of names recalls some of the glamor of that "Renaissance of the Twelfth Century" that encompassed England, with scholars like John of Salisbury (who had studied at Chartres) and Alexander Neckham (who had studied at Paris) with their encyclopedic treatises, or like Gerald of Wales, Gervase of Tilbury, and Walter Map with their more personal anecdotes.

Two of the Latin chroniclers, Geoffrey of Monmouth with his *Vita Merlini* and Joseph of Exeter with his *De bello Troiana*, anticipate Jean de Meung and Chaucer. And the later Anglo-Norman and Middle English political attacks on the corruption of court and clergy are based on the Latin tradition of Alexander Neckham's *De vita monachorum* and Nigel Wirecker's *Contra curiales* and *Speculum stultorum*. Of course, none of these works comes within the orbit of courtly love, except inversely by way of antifeminine satire.

After 1300, for the most part Latin tended to be restricted to what are today termed "nonbooks" in prose: theology, medicine, law, history; and long before 1500, even in these specialized professional areas, French and English translations were becoming frequent.

3. 1200–1350: English Noncourt Literature

During the same period, roughly from 1200 to before 1350, and concurrent with the French and Latin, English secular works begin to appear, largely as translations of French originals and usually directed to the nonaristocratic groups who could not speak French. "Only a small handful of the English romances, then, tell stories which could plausibly have originated with an English poet," writes Robert W. Ackerman. "Yet, in their adaptations and often in their translations as well, the English writers, who were addressing a later audience, tended to create a type of romance quite distinct from the French."[25] The distinction lies in the elimination of the love pastimes.

With minor exceptions (such as *The Owl and the Nightingale*), no English literature touching on courtly love existed before the Black Death. This fact is constantly stressed by critics. For example, Sarah F. Barrow noted that the Middle English romances, even of the "courtly class," "as a rule, contain hardly more than a trace of the system of courtly love. Emphasis is on acting and setting."[26] Derek Pearsall, reviewing the complete corpus of Middle English romances, concluded: "The social context of Middle English romance . . . is overwhelmingly popular and non-courtly. True courtly romance had no real vogue in English, since the audience which could appreciate it, at the time when it was fashionable, was French-speaking."[27]

The typical transition may be illustrated in a specific example. Though *Golagrus and Gawain* and the *Jeaste of Syr Gawayne* both derive from Chrétien's *Perceval*, the only Middle English translation of a romance by

Chrétien de Troyes is *Ywain and Gawain*. It was compiled between 1325 and 1350. Most critics praise it. Ackerman stated that its excellence "must be ascribed to the fact that the composer possessed a literary mind of rare independence,"[28] and more recently Helaine Newstead has written: "The romance is generally acknowledged to be one of the most successful in Middle English."[29] John Edwin Wells in his *Manual* had written that "the admirable verse puts the writer in the class of Gower and Chaucer"[30]—not surprising if (as I indicated earlier) Chaucer borrowed two of its lines. But all critics agree with Wells that "the [English] poet is not the courtly Frenchman"; rather (as Albert B. Friedman notes) he is "a minstrel catering for the sober, realistic audience of a provincial baron's hall, an audience whose sensibilities and sympathies were not adjusted to Chrétien's elaborate and subtle representation of courtly love or to high-flown chivalric sentiment."[31] Precise illustrations of the deletion of court characteristics include the paring of the original 239-line description of Yvain's infatuation with Laudine to 39 lines; the substitution of "dedes of arms and of veneri [hunting]" in the series of opening stories to replace the "dolors," "angoisses," and "granz biens" of love; the omission of the "detailed distinction between the false. . .and the true lover" (by Laudine's damsel); and the passing over of "the fine points of chivalric behavior."[32] Friedman sums up: "Here, as in almost every other instance where his source includes a discussion of courtly love or etiquette, [the English poet] shows himself stubbornly indifferent."[33] To appreciate the contrast between the Middle English romance of 1325 and the reversion to the "discussion of courtly love" fifty years later, one need but glance at Chaucer's *Troilus and Criseyde*. The earliest works written in English, then, were mainly translations from the French, especially romances, minus the court interest in love's finesse.[34]

The Black Death marked the watershed for medieval literature in England, and the year 1350 introduced new trends. Of the three streams that existed prior to 1350, Latin continued, but more and more as the language for specialized and technical subjects; French continued after 1350, but mainly in a literature imported from the mainland of Europe rather than an indigenous literature; and English writings for the noncourt "lewed" continued and increased. On the other hand, two new English streams developed for the court groups,[35] in addition to the previously dominant French literature, which after 1350 became exclusively a palace literature: these two new English streams may conveniently be typified by *Sir Gawain and the Green Knight* and by Chaucer's *Troilus and Criseyde*. For the first time in English writings, the cultural traditions of Queen Eleanor's court were influential.

4. 1350–1500: French Court Literature (Continuing)

The court circles continued to read French literature, although by 1300 the use of Anglo-Norman as a literary medium was disappearing.[36] The London court was French-speaking throughout the fourteenth century. Henry V was the first king "to popularize consciously the use of English,"[37] but there is ample evidence to show the continued use of French throughout the fifteenth century. "French visitors to England," writes P. Rickard, "no doubt found, at least until the fifteenth century, that as long as they kept to the upper classes they did not particularly need to know any English."[38] One might observe that, from the reign of Henry II to that of Richard II and (with the exception of that of Henry IV) on through Henry VI, some three hundred years, all the English queens were French-speaking by birth.[39]

However, after the Black Death it was no longer the traditional, Eleanor-inspired French literature of Chrétien that delighted the English royal courts, but the new French literature (only remotely inspired by her) of poets like Guillaume de Machaut and Eustache Deschamps, which is based more on *Le Roman de la Rose* than on *Yvain*. In France, the change had taken place a little earlier. "C'est le moment où," writes Jacques Ribaud in his recent study of Jean de Condé, "de même que l'ancien français tend déjà vers le moyen français sans en être encore, de même les anciens genres—romans courtois et fabliaux—achèvent de mourir pour faire place à des formes nouvelles, tels le dit moral ou la fantaisie allégorique, peu étudiées et qui mériteraient pourtant de l'être, car, n'en déplaise à certains, entre celui qu'on a nommé 'le grand siècle,' le XIIIᵉ, et ce qu'on a appelé un peu abusivement la Renaissance, il y a tout de même eu autre chose que le lyrisme grinçant de François Villon."[40]

These works, familiar enough in English court circles, formed the *nouvelle vague* that so influenced Chaucer and the Chaucerians.

5. 1350–1530: English Noncourt Literature (Continuing)

Both before and after 1350, meanwhile, the "lewed" translations continued; new native works appeared. By the later fifteenth century, cultivated romances were again being read; and William Caxton was attempting to recapture an educated and sophisticated audience which thought the tensions of the times might be removed by a return to the ideals of chivalry. Close translations of Burgundian romances proliferated.[41] This is the period when English finally replaced Latin and French as the normal medium of expression for the inhabitants of England. Secular writings were, of course, by no means as extensive as religious and didactic works.

Courtly love, relevant only to a miniscule elite group which had money and leisure for idle hours, was naturally absent from the literature for the growing noncourtly reading (and listening) public. The gap between the castle interests of the earlier French romances and the noncourt interests in earlier English literature was illustrated by a comparison of Chrétien's *Yvain* and the anonymous Middle English *Ywain and Gawain*. A similar comparison can be made for the period after 1350, this time between two English romances, the original courtly poem, *Sir Gawain and the Green Knight*, and its later popular variant, *Syre Gawene and the Carle of Carelyle* (in the Porkington manuscript, ca. 1400). The rationale of the beheading scene is clearer in the popular version: the carl is enchanted by "false witchcrafft," and only complete obedience to his orders will ever deliver the carl from his curse (to slaughter his guests). Gawene's obedience not only liberates the carl but preserves Gawene himself from slaughter. Gawene is still spoken of as a model of courtesy, as shown by his cooperation with the giant carl; but it seems to me he is more of a model for a fabliau, appreciated best by a beer-drinking audience in a great hall or tavern, happily tossing "Wassail" and "Drink-hail" from one to another. Sir Gawene falls in love at first sight with the carl's wife; after supper, the "imperious host" conducts Gawene into his own bedroom, has him undressed, and then orders Gawene to embrace his wife three times in the *lit périlleux*:

To the bede he went full sone,
Fast and that good spede,
For softnis of that ladys syde
Made Gawene do his wyll that tyde.[42]

At the climactic moment, the carl interposes: "Whoo there / That game I thee forbede." However, as Gawene has obeyed him without hesitation, the carl promises him an even more beautiful "lady bright." He produces his daughter to "play wytt thee all this nyghte" and leaves the pair alone. The narrative at once passes to the morning after, when the carl "fond his byddynge reddy done." The host is now freed of the enchantment, and that same day the bishop marries Sir Gawene and the carl's daughter. King Arthur knights the carl and bestows on him the county of Carlisle. Not much of courtesy here, just "lack of sophistication and refinement of feeling,"[43] and clearly, as Auvo Kurvinen notes: "The subject matter and the style imply that the story was composed to be recited in public, to the common people rather than to educated audiences."[44]

One could fill many pages with illustrations showing how changed social conditions affect artistic fashions. The clearest examples are found in romances, but all literature, including the religious, is involved. Just as in the period before the Black Death, in the following period also the class basis of literature is clearly evident, and the knightly duel and banquet become the burlesque of apprentices in the *Turnament of Tottenham* and the *Feast of Tottenham*.

6. 1350–1400: English Court Literature—the Alliterative Revival

The last two kinds of literature produced in England are much more closely linked, at least in the spirit of "fine lovynge," to Eleanor's court. Together they formed the "new two-fold literature" of the late fourteenth century, "two great schools of poetry thus existing side by side, aloof but respectful."[45]

About 1350, what with developing knowledge, travel, comforts, leisure, a hankering perhaps after English combined with the decline of Anglo-French throughout the country (as various contemporary writers testify), a native court-coterie literature was developing among sophisticated circles outside the royal palace influence in London: it drew from French literature all the rhetorical and amorous conventions originally established by the writers around Queen Eleanor and developed in the preceding two centuries. It had its base in the west and north, not necessarily (as James R. Hulbert[46] once suggested) in cultural opposition to the French-dominated courts of Edward III and Richard II, but in the deliberate rendering of long-familiar French conventions into traditional English poetic diction that was surfacing for the first time since Anglo-Saxon days.[47] The later-fourteenth-century Alliterative Revival, as it is called, forms by far the most important group of poems of the mid-century. And it antedates the comparable Chaucerian school. I see no reason to suppose that the nobles (like Humphrey de Bohun; Henry Percy, earl of Northumberland; Richard Beauchamp, earl of Warwick—or even John of Gaunt, duke of Lancaster, as Elizabeth Salter[48] hints), who appreciated *Sir Gawain and the Green Knight* in the diction of the West Midlands, did not also appreciate (while attending the court of Edward III) Machaut in French and later (at the court of Richard II) Chaucer in East Midland. And probably the author of *Sir Gawain and the Green Knight* was of similar social status to Chaucer.[49] *Sir Gawain and the Green Knight*, with its conscious archaic literary diction, could not be understood by French-speaking nobles at the court, or by London aldermen speaking in nonarchaic East Midland. Nevertheless, *Sir Gawain* is as mannered and courtly as anything Deschamps or Chaucer ever wrote, and it shows complete awareness of the game of love. This is not surprising, for its author actually followed his French source closely—*Le Livre de Caradoc*, part of the first continuation of Chrétien's *Perceval*. Larry D. Benson has recently commented: "We have seen how much the poet owes to the French tradition for his materials, and certainly in tone *Sir Gawain* is the most continental of English romances; but England provided the poet with his style."[50]

Without the counterinfluence of Chaucer, this alliterative tradition might, with some modifications and concessions to the speech of London, have remained the dominant English pattern.[51] But, because of the power shift to the City of London away from the magnates in the provinces, the Chaucerian alternative style and speech prevailed; and the Alliterative Revival was over by 1400, though it reappeared in the north of England sporadically into the sixteenth century. Indeed, it has continued an underground existence to the present day, as in the verse of Hugh Macdiarmid.

Despite some recent critical emphasis on *Sir Gawain and the Green Knight* and other poems of the Alliterative Revival as sophisticated French-oriented poetry, redolent with the lessons of Geoffrey of Vinsauf (an Englishman) and Andreas Capellanus, I think most readers of this poem still think of it in terms of an adventure involving terror and combat. Wells, in the original *Manual*, lent support to this traditional position, noting "the very spirit of nature in her wilder aspects, the biting winter, the icy rain, the dreary forest, the rugged rocks, the snow-covered country, and the cold hills lost in mist."[52] The student habitually associates alliteration with the heroic age,[53] when knights were bold and women were not invented, and finds this preconception even supported by Chaucer's excursus into prolonged alliteration in the battle scene in the *Knight's Tale*:

The helmes they tohewen and toshrede;
Out brest the blood with stierne stremes rede;
With myghty maces the bones they tobreste.[54]

More compelling is Chaucer's less-known use of alliteration for a sea-battle scene in the idyllic, Frenchified *Legend of Good Women*:

Up goth the trompe, and for to shoute and shete,
And peynen hem to sette on with the sunne.
With grysely soun out goth the grete gonne,
And heterly they hurtelen al atones,
And from the top doun come the grete stones.
In goth the grapenel, so ful of crokes;
Among the ropes renne the sherynge-hokes.[55]

Everybody knows that in Anglo-Saxon alliterative poetry there is really very little lyric or love poetry—*Deor* and *The Wife's Lament* are insignificant beside *Malden*. Consequently it comes almost as a shock to find in the poems of the Alliterative Revival passages as courtly and rhetorical as any in Chaucer's love poems, and moreover earlier. They present a viable alternative as court poetry to the nonalliterative verse of Chaucer and his followers. These alliterative poets are working out of a tradition, and the only source of that tradition is French romance.

Winner and Waster is a very early example of alliterative court poetry, with a dream vision and garter knights whose motto is not "Honi soit qui mal y pense [evil be to him who thinks evil]," but "Hethyng have the hathell· that any harme thynkes [may he have scorn, the noble who thinks any evil]." Only four years earlier, in 1348, Edward III had given a French device to his new order because the knights spoke French! *Winner and Waster* may be placed with some precision between 1352 and 1353, antedating Chaucer's first English court poem, the *Book of the Duchess*, in octosyllabics, by almost twenty years. But there is a typical May morning opening with the *locus amoenus*—all in alliterative lines:

Als I went in the weste, wandrynge myn one,
Bi a bonke of a bourne, bryghte was the sone,
Undir a worthiliche wodde by a wale medewe;
Fele floures gan folde ther my fote steppede.
I layde myn hede one ane hill, ane hawthorne be-syde;
The throstills full throly they threpen to-gedire,
Hippid up heghwalles fro heselis tyll othire,
Bernacles with thayre billes one barkes thay roungen,
The jay janglede on heghe, jarmede the foles;
The bourne full bremly rane the bankes by-twene.[56]

Elsewhere *Winner and Waster* stresses the ennobling effects of courtly love:

It lyes wele for a lede his leman to fynde,
Aftir hir faire chere to forthir hir herte.
Then will scho love him leley as hir lyfe one,
Make hym bolde and bown with brandes to smytte,
To schonn schenchipe and schame, there schalkes ere gadird.[57]

As John Gardner notes, "One finds the same view of courtly love as a morally uplifting force almost everywhere one looks in medieval literature—in Chaucer, for instance."[58] And Gardner quotes *Troilus and Criseyde*, written over thirty years later:

And worthi folk maad worthier of name,
And causeth moost to dreden vice and shame. (I. 251–252)

The Quatrefoil of Love, a decidedly antilove poem, seemingly (as its editor, Sir Israel Gollancz, believed) the work of a clerical moralist attempting "the sublimation of the sex instinct,"[59] is nonetheless familiar with the French conventions of secular love. It was written about the middle of the fourteenth century, once again antedating Chaucer by a couple of decades. Its opening stanza introduces the typical spring opening:

In a moruenyng of Maye when Medowes sall spryng
Blomes and blossomes of brighte colours,
Als I went by a welle, on my playing,
Thurgh a mery orcherde bedande myn hourres,
The birdis one bewes bigane for to synge,
And bowes for to burgeon and belde to the boures,
Was I warre of a maye that made mournyng,
Sekande and syghande amange thase floures
So swete.[60]

How close are the passages from *Winner and Waster* and *The Quatrefoil of Love* to Chaucer in his *Parlement of Foules*:

A gardyn saw I ful of blosmy bowes
Upon a ryver, in a grene mede,
There as swetnesse everemore inow is,
With floures white, blewe, yelwe, and rede

. . . .

On every bow the bryddes herde I synge,
With voys of aungel in here armonye.[61]

The alliterative poems show other examples of courtly love devices, like the *salut d'amour* in *The Parlement of the Thre Ages*:

My lady, my leman, that I hafe luffede euer,
My wele and my wirchip, in werlde where thou dwellys,
My playstere of paramours, my lady with pappis full swete,
Alle my hope and my hele, myn herte es thyn ownn![62]

Had Chaucer not flourished, it is conceivable that English poetry would have continued in the alliterative tradition, and love lyrics in succeeding centuries would have resembled the foregoing salutation or the two-line complaint added to a contemporary illustration in *Sir Gawain and the Green Knight*:

My minde is mukel on on that wil me noght amende;
Sum time was trewe as ston, and fro scham couthe hir defende.[63]

Kenneth Sisam could rightly conclude that the alliterative poets, from about 1350, had "turned to French for their subjects and often contented themselves with free adaptations of French romances."[64] His following statement, while it describes the situation, does not completely elucidate it: "But time and distance had weakened the French influence, and the new school of poets did not catch, as the southern poets did, the form and spirit of their models." This opinion will be discussed in connection with the third type of court literature produced in England, that of the Chaucerian School.

7. 1370–1530: English Court Literature: Chaucer and the Chaucerians

Chaucer did not appear on the literary scene until after 1368 or 1369, by which time the European pattern of love in rhetoric and theory, in Eleanor's sense, had been established through some of the poems of the English Alliterative Revival. Can we agree with Sisam that Chaucer's versions of the same rhetoric and theory were triumphant because, as a southern poet, Chaucer caught "the form and spirit of their models"?

The reason Chaucer, the court poet of love, was accepted and became more and more popular in the fifteenth century, was not only (as Sisam implied) that he wrote in what was becoming standard English, free of dialectisms (though that was an important factor, since Chaucer had a romance vocabulary of four thousand words), or that he better caught the spirit of the "models" than did the Alliterative Revival poets. The fact is that Chaucer did not even go to those models, which were mainly the French romances, particularly the dwindling high-society romances. Rather, he went directly to different models, not used by the alliterative poets.

From before the middle of the fourteenth century, the leading French writers, like Guillaume de Machaut, Jean Froissart, Oton de Graunson, and Eustache Deschamps, were using a new genre that eventually displaced the romances. The new genre was the *dit amoureux*, or love adventure, essentially a skeleton or implied narrative that structured a series of lyrics, comprising two principal types: the *salut d'amour*, or praise of the poet's lady, and the *complaint d'amour*, lamenting the lady's lack of pity. In addition the *dits* embraced lyric set passages, or *topoi*, which might include the spring opening, the garden of delights, allegorical figures, descriptions of the lady, lords and ladies attendant on the God of Love, courtly games, temples, painted figures, statues, or even tales or catalogues of famous lovers. The spirit of the Guillaume de Lorris part of *Le Roman de la Rose*, at its face level, was ever present, and took precedence over Chrétien de Troyes, by then becoming outdated.

Chaucer's first poem, *The Book of the Duchess*, is not based on any French romance (as was *Sir Gawain and the Green Knight*), but on French *dits amoureux*, among others on *Le Jugement dou roy de Behaigne*, the *Dit dou Lyon*, the *Dit du vergier*, the *Remède de fortune*, and *La Fonteinne amoureuse* of Guillaume de Machaut; *Le Paradys d'amour* of Jean Froissart; and the anonymous *Le Songe vert*.[65] Chaucer thus profited by new directions, by the trend toward what was becoming the king's English, and by what had become the major French poetry of French society itself.

With the exception of Machaut, for whom there is no evidence of personal contact, Chaucer was either in communication with or personally known to the leading French poets. Deschamps was familiar enough with his work to send Chaucer a eulogy as one writer to another,[66] and earlier he had written for Queen Philippa a ballade that "may well have been seen by Chaucer."[67] Froissart was in England from 1361 to 1366, first as secretary to Queen Philippa, wife of Edward III, and later as secretary to King John of France during his technical captivity in England—a member of the same royal familia (and payroll) as Chaucer. There is some suggestion that both Froissart and Chaucer were in Italy with Lionel, duke of Clarence, for his marriage to Violente Visconti.[68] Sir Oton de Graunson, who resided some twenty years in England, sent French valentine verses to Princess Isabel of York and, according to the Shirley manuscript (Trinity College, Cambridge, MS 600), Chaucer translated them, changing the sex of the speaker, in his *Complaint of Venus*.[69]

This vintner's son was not the first to put French spirit into English bottles—that had been going on for nearly two centuries;[70] but Chaucer was the first to establish "Chateau Geoffroi" as a mark of international excellence, as a recommended selection of Machaut et Deschamps et Compagnie, *importateurs*.

The *dits amoureux* developed much further the social tendencies inherent in the aristocratic romances. Essentially, these later love poems were occasions for social diversion—they were the fripperies, the added attractions, all subordinated to the pastime of pleasure. The fashionable *beau monde* would continue its dalliance with or without poetry. Rather than reflect that society, the poems became a part of it. It was quite a different matter if a group of lords and ladies assembled in a garden for the specific purpose of hearing Chaucer read his *Troilus and Criseyde*, a sort of publication party, as depicted in the Corpus Christi manuscript, in an illustration "rather French than English in feeling."[71] The gathering would not have been the same if Chaucer had read, say, his *Complaint of Venus* at an assembly where the same lords and ladies danced, played courtly games (like Ragman's Roll), heard music, enjoyed a picnic, and indulged in a little flirtation. In the former case, the party is incidental to the poem; in the latter, the poem is incidental to the party. Under both circumstances, the poem is still occasional, either as *the* occasion or as one of a number of occasions. To this extent, the criticism of all these French and English *dits amoureux* belongs not to literature but to sociology; only in so far as they rise above incidental entertainment do they become a part of literature.

From the twelfth century, many French poems described the conventions of courtly love, loosely adapted by Chaucer in the *Parlement of Foules*, the *Hous of Fame*, and the prologue to the *Legend of Good Women*.[72] One set of Old French *demandes d' amour*, for example, extant in a dozen manuscripts, including several originating in England, started in the mid-fourteenth century and remained popular until after the invention of printing.[73] In 1400 the duke of Burgundy actually promoted courts of love and drew up a series of ordinances for them, giving thereby his official approval to a courtly game.[74] The tradition of the "courts" and ritualized questions underlie both the *dits amoureux* and Chaucer's minor poems. For example, in Froissart's *Le Paradys d'amour*, while the dream framework centers round a complaint (lines 1025–1354) and a salutation in honor of Marguerite (lines 1595–1685), the philosophic substructure is this: How long should a lover reasonably serve without hope of reward? Machaut's *Jugement dou roy de Behaigne* illustrates even more clearly the control of *Liebenfragen*: the core of the poem debates whether the lover whose partner is dead or the lover whose partner is false has the greater cause for sorrow.

Chaucer's early poems simply transfer into the court English of the royal palaces the fashionable French genre of *dit amoureux*. In the *Book of the Duchess* any implied *demande d'amour* is aborted: with a man in black whose lady is dead no sorrow can compare (not when the man in black is the poet's patron); but Chaucer's audience would surely be reminded of Machaut's *Jugement dou roy de Behaigne*. The *Parlement of Foules* is clearly a *demande*: of three suitors, all eminently suitable as mates, all similar in rank, which is the most worthy? But Chaucer introduced more realistic *demandes*, expressed in the parliament of birds, which some suitors at least would have to face, and which came close to wrecking the fragile artificial form: If a lover vows fidelity to a lady, must he remain loyal for an indefinite period (an echo of Froissart's *Paradys d'amour*)? One might take the double sorrow in *Troilus and Criseyde*, an intricate and closely worked *dit amoureux* with numerous isolable *complaints* and *saluts*, to indicate such a problem: Is it more painful to have a mistress who does not even know of the lover's existence, or to have a mistress who does know and who turns out false?

So far as aristocratic literature is concerned, the whole fifteenth century is occupied with the imitations of Chaucer's court love poetry. Very early come the love *dits* attributed to John Lydgate. For Chaucer's *Book of the Duchess*, Lydgate offered *The Complaint of the Black Knight* (with overtones of Machaut's *Dit dou vergier*), which appeared as Chaucer's in the black-letter editions, and also *The Floure of Courtesy*; for the *Hous of Fame*, Lydgate offered the *Temple of Glas*; for the *Parlement of Foules, Reason and Sensu-*

ality; for the *Knight's Tale*, Lydgate substituted *The Siege of Thebes*; and for *Troilus and Criseyde*, Lydgate produced *The Troy Book*.[75]

Whatever fifteenth-century love *aunter* one looks at will almost certainly evoke memories of Chaucer. Here is a spring description from Chaucer's *Troilus and Criseyde*:

In May, that moder is of monthes glade
That fresshe floures, blew and white and rede,
Ben quike agayn, that wynter dede made,
And ful of bawme is fletyng every mede;
When Phebus doth his bryghte bemes sprede,
Right in the white Bole [Taurus]. . .

                    (II. 50–55)

And here is Lydgate's version (with further borrowings from the *Romaunt of the Rose*) in *The Complaint of the Black Knight*:

In May, when Flora, the fressh[e] lusty quene,
    The soyle hath clad in grene, rede, and white,
And Phebus gan to shede his stremes shene
    Amyd the Bole wyth al the bemes bryght,
    And Lucifer to chace awey the nyght
Ayen the morow our orysont hath take
To byd[de] lovers out of her slepe awake. . .[76]

Like Chaucer's *Book of the Duchess*, Lydgate's *Black Knight* is a mosaic.

And one must remember that a good part of the verse of Sir Thomas Wyatt is derived from Chaucer, even to the extent of Wyatt's composing pastiches of separate stanzas from Chaucer and signing them with his own initials.

Chaucer's *Canterbury Tales* were a departure from the main tradition of English court poetry—actually the only English tradition—though throughout the tales many echoes of the *dits amoureux* unexpectedly and perhaps incongruously remained (as in the *Franklin's Tale*, the *Knight's Tale*, and the *Wife of Bath's Tale*). The *Canterbury Tales*, no matter in how many manuscripts they have been preserved, were *sans issue*; apart from Lydgate's *Prologue* to the *Siege of Thebes*, there is no imitation or even influence manifested except in rough "pop" writings, like the late-fifteenth-century ribald tales, or like the mixed prose and verse *Cobler of Canterbury*.[77]

In the fifteenth century, the Chaucerian palace tradition of the court *dits amoureux* was reinforced by new French models, like Alain Chartier's *La Belle Dame sans merci*, translated by Sir Richard Roos; the *Debate between the Eye and the Heart*, from the French poem attributed to Michault Taillevent; *King Truth-teller*, a courtly game, from *Les Voeux du paon*; and

Lydgate's *Reason and Sensuality*, from the anonymous *Les Echecs amoreux*. But there were many more, probably not translated directly, but all building up that reservoir of tradition that vivified the followers of Chaucer. These poets are now little read, even by *romanistes*, but I would suggest that minor French writers of the fifteenth century might be worth investigating further for influences on Middle English palace poetry.[78]

I suggested at the beginning of this essay that it might raise more questions about Chaucer than about Queen Eleanor. Here are just a few.

One major question: How does it come about that a man, trained as a squire in several royal households where such training would include singing and writing poems, waits until he is about thirty before "publishing" his first poem?

And another: If his first original poem is a highly skilled, finished product, certainly not a beginner's effort, where then are all his earlier poems? Are they lost, like the *Boke of the Lyon*? Of his lyrics, of which he said he wrote many, few remain, and most of these are late, save for a few experimental pieces like *Womanly Noblesse*, *A Balade of Complaint*, and *A Complaint to his Lady* (ca. 1373–1374). Where are the others?

Yet another: If Chaucer had not established some kind of poetic reputation before 1368—and there is at present no evidence that he had—why was he the one selected to compose the memorial to Blanche, duchess of Lancaster?

And an even more pointed question: In a French-speaking court,[79] why was not the memorial for Blanche written in French—by one of the already established French writers familiar to the court, like Froissart?[80]

I believe there is an answer that satisfies all these questions, one which I will not develop fully here: Chaucer, following the court fashions, was steeped in the new French poetry; he composed his early verses in French; through these French verses he acquired a court reputation as a poet; he later simply transliterated the French techniques and devices into English. What else was Chaucer really doing with the *Romaunt of the Rose*, which may be as early as 1360, or his "close copy" of Deguileville's ABC hymn to the Virgin in his *Pèlerinage de l'âme*? If we accept these proposals, we are forced to believe that the traditional Father of English Poetry started his career by speaking French and writing French love poems. Incidentally, were I making this proposal about John Gower it would be quite acceptable, for Gower's works in French remain. Why not then Chaucer?

This very tentative suggestion provides the rationale for the title of this essay. The vintner's son started with French wines in French bottles (in *The Book of the Duchess*, for example), continued experimenting, and ended, as in *The Merchant's Tale*, with English wines in English bottles. Throughout his writing career there were occasions for many combinations. But the stock of Chaucer's wines, no matter to what extent transplanted or grafted, was brought from the fields of Blois or Saumur, which the Queen of Courtesy herself had nurtured, as might be expected, with tender, loving care.

NOTES

1. Rita Lejeune, "Rôle littéraire d'Aliénor d'Aquitaine et de sa famille," *Cultura Neolatina* 14(1954):5. "All the Romance-language specialists know her name from having often seen it prominently featured in very diverse writings, about troubadours, chroniclers, writers of romances or courts of love." (All translations are mine unless otherwise indicated.)

2. Charles Muscatine, *Chaucer and the French Tradition* (Berkeley: University of California Press, 1964), p. 54.

3. P[atricia] M. Kean, *Chaucer and the Making of English Poetry*, 2 vols. (London: Routledge & Kegan Paul, 1972), II, 61.

4. P. Rickard, *Britain in Medieval French Literature 1100–1500* (Cambridge: At the University Press, 1956), p. 107, notes detailed descriptions of London in *Perceval* (lines 5754–5782) and in *Cligés* (lines 1484–1489).

5. D. S. Brewer, "Chaucer and Chrétien and Arthurian Romance," in *Chaucer and Middle English Studies in Honour of Rossell Hope Robbins*, ed. Beryl Rowland (London: George Allen & Unwin, 1974), pp. 256–257. R. M. Wilson, *The Lost Literature of Medieval England*, 2d ed. (London: Methuen, 1970), considers the allusion in the *Nun's Priest's Tale* to be "presumably to a French romance, or perhaps an earlier version of the extant *Lancelot of the Laik*" (p. 118). Wilson believes that references in wills to books of Lancelot are probably to French poems, and likewise for references to Tristan (p. 120). (All references to Chaucer are to *The Works of Geoffrey Chaucer*, ed. F. N. Robinson, 2d ed. [Boston: Houghton Mifflin, 1957].)

6. P. J. Frankis, "Chaucer's 'Vavasour' and Chrétien de Troyes," *Notes and Queries* 213(1968):46–47.

7. Henry Barrett Hinckley, "Chaucer and *Ywaine and Gawin*," *The Academy* 8(1906):640.

8. Eleanor Prescott Hammond, *English Verse between Chaucer and Surrey* (1927; reprint, New York: Octagon Books, 1969), p. 31; quoted by Muscatine, *Chaucer*, p. 255.

9. Thomas A. Kirby, *Chaucer's Troilus: A Study in Courtly Love* (1940; reprint, Gloucester, Mass.: Peter Smith, 1958), p. 230.

10. Ibid., p. 240.

11. R. M. Lumiansky, "The Story of Troilus and Briseida according to Benoit and Guido," *Speculum* 29(1954):727–733.

12. G. G. Coulton, "Nationalism in the Middle Ages," *Cambridge Historical Journal* 5(1935):32.

13. R. M. Wilson, *Early Middle English Literature* (1939; reprint, London: Methuen, 1951), p. 289.

14. S. J. Herrtage, ed., *Charlemagne*

Romances II, Early English Text Society (EETS), Extra Series 35 (London, 1880), pp. 107–136.

15. V. H. Galbraith, "The Literacy of the Medieval English Kings," *Proceedings of the British Academy* 21(1935):214.

16. Charles H. Haskins, "Henry II as a Patron of Literature," in *Essays in Medieval History Presented to T. F. Tout*, ed. A. G. Little and F. M. Powicke (Manchester: Manchester University Press, 1925), pp. 71–77. The court patronage has been extensively surveyed by Walter F. Schirmer and Ulrich Broich, *Studien zum literarischen Patronat im England des 12. Jahrhunderts*, Wissenschaftliche Abhandlungen der Arbeitsgemeinschaft für Forschung des Landes Nordrhein-Westfalen, no. 23 (Cologne: Westdeutscher Verlag, 1962).

17. Constance West, *Courtoisie in Anglo-Norman Literature*, Medium Aevum Monographs (Oxford: Blackwells, 1938), pp. 3–4.

18. Ibid., p. 2. Of course, all these French compositions were made exclusively for an aristocratic group. The contrast between the Anglo-Norman *Tristan* of Thomas of Britain and the Continental version by Béroul for a wider, nonaristocratic audience is clear.

19. The influence of Marie de France on later English literature has perhaps been slighted (apart from the Middle English translations of two of her lais). In her works, the Breton folk tales she took for sources were transmuted into examples of courteous behavior in love, almost becoming *demandes d'amour*.

20. M. Dominica Legge, *Anglo-Norman Literature and Its Background* (Oxford: Clarendon Press, 1963), p. 128.

21. Gaston Paris, "Le Donnei des amants," *Romania* 25(1896):508, lines 445–452. Translation by Legge, *Anglo-Norman Literature*, p. 130: "Know well in truth that I would have done all your will without turning back, had I not feared to lose my honour. I shall do it when I can, and nothing shall make me withdraw; but one must look well for the right time and place if one wants to undertake some great action."

22. *Craft of Lovers*, London, British Museum, Harley MS. 2251, f. 53v; another text is in *The Works of the English Poets from Chaucer to Cowper*, ed. Alexander Chalmers (1810; reprint, New York: Greenwood, 1969), I, 558. "To serve your pleasure I would be at your beck and call, /But I am always afraid of casual encounters, /Of wicked deceiving, and improper speech; /Then were I sure my virginity would be destroyed."

23. Legge, *Anglo-Norman Literature*, p. 333–334.

24. Östen Södergard, "Un Art d'aimer anglo-normand," *Romania* 77(1956):289–330.

25. Robert W. Ackerman, "English Rimed and Prose Romances," in *Arthurian Literature in the Middle Ages*, ed. Roger Sherman Loomis (Oxford: Clarendon Press, 1959), p. 481.

26. Sarah F. Barrow, *The Medieval Society Romances* (New York: Columbia University Press, 1924), p. 139.

27. Derek Pearsall, "The Development of Middle English Romance," *Mediaeval Studies* 27(1965):91.

28. Ackerman, "English Rimed and Prose Romances," p. 507.

29. Helaine Newstead, "Arthurian Legends," in *A Manual of the Writings in Middle English, 1050–1500*, vol. 1, ed. J. Burke Severs (New Haven: Connec-

ticut Academy, 1967), p. 65.

30. John Edwin Wells, *A Manual of the Writings in Middle English, 1100–1400* (New Haven: Connecticut Academy, 1926), p. 67.

31. Albert B. Friedman and Norman T. Harrington, eds., *Yvain and Gawain*, EETS 254 (London: Oxford University Press, 1964), p. xvii.

32. Ibid., p. xix.

33. Ibid., p. xxii.

34. Another example: *Sir Tristram*, late thirteenth century, is a rendering of Thomas of Britain's Anglo-Norman *Tristan*, which Lejeune would date earlier than is customary, between 1154 and 1158, written for Eleanor's court. Ackerman calls the Middle English poem "a crude version of its courtly original" ("English Rimed and Prose Romances," p. 516). Newstead writes: "The treatment of the narrative is perfunctory, the expression is undistinguished and clogged with rime tags. . . a much coarsened version of its subtle and moving original" ("Arthurian Legends," pp. 78–79). Incidentally, as noted previously, the Continental version by Béroul, meant for a wider audience, is similarly attenuated.

35. One interesting suggestion for determining the composition of the court class is that implied by J. W. Adamson, "The Extent of Literacy in England in the XV and XVI Centuries," *Library* 10(1929):172—those persons officially privileged to read the English Bible.

36. Larry D. Benson, *Art and Tradition in Sir Gawain and the Green Knight* (New Brunswick, N. J.: Rutgers University Press, 1965), p. 283; Fitzroy Pyle, "The Place of Anglo-Norman in the History of English Versification," *Hermathena* 49(1935):33.

37. Galbraith, "Literacy," p. 228. See also idem, "Nationality and Language in Medieval England, " *Transactions of the Royal Historical Society*, 4th ser. 23(1941):125.

38. Rickard, *Britain*, p. 39.

39. See M. Dominica Legge, "Anglo-Norman and the Historian," *History*, n.s. 26(1941):163–175. Legge says that all English kings to Henry IV could speak fluent French; Edward III knew English; and Richard II probably spoke English as his mother tongue (p. 170). However, Richard II also spoke and read French; see Jean Froissart, *Chroniques*, ed. Kervyn de Lettenhove (Brussels, 1867–1877), XV, 167: "A dont me demanda le rey de quey il traittoit. Je luy dis: 'D'amours.' De ceste responce fut-il tous resjouys, et regarda dedens le livre en plusieurs lieux et y lisy, car moult bien parloit et lisoit le franchois. [Then the king asked me what the book was about. 'Love,' I replied. At this response he was much pleased, and opened the book at random and read several pages, for he spoke and read French fluently.]"

40. Jacques Ribaud, *Un Ménestrel du XIVe siècle: Jean de Condé* (Geneva: Droz, 1969), p. 11. "It was at that time, just when Old French was developing into Middle French without yet reaching it, that the old genres—the courtly romances and the fabliaux—were about to give way to new genres, such as the moral lay or the dream allegory, little studied today although they warrant attention. For, with all due respect to some scholars, between what has been termed the great thirteenth century and what has been somewhat improperly called the Renaissance, there is nevertheless something else than the scratchy lyrics of François Villon." Ribaud notes that Gaston Paris, possibly on linguistic grounds,

set the change at the start of the Hundred Years War in 1328.

41. Occasionally one even sees the influence of Chaucer's earlier poems, as in the late-fifteenth-century romance, *Lancelot of the Laik*, which introduces a preface (lines 1–208) imitating Chaucer's dream visions.

42. Auvo Kurvinen, ed., *Sir Gawain and the Carl of Carlisle in Two Versions*, Annales Academiae Scientiarum Fennicae, ser. B, vol. 71 (Helsinki, 1951), p. 144, lines 461–464.

43. Ibid., p. 53.

44. Ibid., p. 25. See also John Wilcox, "French Courtly Love in English Composite Romances," *Papers of the Michigan Academy of Science, Arts, and Letters* 18(1932):588–589.

45. Basil Cottle, *The Triumph of English, 1350–1400* (London: Blandford Press, 1969), pp. 44, 47.

46. James R. Hulbert, "A Hypothesis Concerning the Alliterative Revival," *Modern Philology* 28(1930):405–422.

47. Pyle, "The Place of Anglo-Norman," p. 41, suggests that it was "only when people of wealth and breeding turned once more to the King's English that the Alliterative Revival was possible, what had survived as a thin and neglected thread now receiving the patronage of men for whose fathers [Anglo-Norman] had been the only language of literature."

48. Elizabeth Salter, "The Alliterative Revival," *Modern Philology* 64(1966):146–150, 233–237.

49. Marie P. Hamilton, "The Pearl Poet," in *A Manual of the Writings in Middle English, 1050–1500*, vol. 2, ed. J. Burke Severs (New Haven: Connecticut Academy, 1970), p. 340, suggests a retainer of John of Gaunt, among others, as a possible author of *Sir Gawain and*

the Green Knight. See also C. L. Wrenn's suggestion of echoes of *Sir Gawain and the Green Knight* in Chaucer, in "On the Continuity of English Poetry," *Anglia* 76(1958):49.

50. Benson, *Art and Tradition*, p. 110.

51. As in *Saint Erkenwald*, for example, the alliterative legend in London dialect. J. L. N. O'Loughlin, "The English Alliterative Romances," in *Arthurian Literature in the Middle Ages*, ed. Roger Sherman Loomis (Oxford: Clarendon Press, 1955), p. 524, considers obstacles to the modern acceptance of the *Alliterative Morte Arthure*, which he places on a par with *Beowulf* and *Paradise Lost.*

52. Wells, *Manual*, p. 57.

53. In the alliterative romances, battle scenes are common; e.g., *Alexander, Destruction of Troy, Morte Arthure, William of Palerne*. See J. P. Oakden, *Alliterative Poetry in Middle English* (1930, 1935; reprint, New York: Archon Books, 1968), II, 28, 34, 37, 40; O'Loughlin, "English Alliterative Romances," p. 521.

54. I. 2609–2611. "The helmets they hew to pieces and reduce to shreds; /The blood spurts out in gruesome red streams; /With heavy war clubs they smash the bones."

55. Cleo 635–641. "The trumpet sounds, and [the sailors] shout and shoot, /And try to attack with the sun [at their back]. /With terrible sound the huge cannon is discharged, /And fiercely they dash at one another all at once, / And from on high, they rain down great stones. / In there go the grapnels, all full of hooks, /The shearing-hooks sever the ropes." A third alliterative description of a battle in nonalliterative verse occurs in *Ywain and Gawain*, ed. Friedman and Harrington, lines 3531–3555.

Hinckley, "Chaucer," p. 640, suggests that this romance gave the idea of alliteration for combat scenes to Chaucer.

56. *Winner and Waster*, lines 32–41, in *A Middle English Anthology*, ed. Ann S. Haskell (Garden City, N. Y.: Doubleday, Anchor Books, 1969), p. 21. "As I went in the west [country], wandering alone, /By a bank of a brook, bright was the sun, /Close by a fair wood, by a pleasant meadow; /Many flowers bent over where my foot trod. / I lay down on a hill, beside a hawthorne, /The songthrushes very actively contended together, /Woodpeckers hopped from hazels to other [trees], /Wild geese with their beaks made the bark resound, /The jay chattered on high, the birds sang; / The brook ran quite noisily between the banks."

57. Ibid., lines 428–432, p. 402 in the Haskell anthology. "It is fitting for a man to provide for his sweetheart, / According to her pleasant disposition to further her desires. /Then will she love him loyally as her own life, /Make him [become] bold and ready to smite with swords, /To shun ignominy and shame, wherever men are gathered."

58. John Gardner, *The Alliterative Morte Arthure* (Carbondale: Southern Illinois University Press, 1971), p. 260.

59. Sir Israel Gollancz and Magdalene M. Weale, eds., *The Quatrefoil of Love*, EETS 195 (London: Oxford University Press, 1935), p. xxiii.

60. Ibid., lines 1–9. "In a morning of May when meadows shall spring up with /Blooms and blossoms of bright colors, /As I passed by a fountain, for diversion, /Through a pleasant orchard saying my prayers, /The birds on boughs began to sing, /And the boughs burgeoning, build their nests, / I became aware of a maid who mourned, /Seeking and sigh-

ing among these flowers /So sweet."

61. *Parlement of Foules*, lines 183–186, 190–191. "I saw a garden full of blossoming boughs /Bordering a river, in a green meadow, /Where sweetness is always abundant, /With flowers white, blue, yellow, and red /. . . . /On every bough I heard the birds singing, /With voices like angels in their harmony."

62. *The Parlement of the Thre Ages*, lines 174–177, in *A Middle English Anthology*, ed. Haskell, p. 416. "My lady, my lover, whom I have always loved, /My happiness and my source of honor, on earth where you dwell, /My medication for passion, my lady with breasts so sweet, /All my hope and my health, my heart is thine own."

63. Henry Lyttleton Savage, *The Gawain-Poet* (Chapel Hill: University of North Carolina Press, 1956), p. 212. "My heart is set on one who will do me no good. /Some time she was true as stone, and could defend herself from shame."

64. Kenneth Sisam, *Fourteenth Century Verse and Prose* (Oxford: Clarendon Press, 1921), p. xviii.

65. The most recent investigation of these French sources is that by James Wimsatt, *Chaucer and the French Love Poets* (1968; reprint, New York: Johnson Reprint Corporation, 1972).

66. Deschamp's knowledge of English was shaky. See Rickard, *Britain*, p. 176. In one or two of his poems Deschamps introduced English expressions, such as *franche dogue* (French dog), *goday* (good day), and *commidre* (come hither). See *Oeuvres complètes d'Eustache Deschamps*, ed. Le Marquis de Queux de Saint-Hilaire, Société des Anciens Textes Français (Paris, 1887; reprint, New York: Johnson Reprint Corporation, 1966), V, nos. 868, 893. See

also T. A. Jenkins, "Deschamps' Ballade to Chaucer," *Modern Language Notes* 33(1918):268–278. The ballade, with the accompanying large manuscript of some of Deschamps's poems, was probably sent about 1386 or later, by which time Chaucer was more a re-creator than a translator.

67. G. L. Kittredge, "Chaucer and Some of His Friends," *Modern Philology* 1(1903):1–18.

68. B. C. Hardy, *Philippa of Hainault and Her Times* (London: John Long, 1910), p. 292.

69. Discussed by Haldeen Braddy, *Chaucer and the French Poet Graunson* (Baton Rouge: Louisiana State University Press, 1947), pp. 71–85.

70. E.g., *The Owl and the Nightingale*. See J. A. W. Bennett and G. V. Smithers, eds., *Early Middle English Verse and Prose* (Oxford: Clarendon Press, 1966), p. 1: "The appearance of this witty and sophisticated poem as early as the twelfth century has been described as miraculous . . . it also reveals a masterly skill in naturalizing French metre. . . The author was clearly familiar with the life of woods and fields, yet equally familiar with the Anglo-Norman culture of the court. . . . His potential patrons would be more familiar with French or Latin verse than with the obsolescent native alliterative metre; and much of his art consists in naturalizing, apparently without help from any models, the French octosyllabic couplet with its easy rhythms and colloquial flavour." Another unexplainable item is an English court lyric, ca. 1200, printed in Carleton Brown's *English Lyrics of the XIIIth Century* (Oxford: Clarendon Press, 1932), p. xii.

71. Joan Evans, *English Art* (Oxford: Clarendon Press, 1949), p. 91.

72. Some critics, disturbed by what Galbraith ("Literacy," p. 201) called the "class conscious arrogance" of the Chaucerian love poems, find their discussions of love remote from their immediate interests and pass them by.

73. See Royal MS 16.F.ii, f. 188, in a collection of French verse (including Charles d'Orléans) executed in England ca. 1500, noted by Sir George F. Warner and Julius P. Gilson, *Catalogue of Western Manuscripts in the Old Royal and King's Collections* (London: British Museum, 1921), II, 203.

74. A. Piaget, "La Cour amoureuse dite de Charles VI," *Romania* 20(1891):417–454.

75. Derek Pearsall, *John Lydgate* (London: Routledge & Kegan Paul, 1970), pp. 84, 126.

76. John Lydgate, *The Complaint of the Black Knight*, lines 1–7, in *The Minor Poems of John Lydgate: Part II, Secular Poems*, ed. Henry Noble Mac-Cracken, EETS 192 (London: Oxford University Press, 1934).

77. See Rossell Hope Robbins, "The English Fabliau before and after Chaucer," *Moderna Sprak* 64(1970):231–244.

78. Only a few court poets were discussed by Pierre Champion, *Histoire poétique du quinzième siècle*, 2 vols. (Paris: E. Champion, 1923). See also Rossell Hope Robbins, "The Chaucerian Apocrypha," in *A Manual of the Writings in Middle English, 1050–1500*, vol. 4, ed. Albert E. Hartung (New Haven: Connecticut Academy, 1973), pp. 1061–1101, 1285–1306.

79. The evidence for a French-speaking court I find overwhelming, and I discuss it elsewhere. For example, in 1365, when Chaucer was about twenty-two, Edward III was writing in French

to his English knights in France to forbid ravaging by their companies (*routiers*); see M. Champollion-Figeac, ed., *Lettres de rois, reines et autres personnages des cours de France et d'Angleterre* (Paris, 1847), vol. 2. In 1377, Edward III's daughter, Isabella, duchess of Bedford, petitioned the young Richard II for restoration of her lands, technically forfeited because her husband, Enguerrand de Coucy, had reverted to his French allegiance (Savage, *The Gawain-Poet*, p.

93). And just toward the end of Chaucer's lifetime, his patron, John of Gaunt, in 1399 wrote his will in French (John Nichols, ed., *Collections of Royal Wills* [London, 1780], p. 152). See also note 39 above.

80. Froissart alluded to the death of Blanche as well as that of Queen Philippa in his *Joli Buisson de jonece*. An elegy by Froissart on Queen Philippa has not survived.

Notes on Contributors

LARRY M. AYRES received his undergraduate education at Dartmouth College. He received the degree of Bachelor of Letters from Oxford in 1966 and continued his graduate education in the history of art at Harvard, from which he took his doctorate in 1970. Since 1970, Dr. Ayres has been a member of the art history faculty of the University of California at Santa Barbara. His area of concentration is Romanesque and Early Gothic painting, sculpture, and metalwork. He is particularly interested in the relationship between English art and the Continental stylistic developments during the emergent Gothic era. He has also written about problems in Parisian manuscript illumination in the time of Maître Honoré. He has received grants-in-aid from the American Council of Learned Societies and a fellowship from the National Endowment for the Humanities to assist his investigations on the decorative program of the Winchester Bible. His published work is primarily concerned with problems in Romanesque and Early Gothic manuscript illumination.

REBECCA A. BALTZER, an associate professor at the University of Texas at Austin, received her A.M. and Ph.D. degrees from Boston University. Her main scholarly interest is in music of the twelfth and thirteenth centuries, especially music of the Notre Dame school of Paris. Her article entitled "Thirteenth-Century Illuminated Miniatures and the Date of the Florence Manuscript," appearing in the *Journal of the American Musicological Society* (1972), won the 1973 Alfred Einstein Award given by that society for the best article published by a young American musicologist in the previous year.

ELIZABETH A. R. BROWN received her Ph.D. in 1961 at Harvard University. Her doctoral dissertation, written under Professor Charles Holt Taylor's direction, was devoted to the history of royal reform and political discontent during the reigns of Philip the Fair of France and his sons. For the past five years, prompted by her interest in the effect of personality on politics, she has studied the applicability of psychoanalytic theory to the history of the Middle Ages. In cooperation with a psychoanalyst who practices in New York City, she has given courses in psychoanalysis and history, and she has recently become a member of the New York Psychoanalytic Institute's Colloquium on Psychoanalysis and the Social Sciences. Dr. Brown taught at

Harvard University from 1957 to 1963. Since 1963 she has been a member of the History Department of Brooklyn College of the City University of New York.

ELEANOR S. GREENHILL, a native Texan, studied medieval comparative literature with Roger Sherman Loomis at Columbia University before going to Germany. She took her Ph.D. at the University of Munich where she studied art history with Hans Seldmayr and medieval Latin philology and paleography with Bernhard Bischoff. Her dissertation was on the *Speculum Virginum* and she has recently given most of her attention to medieval manuscript illumination and Gothic sculpture. She contributed the essay on French Gothic sculpture to the Metropolitan Museum's volume *The Year 1200*. She has taught art history at both the University of Chicago and the University of Texas at Austin.

WILLIAM W. KIBLER is associate professor of French at the University of Texas at Austin. He has been active in the Medieval Studies Program at the University of Texas since its inception in 1970, and it was in connection with this interdisciplinary program that he organized the symposium out of which this volume grew. He is particularly interested in the traditions underlying the development and elaboration of Old French romances and epics, and has contributed a number of articles, particularly on the French epic, to leading journals in this country and abroad.

MOSHÉ LAZAR was born in Rumania and educated in France, Spain, and Israel. He has been a visiting professor at a number of American universities and was on the faculty of the University of Jerusalem from 1957 to 1971. Since 1971 he has been head of the Department of Theatre Arts and dean of the Faculty of Fine Arts and Communications of the University of Tel-Aviv. He is widely known for his work on contemporary poetry, theatrical history, and medieval literature. He has published over twenty-five articles and some half-dozen books, of which the best known to medievalists is his revolutionary study of the courtly love tradition, *Amour courtois et Fin'Amors dans la littérature du XIIᵉ siècle* (1964).

ROSSELL HOPE ROBBINS, one of the world's leading authorities on the Middle English lyrics, is coauthor of the *Index of Middle English Verse* (1943) and its *Supplement* (1965) and translator of *Les Cent Nouvelles nouvelles* (1961). Born in England, he received his doctorate from Cambridge in 1937. He came to America, to New York University, that same year and has held positions at a number of outstanding universities. Since 1969 he has been

International Professor at the State University of New York at Albany. He has written ten books and nearly two hundred learned articles and reviews. In 1974 he was honored with a *Festschrift*, a collection of some thirty-six new essays edited by Beryl Rowland. Although known primarily as a medievalist, by many he is also recognized as a standard authority on witch-craft through his *Encyclopedia of Demonology and Witchcraft* (1959).

Index